D1565150

Ancestors of Worthy Life

Cultural Heritage Studies

UNIVERSITY PRESS OF FLORIDA

Florida A&M University, Tallahassee
Florida Atlantic University, Boca Raton
Florida Gulf Coast University, Ft. Myers
Florida International University, Miami
Florida State University, Tallahassee
New College of Florida, Sarasota
University of Central Florida, Orlando
University of Florida, Gainesville
University of North Florida, Jacksonville
University of South Florida, Tampa
University of West Florida, Pensacola

ANCESTORS OF WORTHY LIFE

PLANTATION SLAVERY AND BLACK HERITAGE
AT MOUNT CLARE

TERESA S. MOYER

Foreword by Paul A. Shackel

University Press of Florida

Gainesville · Tallahassee · Tampa · Boca Raton

Pensacola · Orlando · Miami · Jacksonville · Ft. Myers · Sarasota

This book may be available in an electronic edition.

20 19 18 17 16 15 6 5 4 3 2 1

Library of Congress Cataloging-in-Publication Data
Moyer, Teresa S., 1976– author.
Ancestors of worthy life : plantation slavery and black heritage at Mount Clare / Teresa
S. Moyer ; foreword by Paul A. Shackel.
pages cm — (Cultural heritage studies)
Includes bibliographical references and index.
ISBN 978-0-8130-6046-0
1. Slavery—Maryland—Baltimore—History. 2. Baltimore (Md.)—Buildings,
structures, etc. 3. Historic buildings—Maryland—Baltimore. 4. African Americans—
Maryland—Baltimore—History. 5. Slaves—Dwellings—Maryland—Baltimore—
History. 6. Mount Clare (Baltimore, Md. : Building)—History. I. Shackel, Paul A.,
author of foreword. II. Title. III. Series: Cultural heritage studies.
F190.N4M69 2015
306.3'62097526—dc23
2014027981

The University Press of Florida is the scholarly publishing agency for the State
University System of Florida, comprising Florida A&M University, Florida Atlantic
University, Florida Gulf Coast University, Florida International University, Florida
State University, New College of Florida, University of Central Florida, University of
Florida, University of North Florida, University of South Florida, and University of
West Florida.

University Press of Florida
15 Northwest 15th Street
Gainesville, FL 32611-2079
http://www.upf.com

For you, Baltimore

Contents

Illustrations

Figures

Tables

FOREWORD

About two out of every three museums in the United States are grounded in some form of history—national history, local history, and/or individual history. House museums make up a large proportion of these history museums. Some of these places have interpretive messages that can have a much greater impact on the public than any single history textbook. These interpretations contain themes and messages and are in no way neutral.[1]

Within this context, Teresa Moyer's book, *Ancestors of Worthy Life: Plantation Slavery and Black Heritage at Mount Clare*, provides comprehensive and thorough research that challenges some long-held myths related to one of the most powerful colonial families in America—the Carrolls. At the same time, she provides compelling research that questions some of the long-held narratives of a powerful colonial organization—the National Society of Colonial Dames of America. Moyer implores us, as well as the keepers of the narratives at Mount Clare, to think about the place in different ways and to consider a more inclusive heritage.

Since the 1980s, there has been a radical change in the way museums have been interpreted to the public. Museums have had a long tradition of focusing on the collection of objects and valuing the aesthetics of these objects. This orientation can be perceived as exclusive and elitist, one that reinforces class divisions. The "new museology" critiques these traditional methods and calls for museums to be more accessible by providing more inclusive histories and a more democratic climate for visitors. Objects, which were once collected for their aesthetic value, should be interpreted in their context. "Objects are not signs to be interpreted in a singular manner, but can in fact hold multiple meanings—as many meanings as people who engage with them. It is acknowledged that the individual visitor brings his or her own 'living reality.'"[2] Many museums professionals now see these places as an important stage on which to convey social history to a larger audience.[3]

Moyer's book is about understanding power and the control of knowledge related to the interpretation of the Carroll family mansion known as Mount Clare and the surrounding landscape they once owned. In 1917, the National Society of Colonial Dames of America in the State of Maryland became caretakers of the Carroll mansion, and they developed a historic house museum that celebrates the history of the Carroll family and focuses on the family's importance in U.S. colonial history. (The city of Baltimore maintains and interprets the surrounding landscape.) Today, Mount Clare is located in a majority-black neighborhood in a majority-black city.

Carroll's papers clearly indicate that blacks and whites interacted at the mansion complex; however, the National Society of Colonial Dames of America made a decision about a century ago to not include black history in their interpretation of the house, a decision whose effects continue to be felt today. What is compelling about Moyer's study is her ability to provide an in-depth history of African Americans who were enslaved at Mount Clare, and she also locates many of them in the Baltimore region after emancipation. She amasses some important biographies of the little-known and little-studied African Americans. Moyer's research challenges part of the long-held narrative of a place that has been interpreted as a white household and white landscape. Today, little interpretation is provided about the role of African Americans on the Carrolls' property. The historic house and its surrounding landscape has become, and continues to be, racialized.

Moyer offers an important example of how museums like Mount Clare can change their direction and create new narratives and foster efforts toward making African American history part of the larger official history of the United States. She is also clear that, while African Americans were emancipated, it is important to foster a dialogue about the racism that existed and still exists today in American communities. Facing these difficult histories and making them relevant to contemporary society can be a difficult process. Those who have traditionally controlled the narrative are sometimes reluctant to share control over the development of new histories, the creation of an inclusive heritage. Sites like Mount Clare can become places where conversations about race and race relations and their legacy in the present can take place. Historic plantations have a responsibility to present these difficult histories to visitors. Moyer's work at Mount Clare makes this process doable when the National Society of Colonial Dames of America sees the importance of making Mount Clare inclusive and relevant to the community, the city, and the nation.

Paul A. Shackel, series editor

Acknowledgments

This book is the result of a team effort by administrators, archaeologists, historians, and staff members who most of the time did not know they were working together. I would like to take the opportunity to recognize their roles in enabling the black history of Mount Clare to be told.

Thank you to Mary Corbin Sies, Julia A. King, Cheryl J. LaRoche, Paul A. Shackel, and Psyche Williams-Forson for reviewing earlier versions of this book and providing such terrific feedback.

Reference staff and volunteers at the Maryland State Archives were patient and gracious during marathon pulls of government records. Thank you to all, especially Vicki Allen, Robert Barnes, Brandy Dorsey, Melodie Krauss, Michael McCormick, Edward Papenfuse, Sarah Patterson, Jennifer Petrisko, Matthew Pollard, Amber Robinson, Robert Schoeberlein, and Christopher Schini. In addition, Kim Moreno offered guidance as an archivist and an expert on Margaret Tilghman Carroll.

Staff and volunteers at the Maryland Historical Society gave assistance on using the collections and accessing the minutiae of Baltimore history. Appreciation is extended to Jennifer Namsiriwan, Francis O'Neill, and Marc Thomas. A Lord Baltimore Fellowship from the historical society provided institutional support.

Staff at the Mount Clare Museum House and Baltimore & Ohio Museum provided access to archival materials and history files held in the research library. They also helped me to understand the decorative arts and furniture collections on display. Thanks to Jane Wolterek, Carolyn Adams, Alice Donahue, Elizabeth Otey, and David Shackelford for their assistance.

W. Peter Pearre provided generous assistance with Michael Trostel's book drafts and insights on his research process. His institutional memory provides a unique perspective on one of the classic in-depth histories of Mount Clare.

The Carroll Park Foundation and the Baltimore Talent Development High School provided access to the Carroll Park archaeological collection and organized students to assist me. Thank you to Pamela Charshee and to the students, including Charles Harris, Christopher Harris, Russell Henry, Tashawna Fennell, Jonathan Frazier, Robin Simmons, and Nasha Queen.

Extra-special thanks go to Charles Hall, Maryland Historical Trust; Edward W. Burdeen Jr., Baltimore City Department of Parks and Recreation; and Sara Chaconas, Baltimore City Department of Parks and Recreation for their extraordinary persistence, patience, and problem solving.

Meredith Babb and her team at the University Press of Florida have been exceptionally patient and helpful. Paul Shackel, series editor, has been a heroic reader of every draft. David Palmer and Kirsti Uunila provided useful comments and practical advice on earlier drafts that have greatly improved the final product.

Last, but only because they are the best, thank you to my family. The Moyers are a supportive crew. Much gratitude goes to Matt Burns for his solid insights, unfailing support, and deep wells of patience.

May every writer be so fortunate to have such an exceptional team behind them.

ABBREVIATIONS

Repositories

CPF	Carroll Park Foundation, Baltimore, Maryland
LOC	Library of Congress, Washington, DC
MdHR	Maryland Hall of Records, Annapolis, Maryland
MSA	Maryland State Archives, Annapolis, Maryland
MdHS	Maryland Historical Society, Baltimore, Maryland
MHT	Maryland Historical Trust, Crownsville, Maryland
MCMH	Mount Clare Museum House, Baltimore, Maryland
NARA	National Archives and Records Administration, Washington, DC
NYPL	New York Public Library, New York, New York

Names or Titles within Citations

MHM	*Maryland Historical Magazine*
Dr. CC	Dr. Charles Carroll
CCB	Charles Carroll the Barrister
MTC	Margaret Tilghman Carroll

I

INTRODUCTION

Black history at historic plantations concerns more than slavery and freedom; it also tells the story of why blacks in the past are omitted at places
with so much of their history to tell. Historic plantations offer rich labo-
ratories in which to examine the ways that racism changes and stays the
same through the circumstances that enable black history to be revealed or
hidden. Mount Clare in Baltimore, Maryland, offers a case study of what
this looks like. During its management from 1917 to 2012 by the National
Society of the Colonial Dames of America in the State of Maryland, black
history and slavery were ignored in favor of white ancestry and the material
evidence of whites' ancestors' societal prominence. In the process, the interpretation of Mount Clare failed to address the significance of slavery and
blacks to white plantation owners, the plantation itself, and the region. The
valuable meanings of these stories—such as that racism created struggle
and inequality or that people living on the same property experienced and
perceived life in different, but interlinked, ways—was consequently lost. As
a result, the rich, multicultural heritage that belongs to us all became inac-
cessible, making Mount Clare less relevant or important to people today
as it could be. By studying the interpretation—or lack thereof—of black
history at places like Mount Clare, we can learn from the past and apply the
lessons learned in order to effect change for a more equal and just society.

Today, Mount Clare is located within Carroll Park in southwestern
Baltimore (fig. 1.1). It is one of the industrial and agricultural plantations
established by Dr. Charles Carroll.[1] His son, Charles Carroll the Barrister,
inherited the land and through slavery transformed it into a showpiece
property that he named Mount Clare. In 1917, the National Society of the
Colonial Dames of America in the State of Maryland (Maryland Society)

Figure 1.1. Mount Clare Museum House, Carroll Park, Baltimore. Photo by author.

assumed management of the Carroll mansion for a historic house museum. The members' personal interests included their ancestors' histories, as well as architecture, decorative arts, and gardening. House tours and special events focused on these topics. Archaeological investigations beginning in the 1970s, however, uncovered evidence of enslaved blacks living and working in the vicinity of the plantation. It, in combination with archival material from the Carrolls' papers, demonstrates without a doubt that blacks and whites interacted constantly at the mansion complex. Despite this evidence, the Maryland Society continued to ignore black history and blacks' roles at the plantation and in the Carrolls' lives. As a result, the interpretation of Mount Clare became one-sided and untruthful in a way that was an injustice not only to African Americans but to all people looking to understand the shared heritage of the site.

My purpose in this book is to show a way to think about slavery and black history at Mount Clare. It aims to recover a place for blacks at Mount Clare, as well as to shine a light on the processes that made them invisible in the past and present. One path forward for Mount Clare is to integrate enslaved blacks, who traditionally have been underrepresented, as fully as possible into the site's interpretation. A second path is to recognize that black history is meaningful or relevant not just to African American audiences but to all visitors. Black history is white history, and vice versa; indeed, the Carrolls' history cannot be fully understood without knowledge about the people they enslaved or the Carrolls' attitudes and actions concerning slavery and freedom. A third path is to confront the fact that the relative lack of emphasis on black history is part of the history of historic preservation. These three paths lay the groundwork for historic preservation to support equal access to heritage for all members of society; in other words, historic preservation and archaeology, through the interpretation of historic plantations, can support the cause of social justice.

Social Justice, Racism, and Equal Access to Heritage

Social justice through historic preservation and archaeology emphasizes that equal access to heritage is a social right. A single view of history, such as from the white perspective, privileges one perspective over others. It enables one view to dominate the social narrative and the lessons learned from it. By making multiple perspectives in history accessible, such as those of enslaved blacks, society and all its members have fair access to information that dispels the myths, prejudices, and mistruths of history that carry into the present day and affect its attitudes. Thus, a view of the past that includes multiple perspectives is central to the social services that are at the core of social justice.

Getting at historical truths and creating heritage is a contested and controversial process. Called "insurgent preservation"[2] or "dissonant heritage," the work of promoting diversity in heritage narratives brings attention to the evocative and difficult histories of oppressed or underrepresented peoples. The larger goal of "'restorative social justice' through civic engagement" requires professionals to acknowledge the existence of and do something about the ideological schemes that keep the "other," such as enslaved blacks, in a marginalized and subordinate place.[3] Bringing the heritage of contemporary black communities into public spaces provides opportunities to examine the power of race over things and rights, as well as the ways that race can simultaneously impact the landscape and seem invisible on it.[4] Equal access to heritage through the interpretation of all peoples who lived and worked at historic sites thus furthers the cause of social justice.

Without supporting equal access to black heritage, historic plantations like Mount Clare cannot explore race from different perspectives with their visitors or fulfill the goals of social justice for their constituents. For example, looking at Mount Clare from the black perspective shows that, while the Carrolls had the acumen to create conditions for slavery at Mount Clare, enslaved blacks were the foundation upon which the Carroll empire rested and depended. Blacks are the missing link in the Carrolls' story; their knowledge and skills fueled the plantation, enabled the Carrolls to be social elites, and influenced developments in American labor and social interactions. Visitors to Mount Clare have been unable to learn that blacks on the Carrolls' properties both practiced their own cultural beliefs and values and learned about those of elite whites in order to carry out their daily tasks. The Carrolls and the people they enslaved were not equal in society, because their race and status conferred different rights upon them. Nevertheless, enslaved blacks played as essential a role in sustaining the plantations as the Carrolls. In this way, the people enslaved at Mount Clare were part of a larger process in which blacks became culturally American by negotiating the fallout of a race-based system for ordering society.

The fact that whites did not raise questions about blacks when interpreting Mount Clare is a form of racism. It signifies that the Maryland Society felt that neither blacks nor the foundation of society upon slavery were important to history. In the process, the Maryland Society prevented visitors from finding meaning in the past that could bring new perspectives to their own understanding of the world.

Racism has played a central role in the inequality of interpretation at historic plantations, just as the institutions of historic preservation and archaeology have a history of marginalization and subordination on the basis of race. One lesson from the study of structural or institutional racism, however, is that racism can be invisible to those whom others might label racist. From the perspective of academia, my anthropological training showed me how to recognize and question structural or institutional racism at cultural institutions. Even though I see racist practices at Carroll Park, I know that the Maryland Society and Carroll Park Foundation, two of the key preservation organizations sharing stewardship of Mount Clare, do not share my view.[5] For example, the Maryland Society is interested primarily in preserving the history of its colonial ancestors, who happen to be white. To me, this is a myopic approach to the past that exemplifies structural racism; however, to the Maryland Society, there is nothing wrong or insidious in choosing to focus on the part of history that is of the most interest to them. Making black history difficult to access physically or financially, or erasing it entirely, may not have been intentional or overt to the people preserving Mount Clare. But racism can be a habit of thought whereby whites habitually ignore or forget blacks in their pursuit of promoting their white ancestors, an act that may seem natural and unremarkable to them but is insidious to others.

In my view, structural and institutionalized racism limits the potential of historic plantations when carried out by those who do not recognize racist practices. The preservation, management, and interpretation of historic plantations has been a historically white project that uses interpretation to support structural racism by ignoring the contributions of people of African descent whose work sustained the plantations. Ignoring as central a factor as slavery in the life of a place equates to erasing that history from a place if it is not interpreted. Black life tends not to be interpreted to visitors with depth and breadth, because to do so would threaten whites' ability to argue that past actions justify present ones, including the decision to interpret a place from a white elite perspective. Visitors traditionally have received the most exposure to elite whites' most estimable or admirable accomplishments, social mores, and contributions, and considerably less exposure to the resilience, hard work, and creativity of enslaved blacks. It casts elite whites in a favorable light without providing visitors all of the information they need to form their own opinions. The fantasy of a harmonic landscape peopled by groups of different stations in society teaches people today that inequality is natural—when, in fact, it is anything but. Historic plantations and their landscapes, however, offer rich environments in which to leverage the legacy of slavery for social justice through providing equity and fair access to an interpreted past. The history of Mount Clare, and the history of interpreting Mount Clare, provides a case study on the impact of institutionalized racism on equal access to the past, as well as opportunities for change.

Racial Identity and Recovering Black History

Part of the history of Mount Clare relates to the relevance of racism to American life from colonial times to the present day. Racial identity, meaning perceived differences predicated on race, was an elastic and emerging concept for Europeans in the early colonial era. Britons believed, at first, that Christianity, civility, and rank mattered more than physical attributes. Americans from Europe conceptualized Africa as a savage place outside the narrative of Western progress. Europeans and Europeans in America justified their enslavement of Africans by arguing that, as far as they could tell, Africa lacked civilizations. Dr. Charles Carroll, for example, once expressed in a letter his belief that the "African, Grecian, and Roman Empires are no more" in discussing his concern for his "family and country."[6] His statement reflected the attitude that civilization could not be associated with the race of people enslaved in the American colonies. The concept of race grew out of many factors in relation to one another, among them skin color, space, geography, trends in commerce and agriculture, ethnicity, and social stratification. Meanings grew out of these and were applied to society to create order. The upper and literate classes in the West, for instance, considered physical labor to be a chore best left to slaves, peasants, or servants.[7]

Over time, the courts codified so-called common knowledge about race into law, which then established physical differences and attributed meanings about physical features and ancestry to race. Ultimately, the law was responsible for transforming ideas about the perception of racial differences into material conditions, such as the poverty of the enslaved relative to their enslavers. The intensification of the Atlantic slave trade, the economic and cultural role of plantation America in European society, and Enlightenment notions of human progress embedded and institutionalized racism, creating the belief that members of one race are inherently inferior to those of another race. Racism, in turn, provided a framework for ordering state and civil society and its institutions, as well as human bodies and social structures.[8] It also embedded white privilege in colonial society, whereby to be of European descent yielded certain advantages and freedoms.

Over time, Europeans and Europeans in America increasingly assigned significance to physical attributes as an outgrowth of their conceptual or philosophical attitudes. Europeans believed that a person's complexion reflected his or her climate of origin, which had a long-term, deterministic effect on bodily humors and anatomy. Europeans thought that Africans were "natural slaves" on the basis of the impact of climate on their mental, moral, psychological, and physical attributes. For example, they perceived laziness in Africans, which they attributed to the hot climate from which they came. Scientists compared the physical characteristics of humans from different continents. They concluded that blacks were intellectually inferior to whites, a position that ultimately justified white supremacy. Blacks' skin colors, facial features, and hair textures became characteristics used to justify classifying them as "natural slaves" and promote differences in status between whites and blacks.[9] Such attitudes are important to talk about at places like Mount Clare, because they help visitors both to perceive the circumstances under which people lived in the past and to understand that attitudes change as their historical contexts do. Furthermore, they show the origin of attitudes that continue to shape policies today, such as those concerning the social services most directly linked to social justice.

The context for interpreting race and racism at historic plantations is different in the twenty-first century than it was in the late nineteenth or even early twentieth century, when the foundation was laid for interpreting Mount Clare. Anthropologists have scientifically disproved that race is a differentiating factor in humanity. We all are the human race, and race is not natural or inherent, but a concept constructed by society that "signifies and symbolizes social conflicts and interests by referring to different types of human bodies."[10] Race is today seen to be a social construction, one that has been institutionalized throughout American society. Institutionalized racism means that the concept of race continues to order society. It may manifest through racial prejudice—a set of learned ideas used to evaluate a person of another race. Or it may be seen in racial discrimination, which uses racial prejudice to treat a person unequally on the basis of racial affiliation. Institutionalized racism can also figure in ethnocentrism, an attitude that presumes that one's own cultural, ethnic, or national group is superior to others.[11] White privilege—meaning the advantages gained by people of European descent as a result of their race—is one way to understand what institutionalized racism looked like.

Institutionalized racism manifests at historic plantations through decisions about whose stories to tell or prioritize. It is the reason that black history was not interpreted at Mount Clare. In the mid-twentieth century, however, American society underwent major shifts as a result of the civil rights movement. More people from traditionally underrepresented groups, such as African Americans, gained positions of power to bring about change. They were increasingly able to vote, work in cultural and academic institutions, travel more broadly, and access education at higher levels. As social history became mainstream, it came to be known for emphasizing the diversity of American history and introducing multiple perspectives. More people could find themselves in the past, because social history included cultural diversity and individuals' experiences and acknowledged their agency to think and act on their own accord and in their own interests.

Social history and archaeology at historic sites has had important implications for black heritage and social justice by challenging common beliefs that result from the traditional one-sided view of the past perpetuated by whites. Historians, for example, use sources created by Africans to study slavery from the perspective of peoples from the African continent. They look for women and children, in addition to men, to understand their unique perspectives on racial oppression and black community development. Social history results in new perspectives and challenges commonly held beliefs, such as that slavery was a phenomenon confined to the southern states.[12] It brings complexity to slavery by supporting the agency of blacks, dismantling the idea of a singular "African slave" type, and recognizing slavery as a multifaceted experience. As a result, social history and archaeology brought about a major shift in consciousness concerning the impact of historical methods on the accessibility of the past. It demonstrates that when a telling of history focuses on European American men of means, it isolates them from their historical contexts and social conditions.

One insight from social history and archaeology is that text-based research alone perpetuates white perspectives and does not suffice to uncover the stories of traditionally underrepresented peoples. Archaeology, ethnography, architecture, cultural landscape studies, religion studies, and material culture research provide essential data to complement textual sources. Archaeology, in particular, places people on a landscape and through artifacts creates a primary source record that tracks their activities. For places like Mount Clare, enslaved blacks left no textual records about their everyday activities, thoughts, or beliefs. The nuance of the Carrolls' and enslaved blacks' lived experiences cannot be understood from textual evidence alone. Text-based evidence, such as personal papers or legal documents, offers a narrow and biased view of the past that is restricted to certain activities or perspectives. A picture of everyday activities for enslaved persons can be gained, however, from the distribution of artifacts across a landscape, comparative research with other plantations, changes or renovations to the mansion, and even the absence of artifacts in a space. Whereas textual sources minimize the impact of slavery and enslaved blacks on a landscape, interdisciplinary approaches demonstrate the true imprint of blacks' activities at Mount Clare. Thus, the history of Mount Clare can be broadened to incorporate black perspectives in contrast to those of whites.

History at Mount Clare

Diasporic black communities from the African continent and the Caribbean lived in the Chesapeake region by the mid-1600s, a period when colonial society stratified and tobacco plantations, dependent on slavery, emerged. Charles Carroll, Chirurgeon (a surgeon, or doctor), emigrated from Ireland to America by 1716 and settled in Annapolis, Maryland. Dr. Carroll patented land straddling Gwynns Falls, called Georgia (and later known as Mount Clare and then Carroll Park), in 1729. He conveyed the western portion of Georgia to the Baltimore Company, which he and three partners formed in 1731 to establish the Baltimore Iron Works. Dr. Carroll retained the eastern portion of Georgia for his own use. By 1737, eight enslaved persons lived on Georgia and nine lived at The Caves, another of Dr. Carroll's plantations. Over time, Dr. Carroll amassed significant acreages in Baltimore County for ironworks, shipping, and milling enterprises (fig. 1.2).

Unlike Dr. Carroll, the specific geographic or tribal origins remain uncertain for the people enslaved at Georgia. Their homelands might have been located on the African continent or in the West Indies, Brazil, or interstitial locations along slave trade routes to America. Data about the slave trade suggest that the Igbo from the Bight of Biafra and Greater Senegambia clustered in the Chesapeake region.[13] The experiences of blacks at Mount Clare and in the colonial Chesapeake region were incredibly diverse. Just as no monolithic African culture existed in Africa, neither did

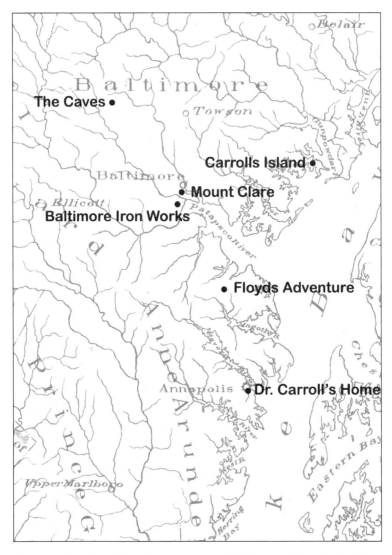

The Caves •

Carrolls Island •

• Mount Clare

Baltimore Iron Works

• Floyds Adventure

• Dr. Carroll's Home

Figure 1.2. Location of Carroll properties near Baltimore and Annapolis. Map by author.

a single, unified enslaved black culture exist in America. They could not typically re-create whole African cultural and societal systems within the political environment of colonial America, but they retained many important aspects of their cultures.

Oppressive conditions and an absence of "pure" African culture meant that they adapted quickly, but it was not a smooth, easy, or welcome process. Africans faced choices about replacing aspects of their identity with an American one. They retained solid senses of African self and culture and determinedly acted on them throughout their lives. The impact of African culture resonated throughout America. For example, southern culture emerged as a mixture of African and English values and behaviors. In the process, enslaved blacks maintained aspects of their homelands' cultures while fashioning a culture that adapted or responded to plantation life. Such cultural adaptations coincided with major changes in colonial society.

Blacks held by the Carrolls in the mid-eighteenth century witnessed fundamental shifts in colonial society. Black slavery became key to maintaining social stratification. Tobacco agriculture was in decline. Black communities, free and enslaved, were growing in size and coherence both on and off the plantation. They developed and carried out methods of resistance, as seen at the Baltimore Iron Works, to push back against their enslavers and maintain personal dignity amid harsh conditions. Blacks enslaved by the Carrolls were also affected by changes in the Carroll family. Dr. Carroll died in 1755, leaving his estate to his son, Charles Carroll the Barrister. Charles became one of the wealthiest men in the Maryland colony as a result of his property, business acumen, and the value of labor that could be extracted from the enslaved. Charles commissioned a summer home in 1760 on the Georgia tract and renamed it Mount Clare upon its completion. He married Margaret Tilghman, herself a wealthy landowner and slaveholder, in 1763.

The black populations on the Carrolls' properties grew by procreation and purchase. At Mount Clare they maintained ornamental and kitchen gardens, orchards, and greenhouse plants; grew grain crops; looked after animals and birds; and did domestic work. Some chose to escape slavery as "runaways," whom the Carrolls attempted to recover. More than fifty enslaved persons lived on the Carrolls' Baltimore County and Annapolis properties, not including children or the very elderly, by 1773. In the

Revolutionary War era, the Carrolls resettled at Mount Clare as wartime activity heated up Annapolis. After Charles died in 1783, Margaret chose from approximately seventy enslaved people to live with her at Mount Clare. This was unique both for the group's size relative to other places in the Baltimore region and for Margaret's wealth in widowhood. A white widow whose wealth eclipsed even that of most men in the region, Margaret's social prominence meant that the people she enslaved practiced everyday tasks and lived in conditions that were relatively unusual for the Baltimore region. Margaret, unlike her husband, freed several people during her lifetime. Upon her death in 1817, most of the forty-nine people she still enslaved were sold and were promised their freedom in the future through delayed manumission. Several were freed outright, but freedom for others was delayed or denied. By the mid-nineteenth century, court records show

Table 1.1. Population statistics for Mount Clare, 1737–1817

Year (Enslaver)	Black	Description of Black Population	White
1737 (Dr. Charles Carroll)	8	8 over age 16	4
1773 (Charles Carroll, Barrister)	18	18 over age 16	2
1774 (Charles Carroll, Barrister)	26		
1790 (Margaret Carroll)	47	47 over age 16	7
1798 (Margaret Carroll)	36	21 age 12–50	2
1804 (Margaret Carroll)	39		10
1813 (Margaret Carroll)	44	10 under age 8, 6 age 8–14, 15 males age 15–44, 6 females age 15–35, 4 males age ±45, 3 females ±36	
1817 (Margaret Carroll)	40	13 under age 8, 6 age 8–14, 12 males 15–44, 4 females 15–35, 1 male ±45, 3 females ±36, 1 unknown age	

Table 1.2. Population statistics for The Caves, 1737–1817

Year (Enslaver)	Black	Description of Black Population	White
1737 (Dr. Charles Carroll)	9		1
1749 (Charles Carroll, Barrister)	15		
1773 (Charles Carroll, Barrister)	19	19 over age 16	4
1783 (Charles Carroll, Barrister)	45	13 under age 8, 7 males age 8–14, 5 males age 15–44, 10 females age 15–35, 8 males age ±45 or females age ±36	
1790 (Nicholas Carroll)	49	49 over age 16	3
1798 (Nicholas Carroll)	37	30 age 12–50	1
1812 (Nicholas Carroll)	31	4 under age 8, 15 males age 14–44, 3 females age 14–35, 3 males age ±45, 6 females age ±36	
1813 (Nicholas Carroll)	45	5 under age 8, 5 age 8–14, 15 males age 15–44, 5 females age 15–36, 6 males age ±45, 9 females age ±36	
1817 (Margaret Carroll)	10	2 under age 8, 4 age 8–14, 2 males age 15–45, 2 females age 15–36	

that only half of the blacks formerly enslaved by Margaret were registered as free in keeping with their manumissions. For the entire history of the Carrolls' ownership, the ratio of white residents to enslaved blacks was at least 1:3, making enslaved blacks the majority population for the duration of Dr. Carroll's, Charles the Barrister's, and Margaret's residence of Mount Clare (Table 1.1, 1.2, and 1.3).

After Margaret's death, her husband's nephew James Maccubbin took his uncle's last name as a condition of his inheritance. James Maccubbin Carroll moved to Mount Clare with a new black enslaved community in

Table 1.3. Population statistics for Carrolls Island, 1783–1812

Year (Enslaver)	Black	Description of Black Population	White
1783 (Charles Carroll, Barrister)	20	10 under age 8, 2 age 8–14, 2 males age 15–45, 3 females age 4–36, 3 males age ±45 or females age ±36	
1798 (Nicholas Carroll)	12	4 age 12–50	1
1812 (Nicholas Carroll)	12	1 female age 8–14, 9 males age 14–45, 2 females age 15–36	

1818. Upon James's death, Mount Clare began to be used as a rental property and slavery ended there. James's descendants rented out Mount Clare to a series of caretakers and boardinghouse keepers for much of the nineteenth century. The gardens and orchards declined; the outbuildings fell into disrepair. The land surrounding the mansion also had new uses. Brickyards scarred the landscape. Rowhouses and developments grew where fields and forests had stood. Mount Clare had changed considerably, from showpiece plantation to rundown hotel, by the time Baltimore City annexed the land in 1851.

Evidence of the impact of slavery on American life continued to affect Mount Clare. The Civil War broke out over slavery. Slavery divided Baltimore during the war. U.S. Army soldiers riding the Baltimore & Ohio Railroad regularly passed the mansion en route to their next engagement. Soldiers camped at two places on the Mount Clare property, at Camp Carroll and Camp Millington.

In 1890, Baltimore City purchased the property from the Carrolls to create a city park. By then, all the outbuildings, including the kitchen, greenhouses, washroom, barns, and mills, had been demolished due to their deteriorating condition. As a result, the central part of the mansion, the space most closely tied to the Carrolls themselves, became the only aboveground evidence of the history of Mount Clare. The erasure of workspaces and living areas associated with enslaved black life set the stage for preservationist groups to focus on the Carrolls alone.

The Maryland Society of the National Society of the Colonial Dames of America reached an agreement with the city in 1917 to care for the mansion as a museum. The Maryland Society set to restoring, landscaping, and furnishing the property as part of its mission to preserve historic houses in commemoration of its members' colonial ancestors. The group focused on telling the Carrolls' story, which hewed to their own frame of reference as privileged whites. Situated within a city park, the house was open to the public as part historic house and part shrine. Interpretation and restoration focused on telling the Carrolls' story with emphasis on their consumerism, fashionableness, and wealth as seen through architecture, furnishings, and decorative arts. The Maryland Society hired professional museum staff and began to introduce African American history at Mount Clare in the late twentieth century. The Carroll Park Foundation became the steward of the acreage comprising the historic easement around the mansion in 1991 through an agreement with the Maryland Historical Trust. It assumed management of the archaeological collection, but its director is not an archaeologist, and there is no archaeologist on staff. The city owns the parkland, which also includes recreational areas beyond the historic easement boundaries. The interpretation has remained consistently focused on the Carrolls.

An indication that black history was not a priority for the site's stewards is that no in-depth historical study included it. The Maryland Society commissioned Annie Leakin Sioussat to write a historical sketch about Mount Clare, which was published in 1926.[14] Sioussat's history focused on the contributions of Charles Carroll the Barrister to colonial society, and she also detailed the efforts of the Maryland Society at Mount Clare, including its work on the refurbished interior, architectural features, and landscaped setting. The Maryland Society next commissioned historical architect Michael Trostel, in 1974, to develop the first in-depth history of Mount Clare.[15] Trostel focused on the Carrolls and the architectural and property history of Mount Clare, with an emphasis on the Carrolls' lives and tastes. The Maryland Society was not alone in focusing on the Carrolls. Historians writing on their own also ignored black history, focusing instead on the Carrolls' lineages, lives, and activities. Biographical accounts portrayed Dr. Carroll and his son Charles as energetic, likeable, innovative, and intelligent members of the wealthy colonial elite.[16] Margaret Tilghman

Carroll was presented as a dutiful wife and mother dedicated to the domestic female sphere.[17] Focus on the Carrolls perpetuated a one-sided view of the past that erased blacks from the landscape and devalued their role in history.

Before my research into black history at Mount Clare, and as of this writing, websites developed for the Mount Clare Museum House and Carroll Park Foundation provided the best information about blacks and slavery on the landscape. The Mount Clare Museum House website includes pages that outline slavery and freedom in Maryland, freedom seekers, Baltimore, industrial slavery at the Baltimore Iron Works, runaway advertisements, and manumissions.[18] The Carroll Park Foundation's website primarily gives information about the vision and plans the foundation has for interpreting the landscape in the future. It provides a brief overview from the perspective of black history and emphasizes that diversity is part of the site's "rich cultural legacy." The website also notes the potential of the archaeological collection to tell the story of black history on the plantation.[19]

Today, Carroll Park is situated in western Baltimore amid several predominantly African American and working-class neighborhoods, but those who live near Mount Clare tend not to visit the mansion. During my visits to Carroll Park, I observed African Americans walking dogs, playing games in the fields or on the basketball courts, or walking for exercise in all areas of the park except for the historic easement section and mansion. I have only observed African Americans immediately around Mount Clare in their capacity as Baltimore park employees or walking the roadways, not as museum visitors. This is noteworthy, because many in Baltimore have very personal stakes in the black history comprising the Mount Clare collections, considering that the city is 63.6 percent African American and 31.4 percent white. In Karen Gurman's study of Mount Clare and its uses, she found that passersby did not pay Mount Clare notice. In her experience, locals were unfamiliar with the museum and its purpose. She argued that making Mount Clare relevant would involve connecting the site to its community by bringing black history into its interpretations and changing the ways it does outreach.[20] As such, the museum is situated in a community that barely knows that it exists, much less feels a connection to the place. Racism in the past has its legacy at Mount Clare, such that discovering a future for black history interpretation will necessitate placing race in historical context to move forward and make black heritage accessible.

Racism and Mount Clare

The uncomfortable truth is that racism, racial prejudice, ethnocentrism, and white privilege are integral aspects of historic preservation, archaeology, and the interpretation of historic sites. They are, indeed, one explanation for the erasure of black history from Mount Clare. Although pushing social justice to the forefront is not a traditional point of emphasis for historic preservation and archaeology, it points to the relevance of sites to a broad audience of contemporary populations. For historic plantations like Mount Clare, a discussion about racism would help visitors understand human interactions in the past and the ways in which they inform racism in the present and impede social justice.

My research for the following study originally responded to the problem that, in more than 120 years of preserving and interpreting Mount Clare, no historical report on the black history of the site had been funded, supported, or completed. My involvement with Carroll Park began in 2006 through a cooperative agreement between the Carroll Park Foundation and the University of Maryland to conduct a survey of the archaeological collections. Upon learning that little was known about black history at the site, but that the Maryland Society and Carroll Park Foundation both were interested in learning more, I created a walking tour.[21] I was surprised to find so little information available about black life at Mount Clare. Nothing comparable to the file folders and books telling the Carrolls' story existed on black heritage. If a visitor wanted to hear about the enslaved persons' lives, or an interpreter wanted to create a program, little information was accessible to them.

I came to believe that the lack of a historical study on black history betrayed not only the bias toward the Carrolls' history but an orientation of those who controlled the interpretation of Mount Clare to perpetuate institutional racism by not funding other perspectives. Historic institutions lay out their paths for preservation and interpretation through mission statements, research projects, development of historical reports and studies, collection of source materials in archives and museum collections, and applications for funding and grants, among other measures. The topics they choose to pursue or avoid create a framework for the future orientation of the institution and the biases or emphases that will manifest through exhibits, public tours, special events, and other interpretive opportunities. I came around to this view as a result of my research into black history at Mount Clare. Except for archaeological evidence and court-registered freedom papers, I reviewed all of the same sources used by historians in the first third of the twentieth century, such as Sioussat and Trostel, to construct a history of Mount Clare. All these sources clearly mention slavery and blacks right alongside information that made it into published histories about the Carrolls.

One major source of information about the history of Mount Clare, however, was closed to me. The Maryland Society has denied me access both to their historical archives, which are kept at the Mount Clare Museum House, and a microfilmed copy stored at the taxpayer-funded Maryland State Archives. Although the Maryland Society's leadership refused to communicate directly with me on this matter, my understanding through archives staff is that my request was denied over concerns about the organization's and members' privacy. Considering the significance of the archives to the history of interpreting black history at Mount Clare, I hope that the leadership of the Maryland Society will one day open their archives to researchers.

Another stumbling block came from the Carroll Park Foundation. When I requested access once again to the Mount Clare Archaeological Collection to photograph enslaved persons' artifacts for this book, the Carroll Park Foundation attempted to implement a restrictive collections access policy. The foundation sought to claim copyright and require researchers to purchase images of the artifacts for a significant fee. Implementing these actions would have effectively closed public access to the collection, which was created from taxpayer-funded excavations and is owned by Baltimore City. Use of the collection for research and publication would have become cost prohibitive for many Baltimoreans, researchers, and students. In response, the Baltimore City's Department of Parks and Recreation, with the Maryland Historical Trust, established a new collections access policy for the Mount Clare Archaeological Collection. It broadens the review of researcher requests and the decision-making process to include multiple stakeholders, including city representatives and professional archaeologists, to ensure fair public access to the collections. The artifacts published in this book were created after the city's and trust's intervention, and under the department's new policies. Clearly, the struggle over presenting and interpreting black history at Mount Clare is an ongoing part of its story.

The Following Chapters

The following chapters address two primary questions: First, what is the black history of Mount Clare? And second, why has black history been erased from the landscape and its interpretation? Chapter 1 has introduced the theoretical and methodological approaches of the project. Chapter 2 outlines the centrality of slavery and blacks to Dr. Charles Carroll's plans to create an interlocking plantation system of fields, mills, and ironworks. Chapter 3 addresses the transformation of Georgia to Mount Clare, a showpiece country plantation owned by Charles Carroll the Barrister and his wife, Margaret, as a result of enslaved laborers. Chapter 4 confronts the contradiction of the Carrolls as American patriots and slaveholders during the Revolutionary era. Chapter 5 discusses black life at Mount Clare within the context of white widowhood and the growth of opportunities for blacks in Baltimore. Chapter 6 addresses the circumstances faced by enslaved persons who were manumitted, freed, or sold after Margaret's death. Chapter 7 outlines the erasure of black history from Mount Clare, particularly since 1917, as a racialized practice of European American historic preservation. Chapter 8 offers recommendations for future interpretation of black history. The following chapters demonstrate that the history of blacks and of slavery is, in fact, recoverable and, furthermore, points to existing architectural and landscape elements to interpret a culturally diverse plantation.

My aim is to demonstrate that access to black heritage is a right of all members of society in that its interpretation is a path to social justice. The history of Mount Clare is rooted in topics that many people find difficult to talk about, even today. Sites like Carroll Park can start conversation about the historical circumstances of race and race relations in the past and their legacy in the present. Before this study, a great deal was known about whites at Mount Clare, and a little about blacks there, but overall nothing was understood about the two groups' everyday interactions. I offer a better historical context for discussion of race at the former plantation and current city park. Historical contexts fill in gaps in knowledge for museums and parks. They provide new perspectives on old problems. Some contexts open avenues for further research. But historical contexts also have a way of facilitating difficult conversations about race and racism. They offer front-line staff, such as interpreters or docents—a basis on which to feel confident about what they say. Visitors can ask for more information and get it. Administrators can use them to improve old exhibits and fundraise for new ones. All these reasons for historical contexts connect with a current ethic in museums and at historic sites to represent all people who lived at a place. Such an ethic draws on contemporary beliefs about citizenship and representation, but it also points to the recognition that a preserved cultural landscape is a forum for all voices to be heard.

2

<hr>

SLAVERY AND IRON AT GEORGIA

A starting point for equal access to black heritage is Georgia's origin story. Reintegrating the history of the ironworks to include blacks reshapes the traditional perception of Dr. Charles Carroll, who established slavery on his Baltimore-area properties by the early 1730s. It challenges the myth that colonial elites developed empires on their own; instead, blacks were the foundation upon which the Carrolls depended. On a larger scale, black history also shows that slavery was a social construction perpetuated by colonial elites. It took place because racism had been institutionalized in Chesapeake society. Black history in this way forces the descendants of white colonial elites to acknowledge that slavery and black history are inseparable from their ancestors' history. The origin story of Georgia thus indicates that, judged in accordance with today's values, the Carrolls were racist, but also that that institutionalized racism persisted in the interpretation of Mount Clare.

The origin story of Georgia can thus be a step toward social justice by facilitating equal access to the past. Blacks on Dr. Carroll's agricultural and iron plantations grew familiar with the repercussions of race and status in America through their everyday lives and labors. Dr. Carroll's practice of slavery belied his belief in a top-down enforcement of societal order, one where slavery was essential to institutionalize a race-based status quo. In addition, blacks helped to create the American-style labor system. Everyday life at Georgia and the nearby Baltimore Iron Works demonstrated that blacks and Dr. Carroll shaped the terms of slavery together, not on equal ground, but through push-and-pull strategies that furthered each group's interests. Finally, enslaved persons had lives of their own beyond labor or as slaves. They created networks of kin, as seen in families, and allies, evident in coordinated escapes, and exercised their limited purchasing power. In these ways, the integration of black perspectives provides multiple perspectives on the past at Georgia that can make it more accessible for visitors to find personal meaning and relevance.

Blacks in Early Maryland

Two ways that black heritage is obscured is by failing to acknowledge its historical origins at a place or by failing to acknowledge the ways that a place and its people are relevant to history. The traditional origin story of Georgia neither acknowledges slavery in the early years of the Carrolls and the plantation nor provides a historical context for visitors so that they can understand the conditions that created slavery in the Chesapeake region. An accurate representation of historical facts and attitudes helps visitors to understand the conditions faced by people in the past, such as by the Carrolls and the people they enslaved.

Much effort had already gone into distinguishing blacks from Europeans, and the form that black slavery should take, by the time Dr. Carroll arrived in the Chesapeake region in 1716. The business of transporting slaves from Africa to the New World had been in place for generations. Africans in the American colonies originated from cultural groups on the African continent, such as the Igbo, Ewe, Bakongo, and Serer. In 1664, the Maryland Assembly declared "negroes" imported into the colony to be slaves for life. The Assembly took measures to separate Europeans from blacks and mulattoes in the 1670s and 1680s, including prohibitions on interracial marriage, assembly without whites present, participation in the militia, and carrying weapons. In addition, a distinction developed between labor and the enslaved body, wherein the value of labor might be limited but the body offered significant potential wealth at resale. A slave became a valuable part of an estate, because the individual was more than the means of acquiring wealth, but was in fact wealth itself, as part of an enslaver's property holdings. Such shifts became the basis for slaveholders to use race to assign enslaved blacks a subhuman and subordinate status in their minds and in society.[1] During class struggles, black slavery helped to distinguish the gentry from other groups. The distinctions between black and white and enslaved and enslaver were particularly clear on plantations.

Plantation slavery, as seen at Georgia, or, later, Mount Clare, developed between 1650 and 1750 in the American colonies. At first, race did not determine where one would land socially in the colonies—e.g., a servant might be European or black. Free blacks in Virginia, for example, extricated themselves from bondage, became landowners and parents with free children, and enjoyed societal rights akin to those of whites of similar stature until their autonomy became sharply curtailed over the course of the seventeenth century.[2] Several factors came together in Maryland that made basing status and labor roles on race attractive, including an increased reliance on labor-intensive tobacco, a need for labor due to fewer European immigrants in America, and the recognition of the connection between tobacco and status. Black slavery provided an answer in Europeans' minds to these issues.

Importation of human chattel to Maryland increased in response. One estimate had at least 1,800 Africans being taken to Maryland alone between 1700 and 1708 and another 1,330 between 1720 and 1749.[3] By 1750, blacks born in the colonies were increasingly the majority among enslaved populations in the Chesapeake. Male-to-female ratios evened out. Women began bearing children at younger ages than their immigrant mothers. Settled family life gave rise to a more autonomous culture.[4] Blacks were not complacent in slavery. They negotiated with slaveholders for advantages and improved circumstances for themselves and their families; escaped for short periods or on a permanent basis; and practiced cultural traditions passed from their homelands and adapted for life in the colonies. Chesapeake culture, as a result, became defined by economic, cultural, and labor struggles within and between African and European groups.

Part of the struggle involved blacks' application of skills and knowledge from African homelands to a new place and climate, while adapting to enslavers' enforcement of work discipline and control. Blacks arrived in Maryland with skills as farmers, cattle herders, weavers, boat makers, healers, architects, cooks, and more. One study of ironworks during the period in western Maryland found that enslaved persons may have transferred traditional African ironworking technologies to the ironworks.[5] Upon arriving in the colony, they learned to use available materials and adapt their expertise to create buildings and farmlands and carry out other tasks. The use of material culture to denote status, at least, was familiar. Elites in both West Africa and America had chairs, tables, raised bedsteads, and fine textiles. Ordinary West African and Chesapeake households had similar contents in the early eighteenth century, including one or two pots for cooking, wooden bowls or trays for eating, mortars for grinding corn and grain, simple bedding on the floor, stools for seats, and chests or baskets for storage.[6] Once in the colonies, blacks learned to adapt their abilities to different tools and materials, but around them lay the evidence of the inequalities between them and the people who enslaved them. Such differences, and the Carrolls' role in them, are part of history at Mount Clare.

Dr. Charles Carroll and Slavery

The circumstances of Dr. Carroll's emigration could not have been more different from those of peoples from Africa and the Caribbean, with the greatest difference being that he chose to leave Ireland for America. The Penal Laws, the persecution of Catholics, famine, and rebellion distanced the Irish from development as it occurred elsewhere in Europe. The Penal Laws, fully developed by 1691, sought to repress Catholics by taking their land. The first group of Catholics fled Ireland to Barbados in 1649; they were followed by William Penn's settlement in America in 1699. The new colonists were interested, according to Thomas D'Arcy McGee, in civilizing the "red men" and joined "whites" in taking their land.[7] Dr. Carroll was distantly related to other Carrolls who already lived in Maryland. They provided a cushion for him, both socially and economically. Upon his arrival, Dr. Carroll shifted his allegiances to gain a foothold in his new home. Already a wealthy man with a venerable genealogical background in Ireland and good connections in Catholic-unfriendly colonial Maryland, he converted to Protestantism to further ease his transition to life there.[8]

After emigrating to the Maryland colony in 1716, Dr. Carroll lived in Annapolis while amassing property in the Baltimore and western Maryland regions. Although no evidence of his entry into slaveholding remains, the historical record shows that slavery immediately became enmeshed in everyday life for him. For example, Dr. Carroll hired out blacks, such as the woman taken by Edward Smith for three months in 1716. He also cared for blacks and slaveholders as part of his medical practice. William Fitz Redmond was charged £6 for his "Negro womans Board, & Chyrurgicall Aplycations." Robert Myre Sr. was charged £8 for medicines to treat servants.[9] Dr. Carroll used blacks in his business transactions, such as selling or collecting them when mortgagers defaulted on their loans. In one case, Dr. Carroll had already confiscated an unspecified number of people when he called in Mary Wolsen's debt. Although Dr. Carroll left Wolsen to decide which enslaved persons to use as payment, he specifically mentioned "Mulatto Nell and Negro Girle Moll" as still being in her possession. In another case, he claimed "some Negros and household goods" due to him by Stephen Higgins.[10] Dr. Carroll also sold individuals, such as a mulatto fiddler named either John Stokes or John Collins.[11] Blacks purchased by Dr. Carroll in 1730 and 1731 may have worked on his Baltimore properties or at the ironworks. In October 1730, Olliver (age thirty) and Nann (age thirty-two) were acquired, along with a copper still, a feather bed and furniture, six steers, three cows and calves, and a bay horse, for £81.[12] In March 1731, Dr. Carroll purchased Coffee, Tom, and Jemmy for £90, in addition to ropes for traces, grubbing hoes, plows and plow irons, plows for horses, "2 Collars of Tootte," a bucket and pail, stock lock, hilling and weeding hoes, and a small hatchet.[13] Blacks were thus an everyday part of Dr. Carroll's business transactions before he established operations in the Baltimore region.

Dr. Carroll patented "Georgia," a tract of land outside the tiny town of Baltimore, in 1729. The property encompassed more than two thousand acres of gentle hills covered in black and white oaks. Its marshy coastlines skimmed the Middle Branch of the Patapsco and Gwynns Falls. Georgia was rich in timber and iron ore; the Patapsco was deep enough for shipping; and Gwynns Falls offered plenty of waterpower for milling.[14] Dr. Carroll purchased additional properties that together formed a strategic system of exploitable resources and transportation networks. Dr. Carroll patented The Caves in 1738 (surveyed in 1734) in the Green Spring Valley and Carrolls Island on the Gunpowder River in 1746 (surveyed in 1744).[15] Together the properties formed the Carroll empire for the doctor and secured the futures of his sons, Charles and John Henry. Dr. Carroll's land purchases furthermore established places for the Carrolls to root and sustain slavery to support their empires, starting with iron.

The Baltimore Iron Works

The Baltimore Iron Works was organized at a time when the American colonial iron industry was expanding, and when there was a shift from wage-based European to enslaved black labor. Dr. Carroll's and, later, his son Charles Carroll the Barrister's, sanctioning of slavery on a large scale is clear from their integral involvement in the iron industry at the Baltimore Iron Works. The Baltimore Iron Works was, indeed, unusual among Chesapeake-region iron companies for the size and scale of its enslaved population. It was also the first of the ironworks built in Maryland to have Maryland owners.[16]

Dr. Carroll began planning for an ironworks by 1730, including lobbying England to open its iron trade with Maryland. Dr. Carroll, along with other Maryland gentrymen, named Daniel Dulany, Benjamin Tasker, Charles Carroll of Annapolis, and Daniel Carroll, formed the Baltimore Company in October 1731 to create the Baltimore Iron Works.[17] All the partners had extensive land holdings and relied on plantation slavery to build wealth. Dr. Carroll and his son, like their partners, became increasingly powerful as the vanguard of colonial enterprise due to their diversified and innovative approaches to investment.[18] Dr. Carroll conveyed sixteen hundred acres of Georgia located to the west of Gwynns Falls to the Baltimore Company in 1731 for £540. He released the tenements for £125 plus five years' rent at £26 per annum. The eastern section of Georgia remained in Dr. Carroll's ownership.[19]

The first Baltimore Iron Works furnace was on Charles Run, today located south of Washington Boulevard on the west side of Gwynns Falls (fig. 2.1). In January 1731, Dr. Carroll became the ironworks manager.[20] His planning responsibilities included a calculation of "hands," including enslaved persons, for which he consulted with ironmasters at the Principio Iron Works near modern Havre-de-Grace, Maryland, and others in Pennsylvania and Virginia.[21] The Baltimore Company, like the owners of the

Figure 2.1. Location of the Baltimore Iron Works relative to Mount Clare. Detail from Lucas Fielding, Plan of Baltimore, 1836. By permission of the Geography and Maps Division, Library of Congress.

Principio Iron Works, saw slavery as the answer to both the problem of a shortage of free and indentured laborers and to the cost of wages. They also believed that slaves offered a more stable workforce than European convict and redemptioner laborers, who were considered unruly and unreliable.[22]

Dr. Carroll's first prospectus calculated the contracting of six enslaved persons for six months at £20 per month and the purchase of twenty-six people at £30 apiece. He calculated that ten would work as cutters, four as mine diggers, four as colliers, two in the "flatts" (flatboats, used to bring ore to the furnace by water), two at the furnace, and two at the sloop; and the remaining two would be women.[23] Another list calculated the charges on one thousand tons of metal. It included fifty-five enslaved persons at a cost of £30 per head and "3 years wages" at £15 per head, by which he meant food and supplies. He also calculated £15 for each of the estimated ten white hands.[24] With a plan in hand, Dr. Carroll asked his friends where he could find blacks to purchase at low cost. His calculations proved judicious: in 1732, one correspondent responded that men and women could be purchased for £20 in Williamsburg, Virginia, a lower price than he had estimated.[25]

Each partner, including Dr. Carroll and later his son Charles Carroll the Barrister, contributed a fifth of the enslaved persons and supplies. Each partner, in turn, owned a fifth share of the company's property and received a fifth of the product to turn into profit. Each provided a fifth of the food supply, cooking implements, clothes, and necessities. The people who worked Dr. Carroll's eastern portion of Georgia yielded his share of supplies to the iron plantation. Insufficient evidence remains for gauging the profitability of enslaved labor on industrial plantations. What matters, however, is that entrepreneurs like the Baltimore Company partners believed that enslaved blacks were preferable to hired workers.[26]

Ironmaking was backbreaking work, and blacks were involved at every laborious stage of it, from construction of the industrial complex to moving the product to ships for transport. Enslaved blacks at the Baltimore Ironworks held positions throughout the complex, working as smiths, carpenters, founders, finers, fillers, miners, and cooks. They worked alongside convicts, indentured servants, and hired black and white hands. Stonemasons from Virginia built the two furnaces and three forges, possibly using

Figure 2.2. The Catoctin Iron Furnace near Thurmont, Maryland. By permission of the Historic American Buildings Survey, Prints and Photographs Division, Library of Congress.

enslaved labor (fig. 2.2). A ramp or bridge went up a hill from a wagon road to the top of the furnace, where fillers filled—or charged—the furnace from the top with alternating layers of charcoal, ore, and limestone. The furnaces and forges were meant to be in blast for a few months at a time. Before the furnace could go into blast, colliers made hardwood chips of charcoal for fuel. The master miner "raised the mine." He drilled a hole into the iron-ore bed, packed the hole with black powder, and set it alight to break the ore loose. Miners loaded the ore into carts; they could raise a half-ton of ore per day. Wagoners moved the ore in carts to stockpiles near the furnace. The men moved between work as woodcutters or colliers and miners depending on the needs at the time. Air, or blast, furnaces had high chimneys, about thirty feet tall, for draft. Bellows operated by furnace keepers and powered by a waterwheel pushed "blasts" of air into the furnace to maintain a high temperature. The same process took place at the forge, where reheated pig iron was shaped into bars. Founders regulated the furnace. They made sand molds and cast molten iron in the casting house at the base of the furnace stack. Molten iron was tapped twice a day from the furnace to the casting house. The iron passed into a long sand trench, called a sow, and its side trenches, called pigs. Finers and hammermen pounded the reheated pig iron into bar iron using a five-hundred-pound forge hammer operated by a waterwheel. Over time, the furnace lining would burn out. When that happened, operations shut down while a new interior was built.

The scale of operations at the Baltimore Iron Works was enormous—the furnace required about five hundred fifty loads of charcoal and nine hundred tons of iron ore to run for five months. The result was an average of fifteen tons of pig iron per week.[27] The furnace at the Baltimore Iron Works, however, was in blast only half of each year, because the woodcutters, colliers, and miners did not, could not, or would not supply enough charcoal and iron to run the furnace more. Pacing their own work may explain the difference between Dr. Carroll's initial estimates for the necessary number of enslaved persons and the increasing number of workers held by the Baltimore Company. Ironwork and its support thus transformed black men and women with no experience in large-scale industrial work into laborers and craftspeople with the considerable knowledge and skill necessary both to participate in the Baltimore Company's program and to resist it. Telling the story of conditions surrounding the lives of enslaved craftsmen, families, and laborers enables people today to break apart the traditional emphasis on the Carrolls' business success through confronting the absence of blacks in the narrative.

Peopling the Baltimore Iron Works

Work projects on the Carrolls' plantations and the Baltimore Iron Works may have followed a pattern common in the mid-Atlantic, whereby enslaved blacks worked in gangs in a mixture of "New Negros" and more experienced slaves, rather than individually. In this system, overseers watched and goaded them to work. Sometimes an enslaved person was made foreman and received special privileges. Blacks were encouraged by enslavers to have families. The idea behind this was that families tied enslaved men to a place and, in turn, discouraged escapes and created workforce stability.

Blacks at the Baltimore Iron Works came from the partners' plantations or were purchased or hired from local slaveholders. Each partner contributed "six able hands," meaning enslaved persons, at the outset to clear wood. Seven blacks enslaved by Dr. Carroll went to the ironworks in 1731–32. The partners purchased "negroes" beginning in May 1732 at the cost of £20 apiece. By December each company owner was supposed to contribute thirteen enslaved persons.[28] If all five partners contributed their quota, the enslaved population would have more than doubled in size from thirty in 1731–32 to sixty-five by the winter of 1732–33. Company records, however, show that forty-three enslaved persons worked at the ironworks in 1734. An additional thirty-eight white employees and additional seasonal laborers worked with them.[29]

According to Dr. Carroll's plan, each partner placed between seven and fifteen enslaved blacks at the ironworks at the beginning of a given year to work for nine years, eleven months. Over the course of a year, the number of new enslaved persons diminished, as did their term. By the end of the year, one new enslaved person would be introduced to work one year, four months, and twenty-one days.[30] Dr. Carroll placed seven men and one woman into service on March 1, 1731, to work nine years, eleven months. Four more individuals went on June 20, 1732, to work four years, five months, and fourteen days. No records after 1733 remain to show if the system was refreshed with new people.[31] The Baltimore Company partners may have cycled enslaved workers between the ironworks and their private property, where the work was not as strenuous.

Blacks at the Baltimore Iron Works were inventoried by name in 1733 and 1734 (Table 2.1). The enslaved population in 1733 included twenty-six people placed at the ironworks by all the partners. They were (illegible names indicated by "or"): Hart, Tom, James Lesser or Larson, James, May, Coffe, Peter, Cesar, Johny, Bath or Bash or Bush, Captain, Joe, Mundays Betty, Harrys Betty, Harry, Sampson, Tom, Toms Bess, Jemy or Jerry, Jack, Frank, Calibay, Toby, Dick, Valentine, and Flora.[32] The 1734 inventory lists thirty-four people, which included almost all the names on the 1733 list, plus several new workers. Jack was a blacksmith. The miners at Gorsuch Bank were Colonell, Bush, Guilamalew (?), Coffee, Cezar, Jack, James, and Nero. Hanna cooked for them. Dick Junior, Dick Senior, and Hannah were

Table 2.1. Comparison of enslaved workers at the Baltimore Iron Works from 1733–1734 inventories, showing remaining and new individuals

1733	1734
Hart	Hart, collier at Howards Bank
Tom	Tom, collier at Howards Bank
James Lesser (Larson?)	James, collier at Howards Bank?
James (C)	James, miner at Gorsuch Bank?
May	Man?, collier at Howards Bank
Coffe (C)	Coffee, either miner at Gorsuch Bank or collier at Howards Bank
Peter	Peter, woodcutter
Cesar	Cezar, either a miner or a collier at Gorsuch Bank
Johny	Johny, working boy
Bath or Bash or Bush (C)	Bush, miner at Gorsuch Bank
Captain (C)	Captain, woodcutter
Joe	Joe, woodcutter
Mundays Betty	Betty, colliers' cook at Howards Bank?
Harrys Betty (C)	Betty, cook at upper house?
Harry (C)	Harry, woodcutter
Sampson	Sampson, woodcutter
Tom	Tom, collier Howards Bank? Or Tom, carpenter at Gorsuch Plantation?
Toms Bess	
Jemy or Jerry	
Jack (C)	Jack, either a blacksmith or miner at Gorsuch Bank
Frank	Frank, miner at Howards Bank
Calibay	Calebay, miner at Howards Bank
Toby	Toby, collier at Howards Bank
Dick (C)	Dick Jr. or Dick Sr., woodcutter at Gorsuch Plantation
Valentine	
Flora	Flora, cook at lower house
Caine (C)	
Hannah (C)	Hannah, cook for Gorsuch Bank miners or Hannah, occupation unknown
	Colonell, miner at Gorsuch Bank
	Guilamalew, miner at Gorsuch Bank
	Nero, miner at Gorsuch Bank
	Nephew, miner at Howards Bank
	Quame, miner at Howards Bank
	Qua, miner at Howards Bank
	Lucy, cook for miners at Howards Bank
	Charles, collier at Howards Bank
	Poplar Rom, collier at Howards Bank
	Philip, collier at Howards Bank

Note: Individuals enslaved by the Carrolls in 1733 are denoted by (C).

at Gorsuch Plantation. Their roles were not specified, but Tom was the carpenter. Nephew, Frank, Quame, Qua, and Calebay were miners at one part of Howards Bank, and Lucy was the cook. At another part of Howards Bank were the colliers Hart, Coffe, James, Charles, Tom, Man, Poplar Rom, Toby, Philip, Cezar, and Betty, their cook; woodcutters included Harry, Peter, Jo, Sampson, Valentine, Captaine, plus Negro Ross the basket maker and Bendax and Francie the cook, plus Peter, who was a hired slave. Flora was a cook at the lower house, Betty was a cook at the upper house, and John was a working boy.[33] Thirty-nine people were enslaved at the Baltimore Iron Works in 1736.[34] Forty-two enslaved people over age sixteen and forty-three hired white men worked at the ironworks by 1737 as part of a ninety-six-person workforce.[35] An undated inventory of who worked where indicated that Dr. Carroll owned only four enslaved workers at the complex: Jemmy was a smith at the furnace, Tom's and Tony's positions are not specified, and Guy was a forge carpenter.[36]

Enslaved persons at the ironworks were themselves supported by others enslaved by the Carrolls and their partners. Twelve people lived on Georgia in 1737: eight unnamed enslaved persons, plus Moses Maccubbins, Alexander Drummer, Jacob Lewis, and Barty Fuller.[37] Their main job was to cut cords of wood for the Baltimore Iron Works, for which Dr. Carroll was credited in financial accounts.[38] At the same time, nine enslaved people and William Lewis lived on The Caves.[39] Enslaved workers at Georgia and The Caves felled trees and moved timber by water to the landings; harvested hundreds of bushels of corn and wheat each year; and tended pigs and processed the meat used to feed ironworkers.[40] Baltimore Company records show that enslaved women were cooks for the ironworks. They worked with rations of corn, salted pork, beef, and molasses to feed workers and their families, some of whom came from The Caves and Georgia.[41] Together, twenty-one enslaved blacks provided support for the laborers at the Baltimore Iron Works on Dr. Carroll's behalf. In these ways, Dr. Carroll used slavery to create a chain of supply wherein enslaved blacks produced supplies to support others.

With a workforce in place, the Baltimore Iron Works furnaces were in blast by November 1734. The thousands of tons of pig iron sent overseas was a direct result of enslaved labor; the first shipment included 292 tons.

The Baltimore Company shipped almost 2,000 tons of iron to England by 1738. Between 1734 and 1737, 20 percent of Maryland's and Virginia's output and 20 percent of the total iron went from the colonies to England.[42] Later, British merchants also handled the sale of enslaved persons and the indenture of convicts to the Baltimore Company's partners. The partners shipped 500 tons of pig iron per year to England by the early 1750s. Dr. Carroll's exports of iron to England totaled 245 tons in 1750–1752. Each partner's income was about £400 sterling per year, and each fifth share was worth £10,000, or about $1,934,476 in 2008 dollars. In 1770, a tenth share was worth £7,000, or $1,139,824. The operation included a furnace, three forges, tracts of land, indentured and hired servants, slaves, horses, cattle, and other flocks, as well as thousands of acres of land rich in ore and timber.[43]

Health at the Ironworks

Of all the value placed on property, the health of enslaved workers proved extremely important, because their able bodies were key to production. Although health was a major concern of slaveholders, blacks themselves used medicine to assert control over their own bodies even as Europeans applied their medical practices to them. They treated themselves with plants, roots, charms, and ceremonies, and employed other practices they had carried with them to the New World.[44] Enslaved persons at the Baltimore Iron Works received medical attention from European doctors for various ailments, including blisters, dysentery, illnesses of "New Negroes" during their transition period in America, digestive problems, skin ulcers, and venereal disease.[45] Such ailments directly resulted from the extremely hard labor, poor nutrition, lack of warm housing, and meager living conditions to which Dr. Carroll and the Baltimore Company subjected them.

No human remains associated with the Baltimore Iron Works have been located, but comparative evidence regarding health comes from another ironworks and the Carroll family. Skeletal remains of first- and second-generation West Africans at Catoctin Furnace in Frederick County, Maryland, show signs of fracture, stress injury, arthritic breakdown of neck joints, rickets, softened bones, stunted growth, poor teeth, and infection due to malnutrition and hard labor. The average age at death was between

36.7 and 41.7 for men and 33.1 and 35.25 for women.[46] The Carrolls' bones, in contrast, reflect a less physically taxing way of life. Dr. Carroll remained relatively robust, except for his arthritis, until his death at age sixty-four. The bones of his son Charles Carroll the Barrister show evidence of anemia, possibly as a result of malaria, and arthritis at his death at age sixty. The doctor's younger son, John Henry Carroll, died at age twenty-two. His bones suggest pneumonia and/or pleurisy as the cause of his death. The Barrister's wife Margaret's bones show no malady.[47]

Although ironworkers may have received medical care from Dr. Carroll, no regular doctor attended to the Baltimore Company's enslaved blacks and servants. Health was immediately an issue: one of Dr. Carroll's seven enslaved persons replaced a man named Billy who died in August 1731.[48] Manager C. Daniell wrote in October 1734 about the "death of a negro man called Nero, he was ailing about three days complaining of a pain in his breast, his wife is very much out of order, Jack the Smith and favor of all other of the negroes also, I hope they will do well, a line from you to the doctor to make more frequent visits would be of service."[49] Several enslaved persons fell ill in December 1734 with violent pleurisy. Hazzard and Coffee died. Colonell recovered, but his wife Hannah did not. Harry, Man, and Poplar also got better. One white worker also died.[50] At the same time, Jemy complained of knee pain and took off work due to a cold. The winter of 1737 brought the deaths of Dick, Long Jamy, Short Jamy, Quamey, and Robin, as well as two white servants.[51] A doctor attended to Dick in early August 1737, but he also died.[52] Although feigned illness was one mode of resistance, wintertime at the Baltimore Iron Works demonstrated the very real risk of sickness. The power of enslaved persons' deaths lay in the pressure they placed on the Baltimore Company to keep them alive and relatively well to ensure that production continued.

Resistance and Freedom

Blacks at the Baltimore Iron Works resisted by temporary or permanent escape, work pacing, feigning illness, and refusal in large numbers to work after a traumatic event. Ronald Lewis argues that the daily operation of iron industries constituted a three-way system "founded less on brute force than on forced compromise."[53] Blacks pushed authority enough to receive advantages and gain space within acceptable bounds; employers yielded without losing control altogether; and slaveholders worked to protect and profit from their property.

On the one hand, Baltimore Iron Works managers expected the laborers to obey three major tenets of the American labor system: follow orders, be productive, and stay in place. On the other hand, the laborers used their knowledge of how the American labor system worked to resist their managers and enslavers. Baltimore Company records note the high demand but short supply of slaves, the risks of working or punishing slaves beyond certain limits, and the centrality of laborers' attendance and skill to productivity. If the managers and owners knew these things, their laborers must have, too. James Pennington (1807–1870), a first-rate blacksmith on a nineteenth-century agricultural plantation in western Maryland, wrote of his escape, "I had always aimed to be trustworthy; and feeling a high degree of mechanical pride, I had aimed to do my work with dispatch and skill, my blacksmith's pride and taste was one thing that had reconciled me so long to remain a slave."[54] Enslaved laborers worked the system to their advantage for self-preservation, to maintain dignity within themselves and their communities, and to resist the effects of racism.

One tactic of resistance was simply refusing to work, which led to Dr. Carroll's distrust of the workforce and his encouragement of disciplinary action. He wrote in 1732 that "We have two negros here perfectly useless and only a [burden], to wit one of those bought by you of Woodward and that boy of Mr Dulanys which was with the Smith, and if Mr Dulany will not change him he must be sold and so must the other . . . I find that in common things none here are to be trusted without a watchfull [sic] Eye & Strict hand."[55] Beatings, shackles, and collars enforced managers' decisions about who should work where, and with whom, if enslaved laborers disagreed. Movement during off days could also be curtailed. After one incident, Stephen Onion, the ironworks manager during the 1730s, ordered the "Overseers to let none of the Hands under their care go abroad on Sundays."[56] Physical punishment and a lack of control over one's everyday life proved to be tipping points for escape.

When laborers had had enough and escaped, Dr. Carroll and the Baltimore Company had several tactics for retrieving them. One was to place advertisements in local papers. By the 1750s, the company partners expanded their advertisements to the Pennsylvania newspapers, suggesting that escaped persons were heading north rather than staying in the Baltimore region. For example, an advertisement in a Pennsylvania newspaper in 1754 sought Caesar, "a New-Negro man, about 25 years of age, very tall, and can speak but very few words of English."[57] If any women escaped, the partners did not pursue them through placing newspaper advertisements. Dr. Carroll also paid agents to find black runaways and report their locations.[58] Another tactic was to torture enslaved persons who remained at the ironworks for information. Richard Croxall wrote in 1748 that "Doc. Carroll's negro has been well corrected but confesses no more than before, have set up advertisements about the house where you ordered."[59] Other times, blacks accompanied the company managers to retrieve escaped men, such as when Stephen Onion sent "Negro Johny" with Richard Croxall to retrieve a white man.[60] The partners placed a higher bounty on escaped whites than blacks.[61] Blacks and European laborers also escaped together. For instance, a nineteen-year-old mulatto man named Ben fled with two white convict men in May 1764.[62] Such collaboration suggested that the collective resistance of adversity sometimes broke down racial barriers between ironworkers.

Overwork was one way that enslaved persons supported themselves. The Baltimore Company supplied cheap cloth, buttons, hats, nails, sugar, molasses, rum, and salt from England.[63] Such items were provided along with daily food rations and supplies, but they also stocked the company store. Laborers who worked additional time through overwork, a common practice on Chesapeake-region iron plantations, earned credit at the company store, where they might buy furniture, clothing and shoes, bedclothes, and other items. Lewis writes, "The overwork system was intended to make the industrial slave a disciplined and productive worker by merging his physical and economic interests with those of the ironmaster. In turn, this would reduce the need for physical coercion, which would do more harm than good to the ironmaster's aim of producing as much iron as possible."[64] Inventories from the Baltimore Iron Works show the items purchased by blacks through overwork, such as Scipio's blanket or the crocus bed, two blankets, and rug shared by Captain and his wife, Flora, and their two children. Nephew the basket maker had a tomahawk, a knife, and a wedge. Sampson and Nephew shared a crocus bed and two blankets.[65] There is no indication that overwork led to cash in hand for blacks or that it provided opportunities to purchase freedom.

Rations and overwork, however, never did provide enough supplies or food for the workers. In fact, the poor conditions at the Baltimore Iron Works may have spurred theft so that men could support themselves and their families when their enslavers gave too little to sustain their lives or those of their families with substance or dignity. Evidence of this is shown in the spring of 1771, when an indentured servant named Thomas Plivy and an enslaved man called Anthony were jailed for robbing a store. The goods were found in their possession. William Hammond was dismayed. Anthony was the smith, and Hammond wrote, "we shall feel the loss of Anthony's time very much, I cannot tell how we can carry on the Forge business without him."[66] Although overwork aimed to conform laborers more closely to American labor, it was not necessarily enough to prevent enslaved persons from rebelling when the need became dire.

Slavery and the Carroll Empire

The enslavement of blacks was key to Dr. Carroll's vision of a network of iron and agricultural plantations even beyond the Baltimore Iron Works to form a diversified investment scheme. He wrote to his son Charles in 1753 that, "If such a work was to be gone upon by any other Person not possessed as I am of the situations servants slaves and other suitable Necessaries, it is not the sum of three times seven hundred pounds and for five years that would enable him to purchase land erect and carry on a furnace and forge and bring in the bar iron by land carriage the distance I mention of mine."[67] Dr. Carroll aimed for his ironworks, mills, and fields across Baltimore County and western Maryland to be one big self-supporting system with slavery at the center of its operation.

Dr. Carroll took out writs of condemnation in 1744 for ironworks in eastern Baltimore on a branch off the Back River. The property was in the vicinity of Carrolls Island and was acquired at about the same time. Dr. Carroll sold the property to the Principio Company in September 1751 due to the "stringency of the times."[68] The colony was experiencing an economic downturn, but the particular circumstances surrounding the furnace complex are unclear. Dr. Carroll submitted an order in September 1746 to his

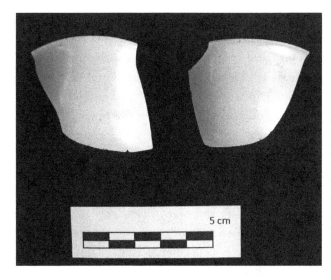

Figure 2.3. Stoneware teacup excavated at the Mount Clare kitchen, Mount Clare Archaeological Collection, Baltimore City Department of Parks and Recreation and the Carroll Park Foundation. Photo by author.

merchant in London for cloth, shoes, hats, construction tools, and other items. He canceled it a few months later.[69] The similarity of the order's contents to those for the Baltimore Company suggested that Dr. Carroll was planning to purchase enslaved blacks to labor at the Back River ironworks. Perhaps his inability to afford them—the lynchpin of the plan—scuttled the project altogether.

Dr. Carroll tried again in 1748. He took out a patent to build a furnace on Gwynns Falls opposite the Baltimore Iron Works furnace. It would be "a furnace for running pigg [sic] iron from the ore with a forge and mill and other conveniences agreeable to said art."[70] A memorandum in Dr. Carroll's papers outlined the kinds of buildings he planned for Georgia. He expected the complex to include a furnace "24 by 26 feet Square" and a "good framed house 50 feet long 20 feet wide, stack of chimneys with 4 fire places," "Ware house, Stables &c Kitchen," and "Cole houses & Corn Room."[71] Architectural historian Michael Trostel dated the list with building supplies ordered by Dr. Carroll at November 1749 and his comments on paying for the supplies at July 1751.[72] Dr. Carroll's plan, with its activity-specific buildings, domestic outbuildings located near the main house and basements, was typical for a Chesapeake plantation. Although his list does not mention them, Dr. Carroll may also have followed Chesapeake tradition by building separate living quarters for blacks and whites. Of additional note is that archaeologists recovered refined white salt-glazed teacups in layers pre-dating the later, permanent kitchens of Mount Clare. These delicate wares suggest that activities associated with the early development of Georgia were not all about construction and industry (fig. 2.3).

In January 1750, Dr. Carroll's partners in the Baltimore Company demanded that he tear down the furnace. They permitted him to run it only once more to recover some of the construction costs. Dr. Carroll then converted the site into a merchant mill. He settled his younger son, John Henry, in 1753 "at Patapsco to build a merchant mill there, and make it a center for my Business, to have Taylor shoemakers and other Supplys for my Quarters there under his Care and Management and allow him one moiety of any Profits."[73] Within a few months, John Henry was living in a "batchelor's house" and Dr. Carroll had commissioned the mill and a bake house to supply bread for ships.[74] While this makes it sound like he was setting up John Henry on Georgia, he may have been referring to another property. In 1753, Dr. Carroll gave him Floyds Adventure on Bodkin Creek at the southwestern coast of the mouth of Patapsco, and all the improvements thereon.[75]

The mill stood just north of modern Washington Avenue and was later known as the Mount Clare Mill. Another mill stood approximately a quarter mile above where Gwynns Run met Gwynns Falls. It was known as Millington Mill in the nineteenth century. Roads enabled carts laden with products to cross Georgia to market. A main road began at a ford at the Mount Clare millrace and ran northeasterly through swampy and low ground along Gwynns Falls until leveling out above the future site of the Mount Clare mansion to head east into Baltimore.[76] Enslaved laborers already on Georgia likely worked the furnace and then the mill. Dr. Carroll gave no indication that he acquired additional persons or that he anticipated financial trouble.

Dr. Carroll purchased property in Frederick County on the Monocacy River for a furnace, plus property in between it and Georgia for a forge and quarters, in the early 1750s. "[I]t would require my whole plantation at Patapsco," he wrote, "as two or three teams must be kept to bring in the bar iron there to be shipped and would so require other quarters where I have meadows and conveniences to keep teams at the force and the furnace [. . .]."[77] Enslaved persons who were knowledgeable craftspeople and laborers in ironworking and other tasks were integral to the scheme. Dr. Carroll indicated in a prospectus sent to his son Charles in London to drum up investors there,

> That the agent here be directed as soon as he can conveniently do it to get young Negro lads to put under the smiths carpenters founders tiners and fillers and also to get a certain number of able slaves to fill the furnace hoist the bridge raise ore and cart and burn the same. Woodcutters may for some time be hired there. There should be but two master colliers one at the furnace another at the forge with a suitable number of slaves or servants under each who might coal in the summer and cut wood in the winter.[78]

Although Dr. Carroll died in 1755 and Charles Carroll the Barrister did not pursue the western ironworks, Dr. Carroll's plans presaged major iron operations in western Maryland and their use of slavery. Among them were the Antietam Furnace (established 1761 on the west side of South Mountain), Mt. Aetna Furnace (on Antietam Furnace), Frederick Forge and Keep Trieste Furnace (established circa 1764 at the mouth of the Antietam Creek), Hampton Furnace (established circa 1765 near Emmitsburg), Green Spring Furnace (circa 1768, near Fort Frederick), and Catoctin Furnace (established 1744, north of Frederick).[79]

Today, Georgia, in the form of Mount Clare, is the best-preserved Carroll plantation, which obscures its historical relationship to the others. The Caves was the prize among the Carroll properties in Baltimore County for its ore deposits, limestone-rich land, location, buildings, and size. Blacks at The Caves grew tobacco; cared for cattle, horses, sheep, mares, and colts; and farmed the land for a mill located on the property. In 1749, Dr. Carroll gave The Caves to his elder son, Charles. The transfer of ownership included fifteen enslaved people, named Jack, Major, Will, Jenn, Pompey, Tom, Sam, Harry, Sabina, Pris, Debb, Bett, Mary, Nelly, and Jacky.[80] Only Sabina, Deb, and Nell may have remained there by 1773, while Tom and Will may have been sent to Mount Clare. Black farmers at The Caves may have been the only tobacco farmers across the Carroll properties. Dr. Carroll was not a tobacco planter by the 1750s, but he managed shipments from The Caves and commissioned a ship to rent to tobacco shippers.[81] In 1751, Dr. Carroll described Charles's holdings as "a seat of very good land here, and two good plantations with a dozen working hands."[82] Black farmers managed by two overseers grew tobacco that dried in two tobacco houses and a barn that was constructed in 1752. At the same time, they witnessed the fundamental shifts in plantation management in the 1750s as a result of fluctuating tobacco prices. They were pressed to work iron and farm grain as a result.[83]

In 1755, changes in the Carroll family reshaped tasks for blacks at Georgia. John Henry died intestate in 1754. After his son's death, Dr. Carroll evaluated his own and Charles's estates and wrote to him in England: "your own Estate in Lands Slaves & Stock is worth 2000ll Sterl and if exposed to Sale would bring the money if [Tobacco] bore a price and upon Valuation of my own Estate in Lands Slaves Debts by Bond Mortgages & other permanent Estate amounts to 10000ll Sterl. & 5000ll Current money wherein is included a List of Debts on Mortgages & Land Security 818ll Sterl & 400oll Current money."[84] An itemized list has not been preserved to the present day. Aubrey Land calculated that 3.9 percent of planters between 1750 and 1759 had estates valued above £1,000.[85] Dr. Carroll passed away in 1755, leaving Charles with thousands of acres of land, enslaved persons, and a warehouse and wharf in Annapolis.[86] Charles became one of the wealthiest men in the colony, due in large part to the empire created as a result of his father's embracing race as an organizing structure for society.

Industrial development in the nineteenth and especially the twentieth century obscured the place where the partners of the Baltimore Company set precedents for the iron industry through their extensive use of slavery. Nonetheless, its significance to colonial history lay in the precedents it set for scaling slavery to the iron industry. The Baltimore Company enslaved one hundred fifty people at the height of its operations in 1764, in addition to hiring wage employees and slaves from local whites. By 1785, when the partners began selling off the company, two hundred people were still enslaved.[87] Enslaved people conducted a broad, diverse, and interconnected set of tasks through hard labor and craftwork.

Although the significance of black history at the Baltimore Iron Works to the origin story of Mount Clare could be easily obscured, to do so does a disservice to people today by keeping them from learning about the conditions under which racism placed blacks in colonial life. While Europeans enforced the distinction between races that perpetuated slavery, they failed to destroy blacks' determination to shape lives for themselves in America that extended beyond their enslavers' constraints. Push-and-pull strategies enabled blacks to influence slavery and shape the American labor system. But such measures only went so far. Ultimately, blacks were unsuccessful in freeing themselves from Dr. Carroll and, as a result, produced a vast family fortune for Dr. Carroll that shaped the next stage of Georgia's history.

3

THE CREATION OF MOUNT CLARE

After Charles Carroll the Barrister inherited his father's estate, he set into motion a vision he had for a showpiece plantation at Georgia. Mount Clare, as the property became known, further became a place where the Carrolls reinforced racism and social inequality to support their own status and privilege. Within the mansion and in its vicinity, however, enslaved blacks and hired or elite whites interacted on a near-constant basis as the everyday business of domestic life took place. Despite the Carrolls' purchasing power and taste being more obvious than blacks' in the material and historical record, Mount Clare was a black place. Enslaved blacks were the majority population, and their knowledge and experience sustained the objects and landscapes of Mount Clare. As a result, the Carrolls' history at Mount Clare is inseparable from that of enslaved blacks. Remembering that fact through inclusive interpretations can demonstrate that historic plantations are places to reflect on past inequalities through preserved objects and sites, rather than places where racist attitudes continue to be reinforced. Part of what historic plantations can contribute to social justice is offering places at which people can learn about the roots of racism-based social inequality as a way to bring about change in society.

A starting point for the story of inequality at Mount Clare is how enslaved blacks came to be there, as well as the Carrolls' attitudes about them. In 1737, Dr. Carroll enslaved seventeen people between The Caves and Georgia, in addition to a few individuals at his Annapolis home. His son Charles, who called himself "The Barrister," inherited his father's estate in 1755 (fig. 3.1). Charles also inherited the blacks enslaved by Dr. Carroll upon his death in 1755, although the exact number is unknown. In 1756, Charles commissioned the mansion that, upon completion in 1760,

Figure 3.1. Charles Carroll, Barrister, painting by Charles Willson Peale, 1770. By permission of the Collection of the National Society of Colonial Dames of America in the State of Maryland, Mount Clare Museum House.

he called "Mount Clare" or "the Mount." In the fall of 1760, Charles brought servants or slaves from his Annapolis house to Mount Clare to join the laborers already living there. When Charles married Margaret Tilghman in 1763, her dowry included enslaved persons, whom she had inherited from a relative. Unlike Charles, who could decide where to live and shape his

Figure 3.2. Margaret Tilghman Carroll, painting by Charles Willson Peale, 1775. By permission of the Collection of the National Society of Colonial Dames of America in the State of Maryland, Mount Clare Museum House.

circumstances through wealth and marriage, enslaved persons did not have the freedom to choose. Major events in white elites' lives—such as moving into a new home, or getting married—meant that enslaved persons were relocated from their homes and separated from their families and communities.

Margaret Tilghman grew up in Talbot County on Maryland's eastern shore in a wealthy slaveholding family (fig. 3.2). Within this environment, slavery was a seemingly natural part of maintaining the social order. Margaret's family passed enslaved blacks through generations to build wealth. Margaret's father, Matthew Tilghman, inherited Bay Side (now known as Rich Neck Manor) and approximately 104 people from his cousin and adoptive parent Matthew Tilghman Ward in 1741. Margaret Ward, Matthew Tilghman Ward's wife, enslaved thirty-seven people at the time of her death in 1746 (Table 3.1). She left them and the bulk of her estate to Matthew Tilghman's two young children, Margaret Tilghman and Matthew Ward Tilghman. Margaret Ward bequeathed to Margaret a seventeen-year-old mulatto girl named Eve.[1] This Eve may be "Old Eve" listed on Margaret's 1817 estate inventory. Margaret assumed the entire inheritance upon her brother's death in 1753, which made her a wealthy young woman. The enslaved people Margaret inherited became part of her dowry; at least some of them went to live at Mount Clare. Charles's order of nails and cloth from England showed a marked increase in 1763 compared to 1760, reflecting the larger size of the enslaved population on his properties and the need to house and clothe them. Margaret's siblings inherited the people still enslaved by her parents when they died in 1790 and 1794.[2] Thus, Margaret and Charles both became wealthier by leveraging their power to treat people as property.

Margaret and Charles wrote little about their attitudes toward slavery or the people they enslaved. Their actions spoke for them. The Carrolls did, however, complain when the people they enslaved were careless with their things. It is possible, however, that the kitchen cooks, farmers, gardeners, and grooms committed crimes on the Carrolls' property to undermine their enslavers. Charles specified in a 1760 order to England for the frame of a hand lantern to be "made strong and the glass well fixed in as our Negros see negligent in carrying them about of night."[3] He ordered a reinforced saddle for Margaret in 1764, because "our Servants here are Careless" and "our workers here are but bunglers at repairing."[4] He complained in a 1765 order that "I would have the Kitchen [roasting] Jack made of the Sort Least Liable to be out of order as our Negro Cooks and Servants are but Careless and Rough Handlers of any thing that may be Trusted to their Care."[5] Beginning in 1766, Charles requested the best of common work

Table 3.1. Enslaved persons listed in Margaret Tilghman Ward's estate inventory in 1747

Name	Age	Value
NEGROES AT GRASSES		
Sarah	an old woman	0
Abraham	24	50
Charles	22	50
Tom	19	50
Matthew	an old man	15
Jenny	25	45
Kate	30	45
Peg	5	20
Billey	2	10
Adam	an infant	5
NEGROES AT HOME PLANTATION (LAW HOUSE PLANTATION)		
Jemmy	54	5
Harry	28	60
Adam	24	50
Dick	35	50
Jo 34	50	
Ned	45	50
Jacob	13, 4'8" high	45
Soll	12, 4'10" high	45
Jere	12, 4'5" high	40
Ambrose	10, 4'3" high	38
Daniel		35
Phill	8, 4' high	30
Jem	5, 3'9" high	30
Rose	50	28
Peggy	45	40
Doll	28	50
Eve	17	50
Moll	10, 4'6" high	38
Ibby	60, gouty	5
Frank	58	20
Mabell	20	50
Beck	9, 4' high	30
Nan	9, 4'1" high	30
Jen	5, 3'3" high	25
Peg	3, 2'6" high	20
Rachel Cancer in Her Lip	18	35
Old Rachel		

tools: "1 Dozen best Scythes," "1 Dozen best Sickles," "6 good grind stones," "4 Best Curry Combs without Brushes."[6] Perhaps Charles believed that the best tools available would be more likely to last despite laborers' misuse.

Mount Clare became a place where the everyday interactions among the Carrolls, the people they enslaved, and white servants drew on past experiences with slavery and an understanding of its role in the future. Mount Clare was set up for slavery and enslaved blacks to be integrated into the entire property. From the built environment to the landscaped gardens, the tools of everyday life to the spaces in which they were used, Mount Clare emphasized the sharp divisions in the social order. Over time, when only the mansion was preserved, visitors' ability to interpret its relationship to the landscape and to enslaved people was disabled. In looking for black history in traditionally white interpretations, a more informed perspective is revealed about the truth of Mount Clare's role in racism and social inequality.

The Lay of the Land

In 1760, the layout of Mount Clare's mansion and outbuildings delineated where enslaved blacks or whites would work, play, live, and learn (fig. 3.3). A kitchen stood to the east of the mansion. Other landscape features likely included barns, a necessary house, a woodshed, quarters, a kitchen garden,

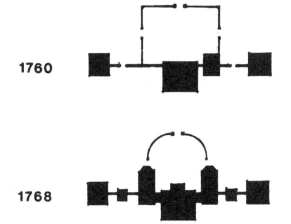

1760

1768

Figure 3.3. The layout of Mount Clare in 1760 and 1768. By permission of Michael F. Trostel, FAIA, Trostel & Pearre, Architects.

and a small orchard. Visitors and residents approached the mansion from the north side from the Frederick Turnpike, a main east-west road from Baltimore to Fredericktown. The south face of the mansion looked across a deep lawn to the Patapsco River beyond. Enslaved blacks were present across the entire plantation on a daily and visible basis.

Housing

Architecture throughout the mid-Atlantic region demonstrated the contrast in housing for enslaved persons and elites, as seen at mid-eighteenth-century plantations such as Northampton and Poplar Grove in Maryland and at Montpelier, Rich Neck, and Monticello in Virginia. The ways in which housing, such as mansions and slave quarters, was constructed represented the belief among the Carrolls and other elites that architecture should reinforce the distinctions between the enslaved and the enslaver. Architecture carved white-only or black-only spaces, or marked routes determined by whites but traveled by blacks.

By the mid-eighteenth century, slaveholders preferred to house blacks in a racially segregated area, the slave quarter, away from the main house. The slave quarter became a black place in the minds of enslaved persons and their enslavers.[7] Plantation owners lived in large, multi-roomed, two-story brick structures. Slave quarters, in contrast, consisted of one- or two-room timber structures, sometimes with a brick chimney, in which multiple activities overlapped in interior spaces and spilled into the yards. Enslaved blacks also slept in kitchens, basements, barns, and sheds in order to be close to their work.

Slave quarters tended to be less permanent structures than plantation owners' houses, both in terms of the durability of building materials and construction and their susceptibility to erasure from the landscape when attitudes about slavery changed over time. When no slave quarter on a plantation is preserved, such as at Mount Clare, the place's black history becomes less accessible, easier to erase, and, consequently, easier to avoid. Historical records may indicate the location of at least one quarter at the eastern end of the mansion complex; unfortunately, earthmoving in the twentieth century carved away its location. Even so, historical records documented characteristics of places where enslaved blacks lived at Mount

Clare. The 1798 tax assessment lists noted structures that were old at that time, but perhaps new in the 1760s. Among them were log and frame wooden structures for quarters, including one-story structures measuring between 16-by-11 feet and 32-by-22 feet. Likely locations for the houses included areas downhill to the east of the mansion, by the Mount Clare mill, and/or north of the Frederick-Baltimore road near the fields. The mansion at Mount Clare, contrary to the frame houses, was brick with plaster inside and large glass windows for ventilation and light. It had separate rooms for different purposes, such as a dining room and bedrooms. Differences in housing were physical manifestations of inequality.

Activity at the Baltimore Iron Works enabled Charles to finance additions to the mansion complex at Mount Clare. Iron production peaked in 1764, and the Baltimore Company sought additional workers to enslave in November 1766 and January 1767. The partners sought unskilled laborers to save money. They wanted twenty-four men between the ages of fifteen and twenty, who were well-seasoned "negroes" or American-born (also called "country born").[8] While it was important to get healthy workers who were acclimated to Chesapeake labor and disease, the partners also wanted to purchase workers cheaply. In August 1767, Charles Carroll of Annapolis suggested purchasing slaves in Virginia, where "young country born negroes" could be purchased "for cheap" at "£25 or 30 sterling." One co-owner cautioned against the plan "this side of winter," because "we shall probably have them all to cloath [sic] with goods bought here for it is very uncertain whether our goods will come in time from England." Charles the Barrister agreed to the plan if slaves could be bought for the terms quoted, thereby demonstrating ongoing support for slavery to sustain the ironworks industry. He authorized £200 of Baltimore Company money to purchase enslaved persons from merchants in London in September 1767.[9] The Carrolls' estimates may have been optimistic, especially for skilled workers or young men. By way of comparison, skilled persons enslaved by Principio were sold at an auction in 1785 for 5 shillings for those over age sixty, £62 for a forty-year-old collier, and £175 for a fourteen-year-old with unspecified knowledge.[10] Charles's strategic planning for increasing the enslaved workforce in a cost-effective way meant that his profits could be put toward sustaining his lifestyle.

Charles was evidently confident enough in his income sources to commission extensive renovations to the mansion at Mount Clare in the late 1760s (fig. 3.4). A reflection of Charles's social standing, the mansion's renovations broadened the impression of Mount Clare as a showpiece. The old kitchen was demolished to make way for a new, enlarged kitchen in the east wing. Additional domestic buildings, including a washhouse, were built in a line east of the mansion. Hyphens were built to connect the mansion to Charles's office in the new west wing and the kitchen in the renovated east wing. The kitchen and office buildings framed a new courtyard or forecourt, which was the main entrance to the mansion, to the north side of the mansion. A bowling green extended along the south side of the mansion. In 1760, Charles ordered bowls and tacks for bowling; perhaps the scythes or sickles purchased at the same time were intended for enslaved persons to maintain the green.[11] Notably, however, eighteenth-century artifacts were archaeologically absent from both the forecourt and the bowling green. The lack of debris suggested that, unlike other areas surrounding the mansion, these areas were for single purposes, such as receiving visitors or recreation, but not for enslaved persons' everyday domestic work. In effect, the forecourt and bowling green were not places where enslaved blacks were visible, unless they were accompanied by the Carrolls or other elite whites.

For enslaved persons' public appearances, Charles purchased cloth and clothing for them in order for them to portray certain roles or functions within the new spaces. While the roles and costumes ultimately reinforced Charles's elite image, cloth and clothing was also meaningful to the enslaved community. Uniforms worn by the butler, maid, and personal valet reflected the wealth of the person served, rather than the slave.[12] Frederick Douglass observed that blacks who worked in the house "constituted a sort of black aristocracy" in their health, dress, and manner.[13] Blacks who worked inside Mount Clare or appeared alongside the Carrolls in public received uniforms of better quality and more colorful cloth than enslaved persons working in the fields or mills. Charles ordered fabric from London for such uniforms. Livery uniforms were made of ticking or coarse fustian (both sturdy cotton or cotton/linen fabrics) lined in scarlet shalloon (a type of twill), with scarlet twist trim. Livery and butler coats might have come from "colored kersey with trimmings."[14] Charles's order for six pairs of men's strong thread stockings, three pairs of boys' thread stockings, and one dozen pairs of women's blue yarn hose may have clad butlers,

Figure 3.4. Mount Clare, painting by Charles Willson Peale, 1775. By permission of the Frick Art Reference Library.

Figure 3.5. Quartz crystal excavated at the 1767 kitchen doorway, Mount Clare Archaeological Collection, Baltimore City Department of Parks and Recreation and the Carroll Park Foundation. Photo by author.

housekeepers, liverymen, cooks, and jockeys.[15] Archaeology at Carroll Park recovered the flat brass buttons ordered from London only in the area immediately surrounding the mansion. Their location indicated that blacks working as liverymen or butlers wore more formal clothes than gardeners, and that they only wore these costumes in the mansion's vicinity.

The East Wing

One substantial expansion that affected enslaved blacks took place in the east wing. Today, much of the east wing's foundation has been destroyed due to earthmoving to create Carroll Park in the late nineteenth and early twentieth century. Visitors see a smaller structure on the site of the old kitchen, as well as a cement outline of the old kitchen as documented by archaeological investigations. Less apparent, however, is the impact of enslaved people on everyday activities in the kitchen and the ways that the Carrolls' renovations affected them. The expansions and increased capacity for domestic labor in the east wing had immediate effects on the enslaved persons who maintained the Carroll household.

The east wing at Mount Clare expanded substantially in the late 1760s as the domestic epicenter. A two-story, two-room brick kitchen was built in the east wing by 1767.[16] Similar kitchens on other southern plantations included living space for enslaved persons. Perhaps kitchen staff at Mount Clare likewise lived in one of the rooms or up above. A new passage into the house kept kitchen and serving staff from going outdoors to deliver food and retrieve dishes. It also made slavery less visible. The Carrolls hired a female European servant from their London merchants to oversee "Cooking Pickling Preserving and the other Requisites for a House keeper" and, presumably, enslaved kitchen workers.[17] Margaret supervised her and the kitchen operations, a common role for the plantation mistress. Her familiarity with the processes of cooking everyday and fancy dishes is shown in her step-by-step recipe book.[18] Enslaved cooks interacted with white servants and Margaret on a regular basis as they went about their work.

Sometime after the brick kitchen was completed circa 1767, a clear, colorless quartz crystal about four inches across was buried at the doorway between the northern and southern rooms (fig. 3.5). The crystal had been heavily reworked or reshaped. Archaeologists who excavated the kitchen in 1986 saw the crystal as an oddity and catalogued it as a rock. Archaeologist George Logan, drawing on his knowledge of caches buried by people enslaved in Annapolis, recognized its significance in 1995. He believed that the crystal had been intentionally buried near a corner of an earlier timber structure.[19] The burial, or cache, also contained one small sherd of a Chinese export porcelain tea bowl, a plain buff-glazed refined stoneware tea bowl, and a press-molded colorless glass vessel, as well as wrought iron nails (fig. 3.6).

Unlike caches at other locations where nails and ceramics have been found, the artifacts in this case may not have been intentionally chosen or included with the crystal. The distinction is important because of the symbolic value interpreted by archaeologists from artifacts found as a group in other caches. Analysis of the stratigraphy of the site indicates a chronology that does not support the ceramics, nails, and glass as intentional inclusions. In the kitchen, postholes marked a wall and either the northeast or northwest corner for the earlier timber structure. The postholes were filled when the structure was demolished. Large pieces of the two tea bowls and glassware found with the crystal, plus another Chinese-export porcelain

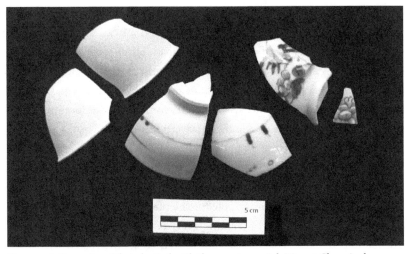

Figure 3.6. Ceramic artifacts buried with the quartz crystal, Mount Clare Archaeological Collection, Baltimore City Department of Parks and Recreation and the Carroll Park Foundation. Photo by author.

tea bowl in a different pattern, were pushed with dirt fill into the holes. The construction of the new kitchen both sealed evidence of the earlier structure in place and dated the artifacts to pre-1767. Furthermore, the stratigraphic sequence of the burial was opposite the postholes. The stoneware teacup appeared in the top layers of the postholes, but it is found in the bottom of the hole containing the crystal. This suggests that soil associated with the top layer of the postholes became the bottom layer of the hole for the crystal. Thus, once the new kitchen was completed, someone removed the flooring in the doorway, made a hole, and placed the crystal in it, and a few scattered artifacts from the earlier period were unintentionally pushed in.

The crystal at Mount Clare contributes to a body of evidence in Maryland that enslaved persons buried materials with symbolic, traditional significance in their work and living spaces. Archaeological finds in Annapolis were particularly relevant to Mount Clare because Charles took enslaved domestic laborers there from his Annapolis house. Perhaps they took cultural traditions with them. Elsewhere in Annapolis, caches dating to 1790–1820 were found in a ground-floor workspace in the east wing of Charles Carroll of Carrollton's house. They were buried between two entryways in the northeast corners.[20] Other caches in Annapolis were recovered from the Slayton House, Maynard House, and Brice House. Caches dating to the mid-nineteenth century have been recovered at the James Brice House in the east wing at a doorway between a kitchen and laundry.[21] Caches have also been found throughout the United States beyond the Chesapeake, such as at the Levi-Jordan plantation in east Brazoria, Texas, and Andrew Jackson's nineteenth-century plantation, the Hermitage, in Tennessee. Together, the caches demonstrate that African traditions moved with blacks as slavery spread.

Comparison of the Mount Clare crystal with caches from Annapolis to African and West Indian traditions suggest its meaning to the person who buried it. The assemblages in Annapolis were similar to African Bakongo *mnkisi* (the plural form of *nkisi*). The Bakongo are from western-central Africa, or the Bight of Biafra, which today includes Cameroon, Gabon, Congo, Angola, and Zaire. Half of the African population in Maryland and Virginia originated in the Bight of Biafra, and people also came from the Gold Coast, Senegambia, and other places.[22] The caches may also point to the Igbo of southeastern Nigeria, on the basis of slave trade patterns from Africa to Virginia, ethnographic studies, and material culture analysis. Some Sierra Leone tribes placed transparent objects above or below entryways as a symbol of ancestral protection over those who walked through.

Caches in America demonstrate the use of *mnkisi* by enslaved West Africans in America, who believed that good fortune and misfortune resulted from humans manipulating spirits. Scholars tend to agree on four general points: first, the caches were created intentionally by blacks; second, they represent homeland traditions practiced in America; third, they consist of available materials appropriated from European American contexts and refashioned for a black spiritual purpose; and fourth, the practices respond to situations taking place in America, like slavery, that also have broad humanistic precedents, such as the need to be protected.[23] Crystals drew on the power of ancestors' spirits to wield control and influence. Burying crystals activated charms or protected them from unauthorized uses. An estimated 83 percent of charms that can be found archaeologically were worn on the body and 17 percent put in the ground.[24] They tended to be found in corners, thresholds, and hearths or arranged across a space in a cosmogram. Caches included common objects, like buttons, ceramics, pins, wire, and nails, appropriated from European American culture. Crystals were more

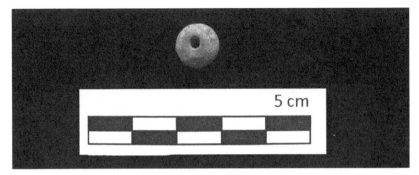

Figure 3.7. Bone bead excavated at the Mount Clare kitchen, Mount Clare Archaeological Collection, Baltimore City Department of Parks and Recreation and the Carroll Park Foundation. Photo by author.

unusual, especially ones the size of the one found at Mount Clare. Organic
or degradable items, such as spices, fabric, or urine, were lost archaeologically. Such items had multivalent properties in that they meant only one
thing to Europeans in America but at least two to enslaved persons: their
value to enslavers and their appropriated significance as spiritual symbols.
Perhaps a cook at Mount Clare buried the crystal to activate its powers of
protection over kitchen laborers against Margaret and her hired servants.

Not all Africans in America practiced these traditions, and the range of
reactions from whites—both in the past and the present—have included
bemusement, fear, and dismissal. Christianized blacks considered conjura-
tion to be a hoax but accepted the validity of associated practices, such as
dreams, visions, and medicines.[25] At Mount Clare, the burial of the crystal
suggested that the Carrolls' Episcopalian affiliation did not displace or over-
power blacks' spiritual beliefs. Beyond Mount Clare, caches found across
the United States have been controversial among scholars, some of whom
have used racist language. Some archaeologists have interpreted their contents as gaming pieces, objects collected and buried by children or rodents,
or as curios. They believe that the caches were accidental and meaning-
less, rather than intentional and purposeful. Those who have doubted the
caches' significance have also felt that too little evidence remained at each
site to explain an African spiritual connection.[26] The preponderance of
evidence today shows that spiritual traditions were perpetuated in black
identities in America, and the appropriation of European American material culture marked the resilience of the traditions.

A bone bead recovered archaeologically from the kitchen may represent another African tradition at Mount Clare (fig. 3.7). Beads in Africa adorned the body and hair as jewelry, as well as ceremonial and everyday clothing. They conveyed social and symbolic meanings about wealth, marital status, and affiliation, and rites of passage, myths, and religious groups. Charms and amulets worn on the body included beads to protect and empower the wearer. Glass beads are often recovered from sites identified with enslaved blacks, as are beads made from bone, ivory, clay, and other materials. No glass beads appear in the Mount Clare artifact assemblage until the mid-nineteenth century, after slavery had ended there. The material and construction of the bone bead suggests that it was made in America from available materials. It raises many questions: Why are no glass beads found at Mount Clare? Could the bone bead represent a generation removed from the transatlantic trade or isolated from African American trade channels in the New World? Does it suggest the inability to participate as consumers in the American economy due to geographic location, cultural isolation, or from not being permitted to overwork or be hired out? Were black cooks after the 1760s practicing homeland traditions, or are there no other beads in the archaeological record simply because none were lost? If the bone bead at the mansion kitchen does represent African homeland culture in America, it suggests two things: first, that the origin or material of a bead was less important than the cultural practices that beads supported, and second, that the role of beads was too significant to abandon.

The persons associated with the crystal and bead may have also witnessed and been involved in the merging of blacks' and European Americans' foodways at the Mount Clare kitchen. The gentry's integration of African ingredients into their meals marked a merging of two cultures in America. Africans brought the knowledge of how to cook and work with food with them to the colonies, but they also used this knowledge to assert influence over their enslavers. Enslaved blacks asserted a collective racial and cultural identity by using available ingredients to reproduce traditional practices. Perhaps rather than viewing food as a way in which Africans were acculturated to America, Africans made foods the way they thought they should be made. Many Europeans who spent time in Barbados, Jamaica, and Antigua acquired a taste for the spicy, African-based food of the Caribbean. Black cooks learned to cook European American dishes that used African or Caribbean ingredients.[27] Charles, for instance, began ordering mace, cinnamon, nutmeg, and cloves only after he and Margaret married.[28] One of Margaret's favorite recipes was a turtle of calf's head: a concoction of tripe, head, feet, tongue, and heart heavily spiced with mace, cayenne pepper, black pepper, and onions. The recipe and its ingredients were popular in the eighteenth century and may reflect the influence of African-inspired cooking on her table. Millet and buckwheat, foods with African associations, were found archaeologically in the kitchen. They may have been ground into flour and made into bread, or used in their un-ground form in dishes. Maryland, unlike the Carolinas and Georgia, did not depend on rice as a food staple. Margaret's recipes instead reflected a creolized French/American cooking style with rice in desserts, rather than the appearance of African dishes on an American table. Rice was fed to invalids, however, such as Abraham in 1809 at The Caves, and baked into treats like pudding and waffles. Rice and coconut are other African or Caribbean foods that mark the broad influence of transatlantic slavery on American kitchens.

In turn, Margaret's recipe book demonstrates the kinds of European and European American dishes that black cooks learned to make. Peaches from the orchard were made into peach cordial and currants into wine. Baked goods included muffin bread, lemon cheesecake made with lemons from the greenhouse, puddings and waffles made with rice; cheesecakes and puddings made with almonds, butter, eggs, bread, and wheat flour; and macaroons.[29] In these ways, the kitchen built during the 1767 expansion of Mount Clare was a place where enslaved blacks and elite whites exchanged cultural knowledge about food, but where enslaved persons may also have practiced their traditions in secret.

Beyond cooking and food preparation, the kitchen hearths were also used for dyeing clothes. Dyer's woad and fig blue dye were used at Mount Clare to color cloth.[30] Blue was a common color worn by enslaved persons starting in the mid-seventeenth century on Chesapeake plantations to differentiate the status of servants and slaves. Home production of woad and indigo supported the color scheme. People who worked in the fields were more likely to wear colorless or undyed clothing.[31] In Charles's orders to London, he usually ordered blue-colored clothing, such as stockings, coat cloth, and bandanas. Dyers in the Mount Clare kitchen also used pokeberry

Figure 3.8. Rib bone with button punched out excavated at the Mount Clare orangery, Mount Clare Archaeological Collection, Baltimore City Department of Parks and Recreation and the Carroll Park Foundation. Photo by author.

and sorrel to make red or purple dye, as well as yarrow, St. John's wort, pear, and lamb's quarters for yellow.[32]

Maintenance of cloth and clothing took place at the washhouse next to the kitchen. Women washed linens and underclothes, a laborious and never-ending sequence of soaking, scrubbing, bucking (a bleaching process using lye from ashes), stain removal, beating, drying, and ironing. Outer clothes, such as gowns, were spot-cleaned or professionally laundered on a more infrequent basis.[33] Archaeology showed that not all activities associated with clothing maintenance took place in the east wing. Although the washhouse was in the east wing, the water pump stood at the west wing. Near it were archaeological concentrations of buttons, pins, and sewing notions in between the orangery and a shed that may have housed its caretakers. The buttons range from center-hole bone discs to four- or five-hole bone buttons to flat metal to glass and porcelain. Launderers may also have made buttons by punching holes in a rib bone, as indicated by one found in the orangery's vicinity (fig. 3.8). Thus, it appeared that washing, sewing, button making, and clothing repair were conducted between the orangery and the office until the west wing was demolished in 1870.

The West Wing: the Office and the Orangery

Whereas the east wing was dedicated to domestic tasks, the west wing underscored the Carrolls' business and political activity and wealth. It included an office for Charles, a shed, and a greenhouse, or orangery. A pinery—a specialized hothouse for pineapples—was under way in 1770. All these places represented either the everyday work of enslaved blacks or the work conducted by Charles to maintain slavery.

The construction of greenhouses reflected the intensification of garden activities at Mount Clare that began in the spring and summer circa 1765. Margaret oversaw the gardens surrounding the mansion. She placed orders through Charles to England for seeds and cuttings. A nineteenth-century writer calculated the western garden as being three hundred feet square.[34] Over the course of each year, blacks planted, weeded rows, pruned, repotted plants, transplanted, divided, and weatherized the plants and trees.

Enslaved persons commonly worked in the ornamental gardens of elite whites. Charles Ball, who wrote extensively on his life while enslaved at another plantation, noted that the gardener where he lived received help from up to a dozen enslaved men and boys in the summer.[35] Likewise, Rosalie Stier Calvert, mistress of Riversdale Mansion in modern Riversdale, Maryland, was assisted by enslaved persons and a hired gardener to do hard labor in her garden.[36] Notably, however, enslaved persons worked for no pay, even though their enslavers might hire and pay white gardeners who generally had similar knowledge of gardening. At Mount Clare, a European gardener hired in 1774 made £25 per year.[37] Despite having similar levels of expertise, whites were paid for their work and blacks were not; the payment of salary quantified the racial and status differences between whites and enslaved blacks.

The inequality of pay extended to the unfairness of who was credited for the gardens. Visitors to the Mount Clare grounds admired the Carrolls, who afforded the gardens, rather than those who actually created and tended them. Mary Ambler described her visit in 1770, saying that she "took a great deal of Pleasure in looking at the bowling Green & also at the . . . very large Falling Garden there is a Green House with a good many Orange & Lemon Trees just ready to bear . . . the House . . . stands upon a very High Hill & has a fine view of Petapsico [sic] River You step out of the Door into the Bowlg [sic] Green from which the Garden Falls & when You stand on the Top of it there is such a Uniformity of Each side as the whole Plantn [sic] seems to be laid out lie a garden there is also a Handsome Court Yard on the other side of the House."[38] Such statements reflect elites' value for erasing laborers from the production of status. Enslaved blacks, however, were key to the maintenance of gardens that spoke to both their own and their enslavers' status.

Gardens were more than displays of wealth or mastery over nature. They were also "inherently political statements because of an integral link between power and nature in the Lockean theory of society, a theory that was accepted as a basic principle of Enlightenment rationalism in the colonies."[39] Charles Carroll of Carrollton's garden in Annapolis removed evidence of the production of the garden in order to further a myth about his identity. Evidence of the enslaved persons and workmen who created the garden were erased so that only Carroll would remain on the landscape as the provider of a bounty with no origin. Thomas Jefferson used his gardens as an outlet for imagination.[40] The issue in focusing on whites' motivations, however, is that it removes enslaved persons' agency: the possibility that they imprinted gardens with their own mastery, pride, responsibility, or decision making. The gardens at Mount Clare did show the Carrolls' status, but they were still as much black spaces as white.

Many plantations had ornamental gardens, but few had orangeries like the Carrolls' did. Orangeries held symbolic value for the gentry as a display of control over nature and of cultural mastery. They provided an outlet for elites to explore science and invention and expand their worldview. But, moreover, they demonstrated the ability of gentry to afford such control, as well as the number of laborers necessary to design, implement, and manage them. Orangeries became increasingly grand, glass-enclosed structures that fell into the gentry's niche market. The Calverts built a 10-by-10-foot orangery in Annapolis circa 1730; it was built over in the 1770s.[41] Margaret's relatives, the Lloyds, built an immense glass-walled orangery at Wye House on Wye Island near Easton in Talbot County in the early 1770s amid upgrades to the gardens. It was completely rebuilt between 1784 and 1786. Enslaved blacks lived in quarters on the north side of the Wye greenhouse from the 1790s until the 1820s or 1830s. Assemblage of ceramics, faunal remains, and personal items associated with clothing present are archaeologically similar to finds at the Long Green slave quarter.[42] Elites developed gardens and associated structures to demonstrate that they could do things that few others could.

The foundations of Margaret's own orangery extended approximately

Figure 3.9. Flowerpot sherds excavated at the Mount Clare orangery, Mount Clare Archaeological Collection, Baltimore City Department of Parks and Recreation and the Carroll Park Foundation. Photo by author.

twenty-seven feet east-west by twenty-five feet north-south, with an addition on the south facade that added eight feet. It contained two rooms and two subfloor heating systems consisting of a complex hypocaust system to deliver year-round heat to the plants. Archaeologists found several developmental sequences, suggesting that the area was edited and reconfigured over time.[43] A shed at Mount Clare between the office and orangery in the west wing may have housed the blacks who tended the orangery firebox and did other maintenance tasks. Margaret's own orangery influenced George Washington. He sought her advice in preparation to construct one at Mount Vernon and later accepted fruit trees from her. Washington may have modified Margaret's design by attaching a slave quarter to his orangery.

Flowerpot sherds along the east side and the northwest corner of the orangery and at the garden terraces and orchard reflect the work of enslaved black gardeners who moved the pots and tended the plants within them (fig. 3.9). Although the stratigraphy at Mount Clare makes dating the flowerpots difficult, similarly decorated pots at Monticello date to the eighteenth century.[44] It is more likely that the Carrolls purchased the flowerpots from local potters than that they were made in a pottery at Mount Clare. Brickyards were later established on the lands surrounding Mount

Clare, which indicates that the clay there was not suitable for constructing vessels. Clay vessels require a different composition of clays than bricks, as well as their own kind of kilns and skills to create.[45] Nonetheless, the flowerpot sherds were significant evidence for the daily crossover and interaction between elite whites and enslaved blacks at Mount Clare.

The flowerpots at Mount Clare provide a way for contemporary interpreters to identify elite white or enslaved black material culture on the basis of who used it, not only by who created or purchased them. Flowerpots were part of enslaved black gardeners' everyday work, but they did not make them; the Carrolls purchased them. At other plantation sites, colonoware offers one "marker" of enslaved communities' expression of culture through ceramics. Colonoware is a ceramic type associated with Native American and African American archaeological sites dating from the seventeenth to the mid-nineteenth centuries. It was first archaeologically identified in the Chesapeake region and then on the southeastern coast, but examples are also found in the Caribbean and throughout America. Colonoware is an unglazed, low-fired, thick walled, hand-built, red earthenware type. Its vessels are globular and may have thick handles, foot rings, or foot stands. Some have makers' marks or cosmographic symbols, such as an X etched into the base. Colonoware has been at the center of debates about the influence of Africans and Indians on each other; who produced the vessels and where; the continuance of African craft and food traditions in slavery; and the value of ceramic typologies in archaeologies of ethnicity.[46]

Flowerpot sherds from the eighteenth and nineteenth centuries exist in abundance in the Mount Clare archaeological assemblage, but colonoware is not represented at all. The gardening pots at Mount Clare were coil-built, thick-walled, red- or buff-colored earthenware clay vessels with a rolled rim and smooth body. They might also have a double roll or bump beneath the rim. In the late eighteenth and early nineteenth centuries, ceramic pots made on engine-turned lathes became popular. They featured shallow, thin, parallel lines on the body near the rim made by holding a comb to the clay as the wheel turned. Other pots had an inverted bead design made by pressing a roulette wheel over one or both of the rolls at the rim. Perhaps blacks at Mount Clare did not carry cultural knowledge to make colonoware with them, or could not make pottery, due to a lack of appropriate clay and equipment. Although colonoware has not been found at

Mount Clare, the flowerpots may constitute a ceramic marker of black life at elites' plantations when found in relation to factors such as the enslavers' elite status and ornamental gardens on plantations. If enslaved persons did build flowerpots at elites' plantation gardens and orangeries, their doing so exemplifies blacks' gardening knowledge intersecting with elite whites' cultural expressions.

Another artifact pointing to a crossover between African and European traditions was an unmodified cowrie shell recovered archaeologically from the orangery area. Unfortunately, it comes from a very disturbed context. The shell, however, can be interpreted within a global context as a single object that represents the mechanisms that brought blacks to America. Cowries figured in economics and trade as currency during the African slave trade and ballast in ships moving among Africa, the Caribbean, and America. Africans in Africa and America used cowrie shells ceremonially in weddings and buried them in caches. Cowrie shells appear archaeologically at slave quarters, such as in the late eighteenth century at Mulberry Row at Monticello, as protective charms. Games also used cowrie shells.[47] Although the precise meaning of the cowrie shell cannot be determined, it holds symbolic significance as an interpretive object for the global significance of the slave trade as it came to Mount Clare.

Beyond the orangery, also in the west wing, Charles conducted business in his office that affected the people enslaved throughout the plantation by placing orders to England for cloth and clothing, as well as making decisions for animals for clothmaking at Mount Clare. England placed severe restrictions on the manufacture of hats, cloth, and shoes in America during the colonial period. Slaveholders preferred to purchase cloth from abroad because it was less expensive than in the country, and then they rationed it. Both Dr. Carroll and Charles, however, purchased their "peoples Cloths in the Country" when shipments failed to arrive ahead of winter.[48] Charles placed one order per year in the 1760s to London that included cloth, sewing notions and accessories, and other supplies. Charles's orders tended to include a piece of gray fearnought for waistcoats and coats; two pieces of blue half thick for waistcoats, jackets, or petticoats; a piece of matchcoat or striped duffel for blankets or heavy coats; two dozen blue and white check handkerchiefs or bandanas; various types of linen; several pieces of white or brown oznabrigg; and one dozen each of men's best felt hats, ordinary hats, and double worsted hats.[49] Oznabrigg was typically used for field hands' clothing, while fearnought and other fabrics uniformed butlers and liverymen. Such items can be seen on the black horseman who is with Charles in Charles Willson Peale's 1775 painting, and who wears a white shirt and vest. In contrast, Charles ordered specially made dresses and outfits for himself and Margaret to be made from fine cloth, such as silk. In addition, Charles ordered sewing notions as well as cloth from Europe, including needles, thread, flat brass buttons, hats, bandanas, and pins. Charles's father's associates James Carroll and Charles Carroll of Carrollton gave similar items to the people they enslaved to reward good behavior, as well as for regular use.[50]

During the Revolution, making one's own cloth became fashionable on plantations as an assertion of independence from Britain. Limitations by England on colonial cloth and hat production before the war placed blacks at a sort of prescient disadvantage when the war began. Blacks could adapt to cloth shortages in the 1770s by intensifying their practice of skills acquired well before then. Colonial cloth production catered to "down market" demand, meaning that it supplied slaves and servants whose clothing was of lower quality than planters'.[51] Flax crops and sheep at Mount Clare and The Caves yielded linen and wool beginning in the mid-1760s. Wool was used for winter clothes. Four pairs of wool cards, plus stock locks and padlocks for sheep pens to secure the animals, were ordered in 1764. Sheep and wool operations expanded two years later, after Charles ordered twelve more pairs of wool cards and six sheep shears and additional padlocks. The wool cards were probably distributed across the Baltimore County plantations.[52] Eddenborough and Jack Lynch, who were enslaved by the Carrolls, both wore clothing made from country-made cloth when they escaped in 1777 and 1780. Leather was also made on the plantation. In 1768, Charles ordered an indentured European servant from merchants in London to tan and curry leather: "Moderately well it will do for me as I shall only want him to Dress my Leather for Negro ware [...]."[53] The English servant and possibly others may have trained enslaved blacks in leatherwork. In 1817, an enslaved black man was identified as a shoemaker according to Margaret's estate inventory. Thus, Charles's office was a place where distinctions were made between clothes that were appropriate for enslaved persons and those that were appropriate for his own family.

Food and Gardens

The architectural changes to Mount Clare, as well as the roles of enslaved persons within them, developed as plans went into motion for the land surrounding the mansion. The Carrolls implemented extensive gardens close to the house and changes to farming and agriculture in the fields farther away. Mount Clare came to have the six essential parts of a country estate as described in garden books: a pleasure garden, kitchen garden, fruit garden, nursery, flower garden, and greenhouse. In addition, Charles shifted agricultural production from tobacco to grain and iron by 1766.[54] As a result, field hands learned to process different crops and perform the cyclical tasks associated with them. Wheat and other grains required attention at planting and harvest but in between required less maintenance than tobacco. As a result of the architectural and land-use changes, blacks at Mount Clare carried out tasks to support the expansion of the property into a showpiece plantation.

A common thread across the mansion, both wings, and the land connecting them is food and access to it as delineated by status. Although enslaved blacks were integrated into everyday life at the mansion and its wings, food and its production for themselves and their families stood as something separate. Blacks' labor in the mansion gardens was only part of their food-growing work, and food signified major ways that the Carrolls' and enslaved persons' lives were fundamentally different. "Peoples gardens"—as a traveler to The Caves called them in 1809—were common on southern plantations. The people enslaved at Mount Clare probably had their own.[55] Charles Ball, who was enslaved at several Maryland plantations, recalled that common crops included pumpkins, potatoes, melons, onions, cabbages, and cucumbers.[56] Perhaps the enslaved population at Mount Clare also acquired seeds or cuttings from the Carrolls' kitchen garden, which grew broccoli, asparagus, celery, turnips, early white cabbage, purple or red cabbage, sorrel, parsley, borage (for cool tankards of wine or cider), cauliflower, six-week and split peas, and beets. Kale or collards, thyme, mustard, and other greens were also grown.[57] In addition, enslaved blacks typically used wild plants to diversify their diets and avoid dependence on one particular crop. "Peoples gardens" served multiple purposes, including supplementation of enslavers' rations, income when sold at market or to enslavers, and fulfillment of emotional needs for independence and a sense of ownership.[58] Thus, not only did blacks at Mount Clare labor to fill the Carrolls' table, but they also worked off hours to fill their own.

The gardens helped enslaved persons to have enough to eat when faced with rations established and enforced by enslavers and overseers. The quantity of food depended on the distributor, but it was never sufficient to fuel hard labor and could not be relied on from week to week. Weekly rations were commonly distributed on plantations at overseer's houses, smokehouses, or corn houses.[59] At Mount Clare, rations may have been distributed at an overseer's house southeast of the mansion, which is shown in Charles Willson Peale's landscape, or the smokehouse near the mansion. Placing the overseer's house and smokehouse close to the mansion safeguarded against theft.[60] Smokehouses were typically packed with bacon and pork from pigs raised on the land, and possibly turkey, making them targets for theft. Blacks, however, also took advantage of the forests and waterways surrounding the plantation to supplement their rations. Gwynns Falls and the Patapsco River provided fish, while the land around them held animals to hunt or trap. Evidence of the area's bounty comes from Charles's purchase of gunflints and fishing gear from London.[61] The equipment may have been for use by him, hunting parties, or enslaved persons.

Enslaved persons' recollections from plantations beyond Mount Clare indicates the scale of rations typical of plantations and gives us an idea what sort of rations were allotted to enslaved persons at Mount Clare. Rations typically included grain, fish, a bit of meat, and sometimes dairy or vegetables. A weekly ration for a southern working slave typically included a peck of corn, three to five pounds of bacon, and a half-pint to a quart of molasses.[62] Bread, peas, potatoes, and milk might replace or supplement part of the rations.[63] Meat constituted a treat or a reward. It was also offered at Christmastime.[64] Several men who wrote about their experiences as slaves discussed rations, offering comparative evidence for Mount Clare. Josiah Henson ate cornmeal, salt herrings, a little buttermilk in summer, and vegetables raised in gardens.[65] One of John Thompson's masters allowed each person a peck of corn, two dozen herrings, and about four pounds of meat. Slaves under eight years of age received nothing. Another master gave meat once per month. One overseer provided one meal per day, consisting of cornbread and two salted herrings, while the master was away.[66] Charles Ball received one salted herring per day and a peck of corn per week to grind with a hand mill. Meat was regularly available when the pigs were killed in December. After that, only bacon was provided, unless it, too, was scarce. Fish supplemented his springtime rations.[67] A nineteenth-century study by abolitionists shows that slave rations tended to be less in quantity than those provided (at least on paper) to soldiers and convicts.[68] Rations were part of the foodways of slavery, meaning that they were specific to a place and time and to resource availability. They also responded to the universal need to eat and the "conditions and constrictions" of poverty, rationing, and surveillance.[69] The lean realities of plantation rations meant carbohydrate-heavy diets lacking in protein, minerals, and vitamins, particularly for those working away from the mansion and its kitchen and gardens.

The extent of grain farming at Mount Clare suggests that oats, rye, and wheat, in addition to corn, played an important dietary role. Hand mills were included in Margaret's estate inventory, but blacks may also have received flours or ground grain from the Carrolls' mills. Margaret's calculations also show the kind of rations she preferred. She calculated totals of corn, rye, wheat, and oats to support The Caves for the period between May 9 and August 1, 1809. A total of 110.5 bushels of corn were at the farm or mill or were owed to the Carrolls. Margaret calculated that 45 bushels of corn would be left on August 1, which brings the total down to 65.5 bushels, or about 262.4 pecks. Slaves and enslavers at other plantations reported that a peck of corn per working hand per week was a standard ration. Presuming that in 1809 there were roughly the same number of working hands at The Caves as in 1812, as per Nicholas Carroll's inventory (twenty-seven people over age eight), who would all work the twelve weeks between May 9 and August 1, indicated a need for about 324 pecks. Inclusion of the mill in Margaret's calculations suggests that at least part of the corn was intended for human consumption. The substantial gap in calculation between available and needed corn suggests that other grains supplemented the corn supplied by the Carrolls.

Copious amounts and varieties of food surrounded blacks at Mount Clare, between the Carrolls' everyday meals and lavish dinners, fruit orchards, hothouse citrus, vegetable gardens, and foods stored in the press house, barns, and icehouse. The ornamental gardens and fields grew several different kinds of grass, as well as rye, scotch barley, and lucerne (alfalfa) for animals.[70] Orchards of plum, pear, peach, and cherry trees, as well as grapevines, were established.[71] The Carrolls obtained apple seeds or seedlings within the colony.[72] Perhaps blacks, like enslaved persons at other plantations, did not wait for permission to avail themselves of the orchard fruits, flours, and table leftovers. Frederick Douglass wrote that the fruits at Wye plantation were a constant temptation to the young and old alike. Colonel Edward Lloyd finally coated the fence around the garden with tar and ordered the chief gardener to whip anyone caught marked by it.[73] Although the interpretation of plantations like Mount Clare tends to focus on lavish parties and decadent teas, the flip side is the modes of production for these meals and the inequality felt by enslaved persons. Cooks, chambermaids, and waiters may have had more plentiful and nutritious meals than field workers. Small children who stayed with their mothers in the kitchen might also have had improved health due to better access to food.[74] Food thus provides a way to make the past accessible and personally meaningful as museum visitors recognize family traditions, the economics of food, and what it feels like to be hungry or full.

Blacks made Mount Clare into a showpiece plantation that emphasized the Carrolls' status in colonial America. Today, the obfuscation of blacks in the interpretation of Mount Clare perpetuates elite values of the past in the present. The reality, however, is that blacks left their mark throughout the mansion and on the landscape immediately surrounding it. The impact they made is important to talk about today, because blacks are integral to the story of Mount Clare. Even though the Carrolls dictated the relationship of status to race, they relied on enslaved blacks to maintain their image by acquiring knowledge and skills in household and landscape maintenance. The Carrolls may have restricted food, clothing, and the movements of slaves, but blacks pushed back through the practice of homeland traditions and by committing crimes against property. As a result, the transformation of Georgia into Mount Clare is as much about the development of enslaved blacks' cultural knowledge at the intersection of race and status as it is about the Carrolls' world as elites.

4

Slavery and Revolution

During the Revolutionary era, Charles Carroll the Barrister aimed to preserve the existing social order, an attitude reflected in his continuation of slavery at Mount Clare. Plantations like Mount Clare demonstrate the ways in which Revolutionary thought did or did not manifest in everyday life for enslaved persons. During the Revolutionary era, the thirteen colonies overthrew Great Britain to become a self-governing republic. Colonial American political theory espoused that a few held power over the many and that the basis of a government's power was in the populace's voluntary surrender of the individual's rights to the leaders of society. Individual liberty and chattel slavery constituted a paradox amid debate about the future of the Maryland colony. A radical social revolution in Maryland by nonlandowners and free blacks sought to overturn the narrow control of the legislature by white, wealthy landowners. Blacks sought to eliminate slavery because they viewed freedom to be their right. Charles is recalled today as an American patriot of the Revolutionary cause, but for whose cause, and for whose patriotism? Charles's political activities were reflected in a fully developed complex consisting of a plantation mansion and outbuildings, whose work was carried out by enslaved persons. The appearance of enslaved blacks' lives at Mount Clare during the Revolutionary era obscured deeper ideological disconnects at the heart of a race-based social order.

Charles, Mount Clare, and the Revolution

Charles aligned himself with other wealthy gentlemen in the conservative faction of the Country party. These conservatives advocated for peaceful protest against British economic policy. They employed tactics such as voluntary compliance with trade boycotts, petitions, and diplomacy. In October 1768, Lord Baltimore had offered positions on His Lordship's Council to Charles Carroll the Barrister and to Margaret's father, Matthew Tilghman, in an effort to gain their loyalty to the colonial government and Great Britain. Both men refused, but the very offer suggests that they were torn between competing personal and business interests. Charles and the Baltimore Iron Works had traded in Britain for decades, and Charles was also a regular consumer of British goods. In May 1769, Charles and others signed a letter announcing the formation of a nonimportation association, which advocated colonial self-taxation.[1] He, however, continued to import wine, cheese, fine clothing, and jewelry from Britain through the American merchants Wallace, Davidson, and Johnson in Annapolis and Joshua Johnson in England until the war began.[2] The other faction of the Country party consisted of landowners who were not as wealthy as the gentry. They believed in direct action, even violence, through public protest by crowds. Radicals' actions garnered more attention and response from Britain—for good or for ill—than the conservatives' tactics. In addition to the conservative and radical factions were colonists who remained loyal to Lord Baltimore and supported British rule. Everyday people gained political power, which threatened the social order championed by Charles and sustained by slavery.

While politicians sought to distance the colonies from British exploitation, Charles perpetuated slavery in the existing social order. Slavery continued apace on the Carroll properties. The Carrolls made Mount Clare their nearly year-round residence in the early 1770s as the tenor of Annapolis changed in advance of the war. The move brought them into more regular interaction with blacks who lived and worked in the Baltimore region. Charles enslaved an estimated fifty people over age sixteen in 1773, a number that may not include the elderly, between Mount Clare and The Caves. Eighteen enslaved blacks lived at Mount Clare: Abram, Dick, David, Charles, Nick, Guy, Timbole, Jingo, Harry, James, Christmas, Ned, Will, George, Charles, Pugg, Lucy, and Tom. Three white males also lived there, possibly Charles, an overseer, and a gardener.[3] The predominance of male names at Mount Clare suggests that hard labor in agriculture, timbering, and farming continued to fuel the Baltimore Iron Works and milling enterprises. Lucy worked inside the mansion, as shown in correspondence at Charles's death in 1783. Twenty blacks were at The Caves in 1773: Sandigo, Millegro, Nedilent, Leslee or Leelee, Deb, Easter, Sue, Nell, Sabinah, Toby, Monster, Natt, Isaac, Mill, Moll, Peg, Cate, Dina, and one more person, whose name is illegible. Four white men also lived on the property.[4] Small children and elderly people may have lived on the properties as well and not been included in the assessments. On the other hand, records have survived neither for Charles's house in Annapolis Hundred nor Carrolls Island in Gunpowder River Lower Hundred. If records from 1783 provided a ballpark figure for 1773, then ten people were enslaved on Carrolls Island and three at the house in Annapolis. Thus, Revolutionary rhetoric advocating for a shake-up of the social order did not appear to affect Charles or slow his slavery apparatus.

In the years leading up to war, Charles continued to purchase blacks. Among them were a boy from Thomas Hammond sold for £10 in December 1770 and a woman bought for £13 from Thomas Rossiter via Captain William Macgachen in September 1774.[5] When Charles hired free blacks, he paid them on a different scale than whites. In 1774, for example, Charles agreed to pay "molatto Joe" £0.35.0 per month for two months, far less than the £25 per year he paid the white gardener Thomas Young. During the same period, he hired enslaved men from other slaveholders, such as Jack from William Ridgeley, or two enslaved persons from another slaveholder for £20 for a year. He also hired "Negro Joe" and "Negro Sam" in February 1782 for a period of eight months. They may have been free blacks. Charles may have paid enslaved blacks to overwork, such as Hager and Beck, who worked at his Annapolis house. Charles purchased Hager for £100 and Beck for £75 as part of an exchange in 1781. In November 1780, however, he had agreed to pay Hager £0.20.0 and Beck £0.15.0 per month to work at the house. Hager and Beck worked for Charles until his death in 1783. Charles's executors paid Hager for two years and six months of wages for the period between October 28, 1780, and April 18, 1784. Beck left to find work in Annapolis after putting the kitchen in order.[6]

The black populations living at, or hired to work on, Mount Clare encountered a showcase property that symbolized Charles's and Margaret's position in society. Charles Willson Peale's painting of the mansion complex captured the landscape as seen by enslaved persons circa 1775 (fig. 4.1).

Figure 4.1. Detail of Peale's painting showing the Mount Clare mansion complex and the surrounding gardens, 1775.

Orchards grew to the west of Mount Clare and terraced gardens stepped south toward the river. Horses grazed meadows on the flat land between the terraced gardens and the river. Enslaved persons tended them; indeed, a black groomsman accompanies Charles and his riding partner (fig. 4.2). From west to east at the mansion complex stood a shed, the orangery, the office, the main house, the kitchen, the washhouse, and a small shed (possibly a necessary house). A house stood southeast of the mansion complex, probably for an overseer. Structures identified as "old" or "fit for fuel" in 1798 may have stood in the 1770s in the fields and at the mills. They included a frame cowhouse (21 by 16, one story), a stone blacksmith shop (53 by 24, one story), a log house (30 by 24, one story), a second stone house (16 by 14, one story), a frame structure (47 by 20, one story), a frame barn (38 by 22, one story), a stone stable (45 by 24, one story), a second log house (32 by 22, one story), a frame stable (24 by 16, two story), a stone potato house (15 by 12, one-half story), a third log house (28 by 16, one story), a brick cooper shop (16 by 13, one story), and a fourth log house (18 by 16, one story).[7] For comparative purposes, old "negro houses" on Nicholas Carroll's 1798 assessment for The Caves included two log structures, measuring 16 by 20 and 20

Figure 4.2. Detail of Peale's painting showing a black groomsman and Charles Carroll the Barrister, 1775.

by 36.[8] The combination of the 1773 assessment with Peale's painting sets the scene for the Revolutionary era at Mount Clare.

Charles's attitudes toward black slavery are not spelled out in his preserved correspondence, but they may be gleaned from his associations with people and committees in Maryland during the war. In June 1774, Charles was among other representatives of Maryland counties at the first Provincial Convention. A Committee of Correspondence in Maryland consisted of Charles Carroll the Barrister and Matthew Tilghman, John Hall, Samuel Chase, Thomas Johnson Jr., Charles Carroll of Carrollton, and William Paca. They or any three of them—all wealthy slaveholders—were empowered to represent Maryland at the Continental Congress in December 1774. Their published statements spoke of the colonies' enslavement to argue for freedom from Britain. For example:

> As our opposition to the settled plan of the British administration to enslave America, will be strengthened by an union of all ranks of men in this province, we do most earnestly recommend, that all former differences about religion or politics, and all private animosities and

quarrels of every kind, from henceforth cease and be for ever buried in oblivion; and we intreat [sic], we conjure every man, by his duty to God, his country, and his posterity, cordially to unite in defense of our common rights and liberties.[9]

Such statements, however, were not meant to include blacks. Charles served until 1776 but resigned when the radical inclinations of his constituents proved incompatible with his own belief in a peaceful approach to good government. Charles served on the Senate from 1775 to 1783, one of the few men in Maryland who qualified. The property requirements were twice for senators what they were for members of the House of Delegates. He served on the Council of Safety in 1775 and 1776. The council was a body concerned with the problem of fugitive slaves joining the British against the Americans. They expressed fears of slave uprisings.[10] They feared, in particular, that Governor Richard Eden of Maryland would, like Lord Dunmore, the governor of Virginia, offer blacks their freedom if they volunteered for the militia. Considering that Charles held meetings at Mount Clare, it is tempting to imagine enslaved blacks overhearing news and strategy from political insiders while carrying out their work.

Charles is credited with framing Maryland's declaration of rights and constitution, which was signed on July 3, 1776.[11] The document focused on the creation of a state government. It emphasized the rights of free men within the state, particularly their qualifications to hold office or to vote. From the position of historical retrospect, several points within the document demonstrated that independence was narrowly conceived. Points included: "[A]ll government of right originates from the people . . . instituted for the good of the whole"; the "people of this state ought to have the sole and exclusive right of regulating the internal government and police thereof"; and "the inhabitants of Maryland are entitled to the common law of England."[12] Enslaved blacks did not count as people or inhabitants.

Interestingly, neither Charles's remaining letterbooks and correspondence nor Maryland papers contain his thoughts on the conflict or reflections on slavery and independence. Furthermore, to prepare for war and wean Maryland from its reliance on England, the convention agreed to increase flocks of sheep and promote the manufacture of woolens in the process and to grow as much flax, hemp, and cotton as each planter and farmer could to increase the manufacture of linen and cotton.[13] Citizens were required to contribute grain to feed the soldiers. The degree to which Charles contributed supplies from his personal plantations to the war effort—notably, it would have been through slave labor—is undocumented.

Americans qualified for leadership and committee positions in the Maryland government based on wealth and landownership. Gentrymen like Charles relied on enslaved blacks to build and maintain the labor-dependent aspects of their wealth. As a result, enslaved persons' labor enabled Charles to take part in the American Revolution and be remembered in history as an American patriot. No record remains to suggest that he or Margaret felt internal conflict over slavery. And yet his enslavement of dozens of people across personal properties and continued partnership in the Baltimore Iron Works suggests that his conservative political stance related at least in part to his desire to maintain slavery and a divided racial system in America.

Slavery and Revolution

No evidence remains about the way blacks at Mount Clare sided during the Revolution, but there were certainly many different sides to take with regard to Revolution ideology. The Revolution brought about awareness of American racial prejudice, the foundations of that prejudice in physical differences between whites and blacks, and its significance as an obstacle to emancipation. Duncan MacLeod writes that the period "was a crucial stage in the development of the debate over slavery and race; that it promoted a real concern over the nature and significance of slavery; and that out of that concern grew a consciously racist society."[14] It was also a formative period for family life and domestic institutions among blacks in Maryland. Increasing numbers of documented escapes from slavery and manumissions suggest a nexus among family, freedom, and power.

Escape was one way that enslaved blacks could defy slavery and the social order. Although escape was not new in the 1770s, it became a tactic associated with Revolutionary-era thought and concepts of individual liberty and race consciousness. It forced white society to recognize, and attempt to contain, black agency through the development of laws, punishment, and violence. Charles recorded an uptick in the number of enslaved blacks who escaped from his properties during the period, beginning with the bold escape of two men while traveling abroad with the Carrolls. It occurred when Charles and Margaret traveled to London in the summer of 1771. The purpose of their visit was to see friends and family—and to shop.[15] Charles placed orders with Joshua Johnson, an American merchant in London and the Johnson of the Wallace, Davidson, and Johnson mercantile company. Shortly before the Carrolls left for Maryland in May 1772, two men, named Adam and Frank, escaped.[16] Adam and Frank fell on hard times within a few months. Adam began to call on Johnson, who agreed to facilitate Adam's return to Maryland. Adam and Frank likely knew Johnson's name, where to find him, and that he and Charles were in regular contact because of their accompanying Charles to his meetings. Johnson wrote to Charles in August 1772,

Sir, This I expect will be delivered you by your Man Adam who comes out in Capt Bishoprick at the request of Mr. Anderson and self, he cal'd on me several times while I was out of town, on my return he cal'd when I saw him, he look'd very thin and simple. I asked him the reason of his leaveing [sic] you he ans'd me in general that he was very sorry for what he had done, that it was not an act of his own but rather the preswaitions [sic] of bad people whom he has since found only ment [sic] to mislead him and that he would most willing by return to your sirvice [sic] if I would procure him a passage and promise you would forgive him, I told him I thought you would but that I would consult Mr. Anderson whom I expected had some instructions from you respecting him and appointed the next morning for him to meet Mr. Anderson at my house. Mr. Anderson told him you would forgive and restore him to favour again on which he agreed to return to you and we got every necessary done which Mr. Anderson will fully inform you of, he was not in the best condition either in Pocket or Health which compel'd us to get assistance for him. The part I have acted I hope will meet with your approbation and that you will fulfil [sic] my promise.

If I can be of any assistance in forwarding the other [Frank] to you, you may rely on it, from what I can collect from this he is on the shift and as the winter approaches its more than probable I shall have a visit from him. I congratulate you and Mrs. Carroll on your return to

Maryland and am with my respectfull compls. To your lady, Joshua Johnson.[17]

The kind tone runs throughout Johnson's letters about Adam, as it does in all his correspondence. Adam feared facing Charles, so Johnson asked Charles Wallace to go with him. He took a letter to Wallace that read,

> The bearer of this [the letter transcribed above] is Mr [Charles] Carroll's Adam who, by ill advisers, left his master here. He has since commenced a penitent and put himself under Mr Anderson's and my direction in procuring his return. He has signified to me that he is ashamed to face his master on which I promised you would go with him and which promise I beg you will fulfill. I have done this with an intent to serve Mr Carroll [barrister] and the poor devil and shall be happy to hear that it meets with his approbation. I know your compassion for the unhappy and willingness to relieve which makes it needless to apologise [sic] for this trouble.[18]

Frank, however, did not contact Johnson. Johnson updated Charles in April 1773: "I could have wished to been able to give you some agreeable news about Frank at this time but have not collected more than that he is in Service at the West end of the Town should I be able to do anything for you with him you may depend on it."[19] Adam and Frank are the first recorded escapes from the Carrolls, but they were not the last.

The decision to escape was not an easy one or a simple undertaking, even if the tide of Revolution lent some ideological support to the action. Violence to personal liberty—be it physical, emotional, or ideological—was the overarching motivation. Escape constituted a means of protest as a condemnation of slavery and the abuse of blacks for the benefit of enslavers. Abolitionist William Still's records of runaway slave testimony indicate that some individuals escaped after prolonged physical and mental abuse by slave owners. Others absented themselves after disagreements with their enslavers over the ability to visit family and threats of being sold or sent away. In other cases, families escaped in order to preserve the unit. Many people expressed their conviction that enslavement was simply wrong. Reactions to abuse, such as escape, represented resistance to slavery.

Some enslaved and free blacks throughout the colonies joined the Continental army or the British army, while others stayed in their communities.

Blacks in the North had more social leeway than their Chesapeake counterparts, and they agitated en masse for rights and abolition for decades
prior to the war. Whites, particularly in the South, were uncomfortable
with blacks joining the Continental army and being armed to defend the
freedom of slaveholders. Rumors circulated that the British were encouraging blacks to rebel. In July of 1775, General George Washington ordered
that no blacks be enlisted in the Continental Army. By November, Lord
Dunmore declared freedom for all slaves who took up arms for the British.
His proclamation was motivated by the British army's desperate need for
soldiers, not antislavery sentiment. Tens of thousands—up to one hundred
thousand by one estimate—escaped from slavery to join an army, while
others seized the opportunity to flee amid the chaos.[20]

During this time, two more men escaped enslavement by the Carrolls.
The August 1777 advertisement for Eddenborough read:

FIVE POUNDS Reward[21]
Ran away from the subscriber, a Negro man, called EDDENBOR-
OUGH, a cooper by trade, about 50 years of age, a little lively fel-
low, active walk, speaks quick, and with a little of the Negro accent,
bald upon the upper part of his head; Had on a country linen shirt,
tow linen trousers, country cloth waistcoat, old shoes, an old straw
hat; It is suspected that he is harboured about Baltimore Town, or in
the neighborhood. Whoever brings him to the subscriber, shall have
Forty Shillings, if taken in this or in Anne Arundel county, and if in
any other county the above reward, and reasonable charges.
CHARLES CARROLL Mount Clare, Aug 15, 1777

An advertisement in 1780 for Jack Lynch read:

FOUR HUNDRED DOLLARS REWARD[22]
RAN away, from the subscribers island plantation, at the Mouth
of Gunpowder, about the beginning of this month, a mulatto slave,
called JACK LYNCH, down look, is an artful rogue, speaks slow, and
appears to be very mild. Had on and took with him, a blue broad-
cloth coat, country cloth jacket, one Irish linen shift, two country
linen ditto, one pair of country linen trousers, a pair of half-worn
shoes, with buckles, an old country made hat, and has lately had a
breaking out on his head. Whoever brings him to the subscriber, or

secures him, so that he may get him again, shall have the above reward, and reasonable charges.
CHARLES CARROLL, Mount Clare July 10, 1780

The two advertisements raise a number of questions. Did only two people
escape from the Carrolls' Baltimore plantations during Charles's lifetime?
If so, why? Why did Charles place the advertisements? Did they have
anything to do with blacks joining the war? Charles's papers, however, do
not discuss any escapes or reveal his reasoning for placing advertisements.
Slaveholders did not always pursue runaways or advertise an escape. Place-
ment of an advertisement was determined by one's ability to afford it, the
proximity of the plantation to a town with a newspaper, and the value of
the enslaved person to the owner. Enslavers also strategically placed advertisements as a scare tactic to dissuade others from escaping.[23] Charles's
residences in Baltimore and Annapolis were proximate to several different
newspapers. He had the wealth to afford advertisements. Did Charles, like
his father, hire bounty hunters? Did he rely on Baltimore's eyes and ears
to produce tips? Did blacks tend to return on their own accord? Even as
they raise questions, Eddenborough's and Jack Lynch's advertisements may
provide some clues about their lives in slavery.

Both advertisements suggest some flexibility in enslaved blacks' movements. Former slaves John Thompson and James Pennington have explained that an absence of a few days was not unusual. Men were commonly permitted to leave on Saturday evening to visit their families on
other plantations until Monday morning. They might use illness as an
excuse not to return until Tuesday. As a result, one did not get alarmed
about an absence until Wednesday.[24] Margaret's estate inventory shows
that Jack had relatives at Mount Clare in 1817. Perhaps Charles was accustomed to Jack being absent as a result of visiting relatives. Eddenborough
may have had friends or family willing to hide him in Baltimore, which was
why Charles noted the city as a place to look. The movement of enslaved
persons around Baltimore was further indicated by an advertisement for
a carpenter named Aaron Pulley. One of Margaret's overseers placed the
advertisement in June 1799. Aaron, too, had been gone several days: "He
left home on Thursday last, and was seen at the races; he often frequented
Fell's-Point." The overseer warned masters of ships not to take him on.[25]

Although the outfits that Eddenborough and Jack escaped wearing were similar to others who escaped slavery to join the Continental army, that does not necessarily mean that the war was their destination.

Effects on the Baltimore Iron Works

During the Revolution, labor became scarcer as free laborers joined the Continental Army. Iron laborers were exempt from enrollment in southeastern Pennsylvania, but the practice was only discouraged in Maryland and Virginia. As a result, the elite partners of the Baltimore Iron Works—some of whom were involved in Maryland's role in independence from Britain—became even more reliant on slavery.

Charles Carroll of Carrollton argued to his partners in 1773 that they should purchase forty or fifty more slaves rather than hire workers.[26] The company agreed to purchase ten convicts and twenty negroes, five of each group at a time. Perhaps based on past experience, they emphasized the need for healthy, country-born negroes ages fifteen to twenty-two. On July 11, 1774, the partners agreed at a meeting at Mount Clare to purchase ten slaves between sixteen and twenty-five years old. On March 30, 1775, they agreed that each partner holding a fifth share should contribute one young, country-born "negro wench" not exceeding twenty-four years old.[27] Clement Brooke complained to the partners when no slaves were acquired by April. Charles retorted, "My two negroes have been some time sent to the works and I have a negro woman ready to send according to our last agreement. Mr. Brook[e] writes me of the 11th that he has purchased 500 bushels of corn for the works in my account to [ill.]."[28] Charles's contributions of enslaved persons did not necessarily work out. Brooke again urged the partners to supply laborers in 1783, because the business was suffering, in part because several people sent in the previous year were unfit. He wrote, "The lad sent in by Mr. Carroll, Barrister in June 1782, very unfit for business, a negro wench from the same 5th sent to Mount Royal Forge Mr Franklin complains of as having a bad leg." Brooke again emphasized the preference for young and able men, as "bad hands are a burden."[29]

Unlike other ironworks, which strove to be self-sufficient, the owners of the Baltimore Iron Works contributed quotas of provisions supplied by their plantations. The owners relied on their plantations to supply their quotas, but there is no evidence that there was a trickle-down effect whereby elites passed their wealth to ironworks laborers in times of need. In 1769, Charles wrote that his overseer at Carrolls Island had been careless and failed to produce enough corn for his share.[30] The owners' internal bickering may have led to each of them attempting to undercut their assigned quota.[31] As a result, enslaved and other workers suffered. The Baltimore Iron Works managers pleaded to the owners for food for the starving workers and animals. Manager Clement Brooke wrote to the owners in 1775 that he could not do his job unless the partners supplied more slaves and more corn.[32] The expansion of the workforce enabled the Baltimore Company to sell iron toward the war effort. Charles was paid £4.12 at least twice by the Council of Safety for iron manufactured by enslaved blacks and others.[33] The message to enslaved and other laborers was that they were expected to be productive for elites' profits, even if they were not supplied with the resources necessary to sustain themselves.

Large-scale use of enslaved labor supported the iron industry in the Chesapeake region. The Baltimore Iron Works, however, was not part of this general trend. Several factors likely contributed to its demise. The seizure of ironworks shares belonging to partners who were Loyalists after the American Revolution and the failure to produce competitively put the Baltimore Iron Works in dire straits by the 1780s. Maryland confiscated Daniel Dulany's share in the ironworks because he was a British Loyalist. Although fewer Baltimore Company records remain from this time compared to earlier years, the end of the Principio Company may suggest some of the reasons why it failed. The Principio Company began to collapse in the mid-eighteenth century due to dwindling timber resources for charcoal and the aging of its enslaved workforce. After the American Revolution, the Maryland General Assembly confiscated all British property in the state, including that of the Loyalist partners of the Principio Company. More than 136 enslaved persons were auctioned with the company's assets.[34]

The Baltimore Company faced similar challenges. Charles Carroll the Barrister died in 1783, leaving a full one-fifth of company ownership to his heirs. Nicholas Carroll, not James Carroll, became part owner and Margaret received a third of his Baltimore Company income for the rest of her life.[35] The fracturing of shares among heirs became more common over the late eighteenth century, which seemed to dissolve any remaining internal coherence of the company's management. In 1785, a one-fifth share was advertised for sale, meaning a fifth of two hundred enslaved people, along with one furnace, two forges, more than twenty-eight thousand acres, and other stock. About seven thousand to eight thousand acres near Baltimore were slated for sale as individual lots.[36] Daniel Dulany's share was confiscated due to his Loyalist ties. Robert Carter sold his share in 1787. The dissolution of the company had disastrous effects on the enslaved community. Blacks were sold as partners peeled away from the company or as their holdings were seized. Sales "shredded families" as men, women, and children were sold.[37] By 1798, the Baltimore Company enslaved no one.

Two Ends to Two Eras

Charles died at Mount Clare in March 1783, months before the signing of the Treaty of Paris that brought an end to the American Revolution. Charles neither freed anyone nor left blacks any clothing or gifts in his last will and testament. Charles did not write of financial worries in his personal papers, and merchant companies did not complain about unpaid bills like they did of his friends. Just before Charles's death in 1783, he intimated to a friend that three-fourths of the debts owed to him had been repaid under the Debt Act.[38] As a result, Charles had considerable wealth and property to pass on to his family, enabling him to leave them a comfortable life, especially his wife. He left all the people he enslaved to Margaret, stating,

> . . . and as my dear wife may probably incline to have in her share of my negroes those or some of them which came to me by Intermarriage with her and their increase I direct and order that she may take the whole or so many and such of time as she may chuse [sic] to have in her said moiety or half part of my personal estate and that she shall further have during her natural life the use of all such of my House servants as may happen not to be included therein but it is intended that the increase shall not be considered as part of the use but to be taken and received into the residue of my estate.[39]

The fact that Charles left enslaved persons to Margaret suggests his confidence in her ability to manage them or to delegate the task to individuals who could do so on her behalf. Charles' obituary called him an "Indulgent

Table 4.1. Charles Carroll's slaveholding in 1783, Mount Clare excepted

	Annapolis[a]	Value (£)	The Caves[b]	Value (£)	Carrolls Island[c]	Value (£)
Males and females under age 8	5	46	13	130	10	100
Males or females age 8–14			7 (males)	175	2	50
Males age 15–45			7	530	2	140
Females age 15–36	1	60	10	60	3	180
Males over age 45 or females over age 36	1	40	8	120	3	75
Total	7	146	45	1015	20	545
Total assessed		1527		5729		3007

Notes: a. General Assembly House of Delegates (Assessment Record) Charles Carroll (Barrister), 1783, Annapolis Hundred, Anne Arundel County, M871-11, MSA SM59-1. Conversion to 2008 dollars: £1527 = $204,295. Nye, *Pounds to Dollars*.

b. General Assembly House of Delegates (Assessment Record) Charles Carroll (Barrister), 1783, Middle River Upper Hundred and Back River Hundred, Baltimore County, p. 3, M871-17, MSA SM59-22. Conversion to 2008 dollars: £5729 = $766,473. Nye, *Pounds to Dollars*.

c. General Assembly House of Delegates (Assessment Record) Charles Carroll (Barrister), 1783, Middle River Lower Hundred, Baltimore County, p. 3, M871-17, MSA SM59-22. Conversion to 2008 dollars: £3007 = $402,301. Nye, *Pounds to Dollars*.

Master," a phrase reflecting elites' belief that their treatment of enslaved people was generous. Blacks, however, did not necessarily share Charles and his friends' belief. Although Charles stipulated that his executors not probate his estate, the 1783 tax assessment provided information about all properties except Mount Clare (Table 4.1). Mount Clare likely had around the same number of blacks as The Caves, because the two plantations had held a similar number of slaves in 1737 and 1773. If so, Charles enslaved approximately 115 people in 1783 on his personal property. He was also accountable for a fifth share of the thirty-one people enslaved at the Baltimore Iron Works.[40]

Charles's will enabled Margaret to choose from two groups of enslaved people to make up her half of his personal estate. The first included the blacks brought by Margaret into the marriage and their children; these individuals likely lived at Mount Clare already. Blacks at The Caves and Carrolls Island appear to have been folded into the Maccubbin brothers' inheritances. The second group consisted of house servants outside the first group. Their children became part of the residue of Charles's estate.

In addition, Charles left to his clerk, Francis Fairbrother of Annapolis, "the negro woman named Sue and all her children or increase that woman I mean who now lives with him."[41] Charles gave Margaret life tenancy on her choice of his Annapolis or Mount Clare properties. She chose Mount Clare. He left her a third part of the residue of his real estate, a full moiety of lands sold after his death, a half part of his personal estate, and household effects from Annapolis. Enslaved persons as property helped to buffer widows from poverty, but other forms of passed-down wealth, such as land and monetary assets, proved to be more reliable support. Charles left the rest of the estate to his nephews, Nicholas and James Maccubbin, provided that they change their names to Carroll. Enslaved women helped to resolve household loose ends. Lucy, who had lived at Mount Clare since at least 1773, boxed Fairbrother's coffee pot and books to send to him in Annapolis.[42] Fairbrother reported on Beck in Annapolis: "Beck is still here and has put the Kitchen in good order and otherwise behaves herself well. She intends to venture out in a few days and thinks she shall be able to get her living. I shall keep my eye on her motions and inform you of them."[43]

Although slavery at Mount Clare appeared in a day-to-day sense to continue unabated, the tide was shifting throughout the Chesapeake. Americans found themselves thinking more about the institution of slavery and the morality of slaveholding. Thousands of blacks from Maryland and Virginia served in armies, were kidnapped as booty, and escaped from masters. Blacks in the 1770s and 1780s engaged with the evangelical movement of the Methodist and Baptist churches and created independent black churches. The movement also persuaded some whites that slavery was un-Christian. That, along with ideological doubts fostered by the contradiction of fighting for white liberty while keeping blacks enslaved, led to increasing numbers of manumissions. Agricultural conditions, such as depleted soil due to tobacco farming, along with postwar economic depression, caused additional disruption in the practicality of slavery. The Revolutionary War laid the intellectual groundwork to end slavery almost a hundred years later, during the Civil War. But in the short term, elites such as Margaret Carroll and her relatives felt their positions as elite slaveholders to be safe. At least through the end of the eighteenth century, they felt a (perhaps misplaced) sense of political mastery and used their power to embed slavery more deeply into the southern half of the republic.

5

White Widowhood

After Charles's death, Margaret chose to live at Mount Clare rather than at their Annapolis house. Although few of Margaret's records and letters remain from her years as a widow, many more sources of historical information from this period are available than previously were about the people enslaved at Mount Clare, especially through government records. Government documents of postcolonial Maryland, in particular, tracked the family relationships, life cycles, skill expertise, and other identifying characteristics of one of the largest enslaved populations in Baltimore County. As a result, details emerge from post-Revolutionary Mount Clare, between 1783 and 1817, about the enslaved population within the contexts of white widowhood and Baltimorean trends in African American life. Such information makes the past accessible in ways that demonstrate the significance of everyday encounters and racial inequality from different perspectives.

Slavery and White Widowhood

Margaret's activities in widowhood were an extension of her responsibilities during Charles's life. Women were active partners in plantation management, even if they tended not to hold equal power to the plantation master. When Charles was alive, Margaret may have acted in a "deputy husband" role that was common for plantation mistresses. Widowhood, however, changed the social structure of plantations; wives were "promoted" from plantation deputy to manager upon their husbands' deaths. Slave management forced white widows to merge their traditional feminine roles and expertise with traditionally male ones. In the process, they shed the image of the pitiable widow in order to establish control and discipline, changing the dynamics among established relationships.

Widows managed and even expanded upon their deceased husbands' estates. They gained new legal power to enter the business world while fulfilling their feminine duty to be trustee of property for the next generation.[1] Margaret followed this model, considering that she used her intellectual and business acumen to sustain her own wealth while keeping Mount Clare in trust for James Maccubbin. Southern white widows reinforced the social order. They tended to be conservative and to endorse gender, race, and class inequality. They also, however, demonstrated that feminine dependence could be a source of power when linked to racial and economic privilege.[2] Although Margaret held traditional roles at Mount Clare, the scale of her slaveholding set her apart from other white widows in the Baltimore area.

The traditional interpretation of Margaret at the Mount Clare Museum House centers on her roles within the domestic sphere as interior decorator, mother, gardener, and wife, but excludes her role in slave management. Furthermore, this interpretation at Mount Clare promotes Margaret as a woman of fine character and does not reflect on Margaret as a slaveholder and how that may affect our understanding of her and her life. For example, visitors to the Mount Clare Museum House learn about Margaret's avid interest in gardening. The gardens were so well known that George Washington sought Margaret's advice in creating his own.[3] Margaret's estate papers, however, indicate that she had help from an enslaved gardener named Richard, but he received no credit for his work. Richard's activities within the domestic sphere and his contact with Margaret are important in understanding Margaret's life in widowhood. Excluding slaves and slavery from the contents of the domestic sphere prevents visitors from learning about the relationships between Margaret and the people she enslaved, especially their own roles in managing the domestic sphere.

What was Margaret like as a person? Men of Margaret's race and status described her as a shy, intelligent woman who became warm and caring as she got to know people.[4] Enslaved persons or white hires, however, may have seen her in a different and perhaps less flattering light. Margaret's particular and status-conscious voice often seeped into Charles's correspondence in the form of requests or complaints. She wanted the best consumables, like tea, and she and her husband articulated the specific qualities and types of persons whom they sought as white servants. In 1802, Margaret confided to an acquaintance that "it is extreme[ly] difficult to meet with young women near this town with [ill.] and capacity—if they have lived in town long enough to learn anything their morals are corrupted, and they are generally so fond of gossiping that you can scarce but keep them at home."[5]

Margaret and enslaved persons are today presented as people of their time: individuals caught in a societal system over which they had limited control. For example, in the fall of 1984, museum chairman Eugenia Calvert Holland wrote that "Those of us who are members of the House Committee have a charming historic personage to emulate. She was a lady of refinement and gentle manners, a woman of property, informed, direct and gracious. I refer to Margaret Tilghman Carroll: bride, wife and widow of Charles Carroll, Barrister—First Lady of Mount Clare."[6] Historians throughout the twentieth century interpreted Margaret as a traditional wife and mother dedicated to the domestic sphere.[7] Presenting women of history in such a way, however, can perpetuate gender inequality in the present by basing it in the past. It also decontextualizes Margaret's attitudes and activities from slavery. More recently, however, a historian has emphasized her business acumen and individuality, especially regarding manumission.[8] No matter what Margaret's personality, the scope of her slaveholding was a significant part of her history and the story of Mount Clare in the late eighteenth and early nineteenth centuries.

The persistence of slavery seemed assured in the years following the American Revolution. The enslaved population of Baltimore County and Baltimore City increased by 60 percent between 1790 and 1810. The number of people enslaved in Baltimore City nearly quadrupled to 4,672. Over the next two decades, slavery declined slowly but steadily until 1830, when the trend accelerated and the free population of Baltimore increased.[9] In 1790, Margaret enslaved forty-seven people over age sixteen at Mount Clare. She was the seventh-largest slaveholder in Baltimore County and Baltimore City. When comparing her with male slaveholders in the region, we find that William Hammond ranked first with one hundred fifty slaves and Nicholas Carroll sixth with forty-nine. After Margaret, the slaveholding women with the next two largest populations held twenty-five and twenty persons. The great majority of Baltimore County and Baltimore City households contained fewer than five or no enslaved blacks in 1790. The few free black households headed by women typically consisted of fewer than five persons and no enslaved persons.[10] Such statistics demonstrate that Margaret and people enslaved at Mount Clare had few counterparts in the region.

Blacks at Mount Clare were in a unique situation for the Baltimore region, due to their community's size, in addition to Margaret's wealth and widowhood (Table 5.1). By 1798, only three female heads of household—all white—were also slaveholders in Baltimore County. Margaret enslaved thirty-six people, twenty-one of whom were between twelve and fifty years old. Her property's total value was assessed at $15,467.52—more than the other women's properties combined. Wealth on Margaret's 1798 property assessment was calculated from slaves, plate, horses, black cattle, sheep, land, houses, and other structures, including mills. By way of comparison, the two white widows in the Baltimore region with wealth closest to Margaret's held significantly less property. Eleanor Croxall enslaved twenty-seven people between twelve and fifty years old. Her property's total value was assessed at $4,977.75.[11] Sarah Smith enslaved forty-five people, seventeen between twelve and fifty years old. Her three properties were assessed together at $5,724.79.5. In 1804, slaves constituted 47 percent of the total value of Margaret's personal property but 14 percent of her total holdings.[12] Thus, human chattel and land were both central to determining Margaret's wealth and her class standing. The relative scarcity of white women as heads of households in comparison with black women, combined with the rarity of white women holding more than twenty slaves, demonstrates the unique position in which blacks and Margaret lived at Mount Clare.

Architecture and Racial Tension

Margaret underscored the uniqueness of blacks' situation at Mount Clare by using her wealth to assuage social tension. The revival of business and trade after the American Revolution precipitated a building boom that intersected with trends toward increased privacy, specialized uses for spaces, and tension between classes and races. Elites like Margaret renovated their homes to create distance between their families and domestic laborers.

Table 5.1. Margaret Carroll's slaveholding, 1790–1817

Year	Total	Males and females under 8 years	Males and females, age 8–14	Males 15–45	Females 15–36	Males over 45	Females over 36
1790[a]	47 over age 16						
1798[b]	36 slaves age 12–50, 21 subject to taxation						
1800[c]	7						
1804[d]	32 slaves over age 12	7 value: 35	5 value: 75	14 value: 550	4 value: 120	2 value: 220	0
1810[e]	39						
1813[f]	44	10 value: 120	6 value: 220	15 value: 1740	6 value: 480	4 value: 160	3 value: 50
1817[g]	49						

Notes: a. 1790 U.S. Federal Census, Patapsco Lower Hundred, Baltimore, Maryland, p. 64.
b. Maryland State Papers (Federal Direct Tax) Baltimore County, Middlesex Hundred, Nos. 2833–3147: Particular List of Dwelling Houses, Particular List of Lands, Lots, Buildings, and Wharves; Particular List of Slaves, 1798. Maryland State Papers. M3469-7. MSA SM56-7.
c. 1800 U.S. Federal Census, Baltimore City, Baltimore, MD, Roll 9, p. 161.
d. Baltimore County Commissioners of the Tax (Assessed Persons List) Margaret Carroll, 1804, CR 39,605-10, MSA CM 1204-1.
e. 1810 U.S. Federal Census, Middlesex Hundred, Baltimore, MD. Roll 113, p. 480.
f. Baltimore City Assessor (Tax Records) Mrs. Carroll (widow), 1813, RG 4. Series 2, p. 73, Baltimore City Archives.
g. Baltimore County Register of Wills (Wills) Margaret Carroll, 20 March 1817, WB 10, p. 297, CR 72,244-2 MSA.

Such distance aimed to ameliorate class and racial friction of the post-Revolutionary era in everyday interactions as it grounded the conceptual social location of enslaved blacks in physical places.

Margaret commissioned a number of architectural changes to the mansion at Mount Clare in the 1780s and 1790s. The results structured the interactions between herself, family and guests, enslaved persons, and hires at the mansion. Some changes to the mansion were precipitated by Margaret's desire to "freshen" its appearance. Others were done to repair damage sustained in a fire on May 18, 1790. The "right wing" of the mansion "was entirely consumed, and much valuable furniture considerably damaged; by the exertions of a number of the inhabitants of this town, the left wing and body of the building were preserved. The fire was communicated by a spark falling from the chimney on the roof." The "right wing" was Charles's former office, which stood to the west of the main house.[13] Additionally, Margaret commissioned eight-foot-wide service passages on the far sides of the kitchen and office wings, which moved service entrances away from the main house. Call bells in the kitchen wing provided additional privacy and distance for Margaret and her guests from house servants. Other changes included a larder built off the hyphen between the dining room and kitchen wing. It had a fireplace and could have served as servants' or slaves' quarters. Also, the scullery became known as the pantry. A number of changes were made inside the main house as well. Margaret converted her husband's office into a drawing room, in order to have the three principal rooms necessary for late eighteenth-century, large-scale entertaining: a room for playing cards, a dining room, and a dancing room. Enslaved persons adapted to the restructuring of their movements and, indeed, gained more privacy in the process. Unfortunately for the interpretation of black history today, the wings were demolished in 1870.

Renovations of the mansion were complete by 1798, but quite a few buildings beyond the mansion were in disrepair (fig. 5.1). The 1798 federal assessment provides a detailed list of structures. No plantation layout map survives to situate them on the landscape. Comparison of the 1798 assessment with Margaret's 1817 estate inventory provides a few clues about where they were located. Even so, an attempt to place their general locations on the landscape is important because the buildings and their activities were

Figure 5.1. Mount Clare in 1798. By permission of Michael F. Trostel, FAIA, Trostel & Pearre, Architects.

integral to blacks' everyday lives on the plantation, their movements about it, and to making black history more accessible to visitors today.

The mansion complex contained Margaret's residence and the two wings. From west to east, it included: a brick addition (18 by 12, one story), a brick shed (39 by 24, one story), a brick greenhouse (the orangery, 26 by 26, one story), the brick service passage to the office or drawing room (28 by 8, one story), a brick-and-stone office or drawing room (51 by 21, one story), Margaret's residence (46 by 36, two story, with piazza, 18 by 8), the brick kitchen (34 by 18, one story), the service passage to the kitchen (28 by 8, one story), a brick addition (14 by 12, one story), a brick washhouse (26 by 26, one story), and a brick shed (39 by 24, one story). A smokehouse and a milk house (both 20 by 20, stone, one story) stood near the complex, perhaps at the east wing to be near the kitchen. Bacon, smoked beef and tongues, and hams were kept in the smokehouse.[14] Hired women likely lived in the attic garret bedchambers or slept in Margaret's room. Hires and enslaved persons may have lived in other spaces with fireplaces, such as the kitchen, pantry, orangery, and basement. The "sheds" and "additions" in the wings of the mansion may also have been quarters. Margaret's 1817 estate inventory lists furnishings in one slave quarter, probably the brick shed measuring 39 by 24. "The Quarter" furnishings included a cot and bedstead and a table and chairs. Also nearby were a bathing tub, an old table, and a teakettle and frying pan. Such items indicate that some of the people enslaved by Margaret lived close to the mansion but in their own space.

Other locations for buildings listed on the 1798 assessment are more difficult to place. Plantation support buildings tended to cluster near work areas, such as fields and mills. Some of the structures at Mount Clare housed sheep, horses, cattle, and pigs or were processing areas for hides, wool, and meat. Structures in the vicinity of the mansion at Mount Clare may have included a "stone &c" house (25 by 16), a stone stable (43 by 26, one story), a second stone stable (25 by 25, one story), a stone corn house (18 by 16, one-half story), a stone press house (45 by 34, one story), a frame house (16 by 11, one story), and an old frame cowhouse (21 by 16, one story) to supply the meat house and milk house. The press house may have been a distillery as well as a juice manufactory. By way of comparison, George Washington's Mount Vernon had a distillery for wheat and corn near the mill.[15] Perhaps a similar arrangement existed at Mount Clare.

The assessor also listed buildings at the two milling complexes and perhaps in the fields. The farming complex included barns, stables, and frame structures to protect wood or act as staging areas. In addition to supporting daily life at the plantation, the fields and agricultural buildings provided grain for the mills. The Mount Clare mill complex may have consisted of a miller's house and an old frame (44 by 16, one story) with a brick shed addition (44 by 16). They might have included an old stone blacksmith shop (53 by 24, one story), a log house (fit for fuel, 30 by 24, one story), a stone house (16 by 14, fit to fall, one story), a frame structure (15 by 15, one story), an old frame structure (47 by 20, one story), an old frame barn (38 by 22, one story), and an old stone stable (45 by 24, one story). Perhaps an old log house (32 by 22, one story), an old frame stable (24 by 16, two story), an old stone potato house (15 by 12, one-half story), an old log house (28 by 16, one story), and an old brick cooper shop (16 by 13, one story) stood by the other mill. A two-story brick mill house (26 by 26, two story) and a stone mill house (50 by 46, three story) sat west of the mansion along Gwynns Falls.[16]

Blacks may have worked between Margaret's two mills and the grain fields. Margaret hired white millers to oversee the milling operations.[17] Such structures connected Mount Clare to broader trends. American agricultural production took on considerable importance in Europe in the 1783–1815 period due to war, famine, and population growth. The Carroll mills were among the fifty merchant mills within eighteen miles of Baltimore in 1799. Beginning in 1815, and continuing for the next eleven years, Baltimore—and enslaved people involved in the milling trade—surpassed all other American markets in its flour inspections. One more old log house

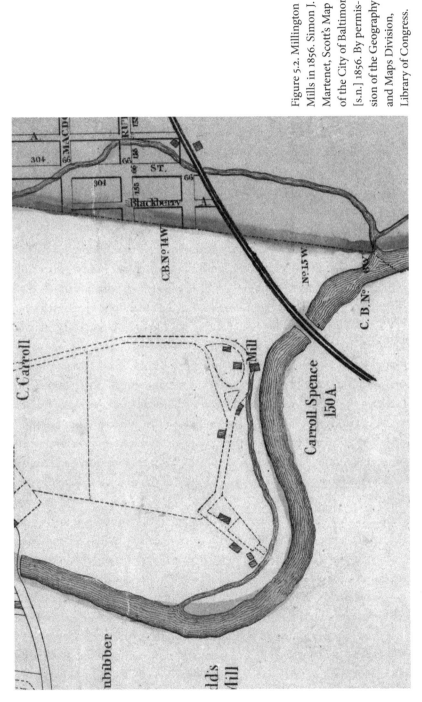

Figure 5.2. Millington Mills in 1856. Simon J. Martenet, Scott's Map of the City of Baltimore, [s.n.] 1856. By permission of the Geography and Maps Division, Library of Congress.

(18 by 16, one story) may have stood near them, or perhaps it was the house pictured in Charles Willson Peale's painting of Mount Clare. Although James Carroll may have expanded it after Margaret's death, the layout gives a sense of the components of a milling complex (fig. 5.2).

Finding the locations of slave quarters at Mount Clare would provide information about the conditions of enslaved persons' lives, as well as shed light on the effect of racism on plantation organization. Unfortunately, the property assessor for Middlesex Hundred (the land hundred in which Mount Clare sat) did not specify which buildings were slave quarters or overseers' housing for Mount Clare or any other property in the hundred. At Mount Clare, "sheds" and "houses" identified by him may have been code for slave quarters. Records across slaveholding states used many terms for housing, such as cabin, hut, quarters, house, double house, dwelling house, or Negro house. Eighteenth-century quarters for enslaved persons tended to be small, one-room, post-in-ground, wooden structures. The number of people per quarter varied greatly, as reported by former slaves, ranging from 260 slaves in 38 cabins to 29 slaves in a long shed to 100 slaves in 27 cabins.[18] One estimate has 5.2 slaves per structure as the average.[19] Assessors in other Baltimore region hundreds, however, did identify slave quarters, and they provided a sense of the proximity, quantity, and character of housing supported at Mount Clare. Quarters at The Caves, a Carroll property, were clustered within two acres of the main house. They were "2 old negro houses, log, each 16 by 20 feet—1 ditto, 20 by 36."[20] Nicholas Carroll enslaved thirty-seven people at The Caves in 1798, and the thirty-six people enslaved at Georgia may have experienced similar living arrangements. The twenty-seven persons enslaved by Eleanor Croxall lived in "one frame negros quarter one story 18 by 18" and "one log negroe quarter one story 20 by 18."[21] Quarters from other places thus offer comparative evidence that suggests the societal norm for slave quarters and indicates what they may have been like at Mount Clare.

James Maccubbin may have followed broader trends in housing during his tenure at Mount Clare by improving the quarters. By the mid-nineteenth century, a building boom in slave quarters throughout the South resulted in larger, better-constructed buildings. Slaveholders believed that upgraded housing could coerce slaves into good behavior and disguise the oppressive nature of slavery. Quarters included a wide variety of architectural configurations, construction materials, and sizes. They might stand near the slaveholder's house, in clusters, or be spread across the landscape. The housing may have reflected the architectural or cultural knowledge of enslaved people. Shotgun-style houses in the South, for example, are a legacy of African and Caribbean cultures in America. Quarters gave enslaved persons a measure of assurance and control over their lives.[22] Although the evidence does not remain for similar upgrades at Mount Clare, the overall historical trend is important for Mount Clare because conditions there were part of a broader mistreatment of enslaved persons that later societal trends aimed to ameliorate.

Material Goods and Social Ceremonies

Within these places and spaces, enslaved blacks witnessed Margaret's changing role in widowhood and the social score she faced. White widowhood highlighted the dependence of an elite woman's social standing on her difference as a white woman from a black slave. Such links between women and race in the antebellum South became a foundation upon which white men built patriarchal ideals. Material culture facilitated the ability of women like Margaret to demonstrate their traditional feminine roles in the home and in society.

Tablewares were considered necessary, in order to both carry out social teas and entertaining, as well as to use the social ritual as an opportunity to display one's wealth and status. Tablewares enabled Margaret to display her standing and carry out a traditional feminine role. On the other hand, enslaved persons gained insight into elites' cultural practices through tablewares. In order to cook, serve, and otherwise do their work, enslaved blacks learned how to wash and store the tablewares, serve courses, set tables, and cook various foods for the event. Enslaved women who worked in the kitchen and in the main house in these ways became familiar with elites' material culture and social rituals.

Complex and labor-intensive meals became popular among wealthy elites in the mid-eighteenth century. Meals came to require special sauces, multiple courses, trimmings, and other elaborate expressions of luxurious abundance. Diners in the early nineteenth century sat down to large serving dishes at the center of a table. Smaller dishes, sauce containers, and pickle dishes sat among them. Water decanters stood at the corners. After the meal, a dessert course was set out, and then women and men separated for post-meal socializing.[23] Enslaved blacks set the table, moved furniture in the house to accommodate large parties, and cleaned up afterward. Unlike in their own homes, enslaved blacks prepared a separate, use-specific room for meals: the dining room, a hallmark of wealthier and larger houses. Enslaved blacks also laid out more complex tablewares for the Carrolls than for their own meals. Charles and Margaret ordered sets of Chinese export porcelain and creamware in graduated sizes; forks and knives; and serving dishes for soup, sides, or everyday dish sets from London and America. The amount of porcelain recovered archaeologically from the mansion area compared to other ceramic types indicates that the Carrolls used expensive, fine tableware for dining on a regular and frequent basis.[24] In the process of carrying out their work, blacks learned white elites' social ceremonies and values, such as the meaning of formal versus informal place settings, the appropriate use of different ceramic patterns, and the service requirements for entertaining or everyday dining.

Beyond meals, tea and the social ceremonies surrounding it presented Margaret and the people she enslaved with another marker of wealth and standing. The Carrolls were particular about their tea, as they could afford to be. When Charles was alive, his letters to tea merchants indicated that Margaret was displeased with the quality of the tea they sent. Her complaints demonstrated her knowledge of tea as well as her concern over having the best of it. Tea—and its quality—enabled Margaret and Charles to distinguish themselves from the less wealthy. In the mid-eighteenth century, drinking tea became less the domain of the elite and more accessible to everyone. By the nineteenth century, tea, like dining, became more complex in its furnishings, which included a tea table, a tray or waiter or tea board, a teapot, a cream jug, a sugar bowl and tongs, cups, saucers, teaspoons, a tea urn, a stand for the urn or pot, a slop bowl, a canister, a strainer, a spoon tray, and plates for snacks. A genteel tea required the right table settings, enough food and drink for each tea-taker, and sufficient familiarity with the ceramics and foods in order to use them correctly.[25] Enslaved blacks acquired knowledge of tea ceremonies and their social meaning in the process of setting up the tea service, preparing snacks and beverages, or serving Margaret and her guests. They were integral elements of the social ritual designed to emphasize enslaved blacks' subordinate position to elite whites.

Cloth and clothing was traditionally another area for white women to manage with enslaved blacks. Mistresses worked with enslaved women to spin thread, weave and dye cloth, and sew clothing. As they did with food, slaveholders tended to ration cloth and clothes in the nineteenth century. Comparative evidence from other plantations provides insight into possible clothing rations at Mount Clare. Robert Collins advised two suits of cotton for spring and summer, two suits of woolens for winter, four pairs of shoes, and three hats per year. Collins observed that neatness was important to enslaved blacks and engendered pride and self-respect. He saw clothing as a way to foster good behavior.[26] One southern plantation owner allotted each adult field hand seven yards of oznabrigg, three yards of check, three yards of baize, and a hat each October. Another provided two cotton shirts, two pairs of pants, a pair of shoes, and a woolen jacket each year in the fall.[27]

Cloth and clothing were made at Mount Clare and The Caves. Flax was grown behind the barn at The Caves in the early nineteenth century, and probably before then. Women gathered it. Moses, the weaver, wove flax at The Caves into linen for trousers and other clothes.[28] Eight to ten hand spinners had to work to keep a weaver occupied full time,[29] which suggests that Moses had help. His equipment included a loom and gears, three flax spinning wheels, three yarn wheels, an iron pot, an unfinished loom with two flax hackles, a cut reel, and an old copper boiler.[30] Eliza Tilghman Goldsborough, Margaret's favorite niece and a frequent guest at Mount Clare, left a diary of her daily interactions with the people on her own property. As part of their transactions, Eliza supplied clothing to blacks who worked inside the house more frequently than to field laborers during the year. She paid enslaved women small sums for extra spinning and weaving.[31] It is tempting to assume that Eliza's practices were condoned by Margaret and even modeled by her, such that the women at Mount Clare had a similar arrangement.

Advertisements for some blacks who escaped from the Carrolls' properties demonstrated that they mixed and matched European and African tastes to create a highly conscious, consumer-aware, hybrid style. Aaron Pulley cut a colorful sartorial picture relative to Eddenborough or Jack Lynch when he escaped from Mount Clare in 1799: "His clothes were a bottle green, coarse cloth coat, a nankin coatee, a orange colored cotton waistcoat, with purple stripes in it, lead colored cassimere breeches, nankin waistcoat and breeches, cotton stockings, a pair of shoes, a new hat, and white shirts."[32] Clothing, when used to express personal style, provided freedom within racism and from one's subordinate position in colonial and antebellum society.[33] But, if Margaret provided some clothes, and others were made at the plantations, where did enslaved blacks acquire such garments? Perhaps they wore hand-me-downs from the Carroll family, purchased them, or modified former uniforms to make them.

Lifetimes at Mount Clare

Amid the routines and rituals organized by architecture, social ceremony, clothing, and work were the roles and expectations assigned to people of various ages, genders, and abilities. From birth until death, each enslaved individual at Mount Clare fulfilled responsibilities both to their enslavers and to their own families and communities. Thirty-two enslaved blacks lived at Mount Clare in 1804, forty-four in 1813, and forty in 1817. Margaret placed the several people she enslaved in 1817 at The Caves after Nicholas Carroll's death in 1812. Nicholas Carroll left significant debt and a complicated estate. Margaret inherited a share of Nicholas Carroll's land, but not slaves.[34] Comparison of the numbers over time demonstrates the ways in which infant mortality, skill acquisition and labor, family life, and freedom took shape at Mount Clare in terms of life stages and gender. Understanding what life might have been like for different people enslaved at Mount Clare provides both insight into everyday life and the inequality of lived experiences of slavery and enslavement.

Infancy

Infant mortality was high in the late eighteenth and early nineteenth century among all populations. Enslaved children under a year old were commonly omitted from tax assessments as part of a slaveholder's wealth and, as a result, are often lost to history. Compared to enslaved women, Margaret's access to prenatal nutrition and care and her ability to ease up on work in advance of childbirth made her experience of pregnancy different from theirs. Her twin daughters, in addition, were born into a world where their white race and class status immediately conferred privileges unavailable to blacks, including and especially freedom. Despite these advantages, Margaret suffered loss nonetheless, when her daughters died in infancy. Infant and child mortality was common in enslaved communities as well. Dolly's son James was about a year old when he was baptized in 1804, but his absence from 1817 accounts suggests that he passed away in the intervening years. Perhaps, then, other gaps between siblings signaled infant and child mortality in the enslaved community at Mount Clare. Dolly and another woman, named Henny, each bore a child every two years. Yet, just as Dolly's son James (b. 1803) might have fallen between William (b. 1802) and Thomas (b. 1806), another child might have been born between Thomas and Sampson (b. 1811). Henny may have lost children between the births of John (b. 1806) and Jim/Sam (b. 1812), or between Jim/Sam and Bill (b. 1816). Infant and child mortality was only one explanation for the timing of infants, however. Enslaved women practiced birth control and committed infanticide; but they also miscarried, or their nutrition was too poor to carry to term. Women and men living apart made conception less likely, and their relationships could be interrupted by escape or sale. Despite these challenges, and even though infant mortality was high, infants at Mount Clare more often than not lived into childhood with at least their mothers if not both parents present.

Privileges afforded to some infants and very small children may have signaled that Margaret had a special relationship with some of the people she enslaved, especially the Garrett family. Richard Garrett was a gardener for Margaret at the mansion, so he came into greater contact with her than enslaved people who worked farther from the house. One Garrett child was baptized at Margaret's church, St. Paul's. James, son of "Richard and Dorithea Garrit" (later Garrett) was about a year old when he was baptized on July 20, 1804.[35] James, according to St. Paul's records, was the only child from Mount Clare who was baptized there, but he was also unusual because he was a slave. Most of the few "colored" infants baptized at St. Paul's belonged to freepersons. Unfortunately, however, James may have died at a young age: he was not named on Margaret's estate inventory in 1817. In addition, the Garretts' youngest daughter was named Margaret, possibly after Margaret Carroll. Upon her enslaver's death, Margaret Garrett and her younger siblings were among the small children who were permitted to go with their parents.

Any joy associated with motherhood and the creation of families was tempered with a lack of control over the fates of children. Given Margaret's own losses, how did she treat enslaved infants' births and deaths? How did the mothers react? Or if infant mortality was lower than demographic analysis suggests, why? What conditions at Mount Clare and in the Balti-more region were conducive or detrimental to the survival of infants into childhood? Such questions tap into why infants play a significant role in black history at Mount Clare.

Childhood and Prepubescence

The number of children under age eight at Mount Clare almost doubled in the nineteenth century: there were seven in 1804, ten in 1813, and thirteen in 1817. The number of enslaved male and female youngsters ages eight to fourteen remained stable at Mount Clare, with five in 1804 and six in 1813 and 1817. In comparison, the number of children declined over time at The Caves after Charles's death. Nicholas Maccubbin enslaved thirteen children there in 1783, four in 1812, and five in 1813. Margaret enslaved two children at The Caves in 1817, but the number then enslaved by Nicholas C. Carroll is not known. Ten children lived at Carrolls Island in 1783 and none in 1812.

Enslaved infants who lived into childhood took on responsibilities both in Margaret's household and their own. The grooming of children to carry out work around the plantation began as early as possible. Healthy children who became accustomed to laboring contributed to production on plan-tations and to the enslaver's wealth. Young enslaved children often grew up working alongside their parents in kitchens or fields. Older children learned to be house servants and were apprenticed to learn trades. They began working fields around eight years old. Records from other planta-tions indicate that boys and girls carried out lighter tasks, tended farm animals, conducted housework or errands, and babysat.[36] If young boys did tend animals at Mount Clare, by 1804 they were responsible for twelve horses, forty-two black cattle, fifty-one hogs, and twenty-nine sheep.[37] By 1813, however, youths tended similar numbers of horses (twelve) and cattle (forty-nine), but half as many hogs (twenty-four) and no sheep.[38] They may also have looked after chickens, turkeys, geese, and other birds and animals. The archaeologically recovered faunal record indicates the consumption of beef, fish, turkey, chicken, pork, and possibly goat, due to the deposition of sawed bones in the vicinity of the mansion.

Children and youths absorbed skills and knowledge from their parents and enslavers about everyday plantation maintenance as well as the power relations that typified relationships between elites and slaves. Plantation mistresses were involved in enslaved children's lives. They might babysit the children, advise their parents on health care, and teach them European American standards of morality and proper conduct. Enslavers' involvement in the children's lives created tension with black mothers.[39] Gifts, attention, special dispensations, and teaching of social standards exacerbated tensions between enslaved parents and their enslavers. Parents took advantage of opportunities that came to their children as a result of slaveholders' paternalistic or maternalistic attitudes, however. Since enslaved children were owned by their enslavers, but the parental responsibility fell to their families, they found themselves situated between two sets of adults vying for their economic worth and emotional development. They were "children without childhoods" as a result of their experiences with separation and despair.[40] James Pennington, for example, described his parents' inability to give him sufficient attention:

My parents were not able to give any attention to their children during the day. I often suffered much from hunger and other similar causes. To estimate the sad state of a slave child, you must look at it as a helpless human being thrown upon the world without the benefit of its natural guardians. It is thrown into the world without a social circle to flee to for hope, shelter, comfort, or instruction. The social circle, with all its heaven-ordained blessings, is of the utmost importance to the tender child; but of this, the slave child, however tender and delicate, is robbed.[41]

Adulthood

Blacks' roles became delineated by sex with the onset of puberty and as physical ability merged with expertise in aspects of plantation management. Men ages fourteen to forty-five and women ages fourteen to thirty-six were the highest-valued groups at Mount Clare and other Carroll plantations. The number of women ages fourteen to thirty-six changed significantly, from five in 1804 to eight in 1813 and then to four in 1817. On the other hand, the male population was larger, more consistent in size, and more valuable. Fourteen men were at Mount Clare in 1804, fifteen in 1813, and twelve in 1817. They outnumbered women about 3:1. Margaret may have purchased men when natural population increase did not result in enough males for hard labor. Jacob Hall and William Coney, for example, appear unrelated to the rest of the Mount Clare population.

Data such as the age at first child's birth, the absence or presence of fathers, marital status, and the number of years between children demonstrate that black mothers at Mount Clare had a typical experience of enslaved persons and families. Women ages fourteen to thirty-six tended to work in fields or in the mansion, but they carried the additional weight of childbearing, too. Childbirth decreased the life expectancy of women and diminished their capacity to work full time and, in turn, made purchasing them more of a gamble for enslavers. A few women go missing between the 1804 and 1813 assessments for Mount Clare; one explanation is that they died in childbirth. Enslavers encouraged women to bear children, sometimes with inducements such as gifts, time off, lighter workloads, or freedom.

Enslaved women in the South typically had their first child by age nineteen or twenty, waited a few years for another child, and beginning with the second bore children about every two and a half years.[42] The patterns held for black women at Mount Clare, as seen by comparing two generations of mothers in 1817. Of the older generation, Dolly bore her first child at age twenty and her second about three years later. Henny had her first at age nineteen. Dolly's daughters bore their first children at ages seventeen and twenty. Henny's eldest daughter birthed her first at age seventeen. If the younger-generation mothers were married, the unions were not recognized in Carroll records. Dolly's and Henny's marriages to men at Mount Clare, however, were recognized. The evening out of the male/female ratio by the late eighteenth century improved the regularity of family units; indeed, the Garrett and Lynch families grew by a child every two to four years. The regularity of births suggests that the families had some stability. It may also indicate that Dolly, Richard, John, and Henny held positions specific to or unique to Mount Clare, compared to The Caves or Carrolls Island, such as cooks or gardeners.

Such circumstances made relationships between men and women a challenge, and they also resulted in stepfamilies. One example at Mount Clare is the relationship between Henny and her husband, John Lynch. Henny bore her first child, Maria, at age nineteen, when John was ten years old; it seems unlikely that John is Maria's biological father. Henny's next child was born eight years later to John. She then bore a child every two years thereafter until 1817. Mothers, such as Mary or Sukey at Mount Clare, like many other enslaved women, raised their children together, due to the absence of their children's fathers on a day-to-day basis. On the other hand, Margaret assigned adult women work away from their children. Mary's young son Jerry lived at The Caves while she was at Mount Clare with her other son in 1817. Perhaps Mary moved among the plantations but not always with her children. Fathers' interaction with their children might be curtailed by their living on another plantation, or they might be sold, find their visits to other plantations rationed, or escape. Although matriarchical childrearing was a cultural tradition in Africa, whether or not enslaved blacks practiced it deliberately or out of necessity remains unclear. The cultural tradition may have been familiar, but in America it was dictated by forces beyond black mothers' control.

Another characteristic of the midlife demographic was that its members had the least stability of any age group. Midlife individuals were most likely to escape, be sold, or be hired out. By 1804, six men ages 14–45 and one woman age 14–36 are unaccounted for. One boy age 8–14, two women ages 14–36, and three men ages 15–45 are missing in 1813. By 1817, no men between the ages of 32 and 43 lived at Mount Clare (the possible exception is Moses, who was ill). What became of them?

A few blacks became free, either on their own terms or through manumission. Aaron Pulley, who escaped in 1799, may account for one of the men absent in 1804. Another explanation is that free or self-emancipated blacks fought in the War of 1812. In 1813 and 1814, an "exodus" of blacks shook the institution of slavery and generated panic among enslavers, even though by war's end many slaves remained on plantations.[43] Whether or not any enslaved persons escaped from Mount Clare to join the British remains unknown, but no exodus took place. Margaret enslaved fifteen males between fourteen and forty-five in 1813. Manumission was another path to freedom. Margaret freed Henry Harden in 1815.[44] Were other men released before Margaret's death? If so, how did they earn money to purchase freedom, or what was the inducement for Margaret to release them? Perhaps he was hired out. Many widows hired out slaves as porters, deliverymen, or in trade labor as a source of income.[45] For example, Margaret hired out Milly, a girl between the ages of fourteen and twenty-six, according to the 1800 assessment for Baltimore City. She had seven slaves in the city as per the 1800 census, but no one there by 1810.[46] Were they typical? Or did Margaret's wealth and a desire to maintain the plantation prevent more people from working off-site? Many blacks from other sites hired themselves out, with or without permission. Black men earned small amounts of cash by overwork around Mount Clare.[47] Other inducements were more subtle. Unpleasant attitudes, threats, and drunkenness pushed enslavers to decide whether to place advertisements to sell a slave or allow a person to purchase freedom.

Males ages thirty-two to forty-three and women who had not yet borne children were most likely to escape slavery or be freed, as shown by Mount Clare records. One anomaly is Nell Williams, who was seventeen years old at the time of her freedom in 1795. Two other individuals, Henny and Fanny, were also freed in 1795, but it is unclear if they were her children, or how their freedom was established. Henny was two years old at the time, but Fanny was not born until 1804.[48] Margaret still bought and sold slaves in 1795. She corresponded with a potential buyer or hirer of a slave named Phillis who was to serve two years more. Phillis may have been willing to serve six more years, but Margaret does not explain why, and the difference was crucial to the amount that the buyers were negotiating. Margaret explained that her intention in selling Phillis was to replace her if she could because hiring was extremely costly and difficult.[49] What motivated Margaret to free Nell? Were Henny and Fanny her daughters? Did a family member purchase Nell's freedom? Was Margaret selling slaves in order to purchase more? Or did it have to do with the liquidation of the Baltimore Iron Works? The remaining Baltimore Company partners manumitted several adults and children around the same time, and company land was being sold then, too.[50] Escape, joining the military, and manumission were the three ways that enslaved blacks at Mount Clare became free during Margaret's lifetime.

The Elderly

The older generation at Mount Clare comprised men forty-five years and older and women thirty-six years and older. Few men remained on the plantation to reach the forty-five-plus age demographic. They and women age thirty-six-plus provided stability and institutional knowledge for each generation. Grandparents cared for their grandchildren in the absence of parents who had been sent away to work, been sold, or passed away. Frederick Douglass writes in his autobiography about living with his grandmother until called to work in the fields. He describes his affection for her and the pain of being separated from her.[51] Elders played important roles in the development of community and the memory of homeland culture. West African cultures provided a context for understanding the roles of older or elderly persons in the New World as they faced racism and oppression as slaves. Elderly blacks passed knowledge of African traditions, social practices, and lifeways to younger generations. Stories and folktales—told in African languages when the storyteller's knowledge remained—were infused with references to animals and foodways in Africa and teachings about African culture. The passing of cultural knowledge came with an ethic for generational respect and community loyalty.[52]

Adult mortality at Mount Clare is difficult to gauge. Nicholas Carroll enslaved thirty-one people at The Caves in 1812, ten of whom were about sixty years old or older.[53] Upon James Carroll's death at Mount Clare in 1832, seven of the nineteen people he enslaved were over fifty-five and three were seventy-five years old. One estimate of slave mortality calculates that more than a third of enslaved persons reached age fifty by 1850. By 1860, the number had increased to half of all enslaved persons.[54] Margaret enslaved one "verry old" woman named Eve in 1817, but the population overall appears to have been relatively young compared with that enslaved by her nephews.

Choices and Manumission in Antebellum Baltimore

Considering the size and demographic scope of the black population at Mount Clare and The Caves, enslaved persons and elites alike faced uncertainty about their futures in a Baltimore so different from how it had been in the colonial era. Margaret and her advisors, Henry Brice and Tench Tilghman, must have considered the factors surrounding black life in Baltimore—or, at least, what they believed about it—as they prepared her last will and testament. Several factors influenced Margaret's choices for manumission in advance of her death. Enslaved people were powerless before the law and when facing elites' choices for them.

Margaret's slaveholding as a widow happened during a period of transition regarding slavery's role in society during the late eighteenth century. Planters in the colonial era tended to keep enslaved people and land in the family for their productive value.[55] After the colonial era, the considerable changes in society included slavery. Between 1790 and 1820, the population of Baltimore exploded. The enslaved population multiplied almost by four and the white population by three. Half of Baltimore's black population was enslaved in 1800, and in 1840 just 15 percent was.[56] Frederick Douglass wrote about his visits to Baltimore from Maryland's Eastern Shore around this time. He wrote that he observed

> . . . a marked difference in the manner of treating slaves, generally, from which I had witnessed in that isolated and out-of-the-way part of the country where I began life. A city slave is almost a free citizen, in Baltimore, compared with a slave on Col. Lloyd's plantation. He is much better fed and clothed, is less dejected in his appearance, and enjoys privileges altogether unknown to the whip-driven slave on the plantation. Slavery dislikes a dense population, in which there is a majority of non-slaveholders.[57]

As Douglass found, everyday life for enslaved and free blacks in Baltimore felt fundamentally different from that in the Chesapeake area hinterland, but it was particularly different from slavery in the southern states. Slavery became a geographically southern phenomenon as the northern states began to abolish it. The number of people enslaved in Baltimore peaked in 1810 and declined afterward. After the War of 1812 and the depression that followed, the transition from enslaved to free labor gained momentum. The number of men enslaved in the industrial or craft labor sector tapered off in the 1820s. Free labor became cheaper and enslaved blacks were less able to extract concessions from employers or owners. The expanding southern cotton market and development of western territories refocused the slave trade away from Maryland. All these factors led to a decrease in enslaved men in Baltimore but an increase in women enslaved in domestic positions, due to the kind of labor required.

Baltimore-area planters were moving away from slavery as a way to build capital, as burgeoning industrial development offered a more stable investment. Short-term hiring became more attractive and cost-effective in the region than slavery. Margaret had developed her own wealth through real estate and banking, but not industry. Slaveholders found the support of enslaved people increasingly difficult, with diminishing return on their investment. Their ability to support their own families diminished, as slavery became a burden without significant financial compensation. Enslaved individuals and families at Mount Clare were not a "burden" to Margaret in this way, because she was elderly and had no family of her own to support. Planters ceased to bequeath enslaved persons to their descendants, but instead directed their executors to sell them.[58] Margaret wanted her property distributed among family members, but she had no living children and her extended family already held sizable enslaved populations. Although Margaret maintained Mount Clare for James Maccubbin, the next owner, she neither owned the property nor passed on the people she managed upon it during widowhood to him. Rather than bequeath her wealth through human property, possibly burdening her relatives, Margaret bequeathed household furniture, clothing, and jewelry to her female relatives and "liquidated" slaves and other property in order to give them cash.

The law provided some structure to Margaret's and her advisors' choices regarding manumission or freedom. Manumission laws regulated the terms of manumission. They aimed to prevent a slaveholder from evading the support of a freedperson during his or her lifetime, protect the public from the responsibility of caring for destitute freedpersons, and limit manumission. The Maryland Assembly passed an act in 1752 to prevent freed disabled or superannuated slaves from becoming a burden to society after emancipation. It limited manumissions to enslaved persons under fifty years old who could work to support themselves. It prohibited manumission by last will and testament, requiring instead that manumissions occur only by deed recorded in the county court. Furthermore, the law required all free blacks to register with the court.[59] An act passed in 1796 liberalized the ability to manumit by increasing the legal instruments that a slaveholder could use. Whereas before slaveholders used deeds in county land records, now they could use wills, chattel records, and other legal records. The act also specified that manumitted individuals had to be younger than forty-five years old and able to work and support themselves. It furthermore required that deeds of manumission be recorded at the court in order to prove freedom.[60] Something of these issues was suggested in Brice's actions regarding other estates for which he acted as executor. Brice petitioned the court in 1813 on an executorship for Margaret's nephew Nicholas Carroll. He hired out enslaved males from the estate but knew "no occupation for the women nor means to support the Children." He argued that they were "an incumbrance [sic] and will if retained involve his wards in much expense and materially lessen their income hardly now sufficient for their reasonable maintenance." Brice asked the court to permit him to sell the women and children.[61] Testamentary manumission and delayed manumission—meaning the promise of freedom at a future date with a last will and testament as the manumitting document—became a common practice.

Margaret's choices would have been influenced by the world as she saw it. For many antebellum southerners of Margaret's demographic, pro-slavery ideology and doctrine transcended race. It provided answers to the problem of ordering society according to labor and capital. Slavery became less socially palatable; manumission became more fashionable, but its practice revealed the internal conflicts slaveholders felt. Manumissions by prominent men such as Robert Carter and George Washington—with whom Margaret had corresponded and admired—inspired others of less status to manumit. They found it not one difficult choice to make but a set of choices. Washington, for example, thought twice about manumission because it would split up families and disrupt the kin networks that extended across his plantations and into neighboring plantations.[62] De-layed manumission protected slave owners' financial interests while appeas-ing ideological discomfort with slavery. Enslavers even told themselves that it was an incentive for enslaved persons to be reliable and provide good service. Margaret's perpetuation of slavery through delayed manumission may suggest her shared belief in the naturalness of slavery, but also that it was an untenable practice. Considering Margaret's request that young children go with their parents, she may also have had difficulty splitting up families.

Another influence on Margaret's and Brice's actions was the Episcopa-lian church's doctrine. Both were members of St. Paul's parish in Baltimore. Margaret was undoubtedly aware of tensions surrounding slavery within the Episcopal Church. Episcopalians, unlike Quakers and Methodists, supported slavery implicitly by not disavowing it outright. The call to free slaves based on religious arguments appeared to attack the morality of large landowners in the church. The records of St. Paul's parish in Baltimore do not capture the congregation's debates about or feelings about slavery, but many of its white members were slaveholders. Blacks were afforded lim-ited participation in church activities. More than half of the people who purchased enslaved persons from Margaret's estate attended church at St. Paul's. Members of St. Paul's were among a group of men who founded the Maryland Society for Promoting the Abolition of Slavery, and the Re-lief of Free Negroes, and Others, Unlawfully Held in Bondage in 1789. Slaveholders could not be members of the society, and only men are listed as participants.[63] Margaret's gender and her slaveholding disqualified her from membership no matter what her beliefs on abolition and emancipa-tion may have been. Bishop James Kemp was against slavery but recom-mended delayed manumission to free slaves. In 1816, he reminded the par-ishes to include blacks in their religious instruction.[64] The influence of the Maryland Society or church leaders over St. Paul's Parish and Margaret's thinking in 1817 is unknown. Few freed or enslaved blacks were baptized or married at St. Paul's in comparison with whites. No blacks were buried in the graveyard. While the church extended some tolerance toward en-slaved blacks, its members tended to perpetuate the institution of slavery, as seen in Margaret's choice to delay manumission for most of the people she enslaved.

Margaret's attitude toward race and betterment may, on the other hand, be indicated by her support of the St. Paul's charity school for girls. Margaret left two lots in Baltimore to St. Paul's for the school. The school was organized in 1799 to educate young, orphaned, or disadvantaged girls in reading, writing, needlework, and other tasks. Girls were then sent out by the school to work.[65] Margaret's support of uplift for white disadvantaged girls did not carry over to enslaved blacks at Mount Clare, as suggested by differences in literacy. The older generation was illiterate, but, according to later census records, their children were not. Dolly Garrett's daughter Margaret was enslaved as a small child, but she and her children learned to read and write by the mid-nineteenth century. Jacob Hall built his family as an older man. He and his wife were illiterate, yet their children were not.[66] Some of the older population may have learned to read later in life or kept their literacy secret. Although formerly enslaved persons may have concealed their literacy from census enumerators, government documents chart a trend for increasing and more reliable literacy among generations further removed from enslavement.

Margaret does not appear to have provided material uplift to blacks, either. Margaret gave specific instructions on the distribution of her property to family members and bequeathed her common clothing to "hireling" Mary Browning. She did not specify any items for enslaved persons. Comparison of two nineteenth-century inventories, however, suggests that Margaret may have given her everyday ceramic tableware and stoneware mugs to enslaved persons before her death. An inventory dating to the turn of the century omits the most valuable household goods, such as the china ordered from England and her jewelry. It included, however, sets of queensware (or creamware) and blue and white plates and dishes, mugs, a redware coffee pot and sugar dish, and water jugs in stoneware, redware, and "brown" that are not listed in Margaret's 1817 estate inventory. Items associated with tea and alcohol, such as teacups or wine glasses, are accounted for on the 1817 inventory. Margaret appears to have considered bedclothes, clothing, and furniture to belong to the people she enslaved, as they were not inventoried at her death.

Margaret's manumission choices aligned closely with those of other wealthy elites who looked beyond slavery for investments. Considering both Margaret's status and her manumission of forty-nine people, blacks from Mount Clare and The Caves were outliers to general trends in the region. Slaveholders of three or fewer people in Baltimore City were three times as likely to manumit than slaveholders who possessed seven or more.[67] In comparison, the most reliable manumitters in Anne Arundel County were women with fewer than twenty enslaved people who did not grow tobacco, hired out slaves, freed on a selective basis, and stipulated delayed manumission.[68] Planters in Baltimore County were turning away from slavery as a way to build capital. Instead, they directed their inheritors to sell the slaves and invest the profits in more stable outlets.

White widowhood emphasized the differences between enslaved blacks and white elite females. Margaret sustained her wealth and added to it. She commissioned architectural changes and social ceremonies to support her position while allowing outbuildings and quarters used by blacks to fall into disrepair. The image of Margaret cannot exist without an understanding of her slaveholder status.

6

Manumission and Freedom

Margaret Tilghman Carroll died at Mount Clare on March 14, 1817, at age seventy-six. Her death brought about major changes for the forty-nine people she enslaved. Some were sold while others were freed, but none were kept at Mount Clare or The Caves any longer. Following what happened to them next in slavery and freedom shows the range of experiences that enslaved blacks might encounter after a slaveholder's death. Their stories show that freed blacks were defined by more than their past and dispel the myth that freedom brought equality. Freed blacks from Mount Clare and The Caves entered the developing working class of antebellum Baltimore. Some raised families and found jobs as gardeners, bricklayers, washers, and laborers; others disappeared. One became a leader in the African Methodist Episcopal Church. It is important to note, as will be discussed in the coming chapters, that black history did not stop at Mount Clare. These "what next" stories are important to tell. For historic plantations to be relevant and of service to society, they must talk about the ways in which slavery and racism continued to affect blacks, even after they had obtained their freedom, because they are at the root of inequalities that inhibit social justice.

Freedom "Deemed Best"

After Margaret's death, the forty-nine people she enslaved at Mount Clare and The Caves must have wondered what would become of them: Would they be sold? Would Margaret manumit them? If so, under what terms? What might life be like as a free black person? Margaret left all her "Negroes and Slaves" to the executors of her estate, Henry Brice and Tench

Tilghman Jr., "in trust that they will set them all free at such ages and in such Terms as they deem best under all circumstances having a view to a provision for the Comfortable support of the aged and infirm with which duty my Executors are charged."[1] This meant, however, that blacks remained powerless to direct the course of their lives. Brice liquidated Margaret's land and slaves into cash for her female relatives, rather than distribute human chattel among them.[2] Manumission at Mount Clare and The Caves was thus not a benevolent act but was a practical way to recoup Margaret's investment in slavery while reinforcing the status of white women.

Margaret gave few specific instructions in her will. She trusted Brice, one of her husband's nephews, to act as he "deemed best," directing him to have "a view to a provision for the Comfortable support of the aged and infirm." The one exception was "the Negro boy Tom," whom Margaret gave to Charles Ross of Annapolis to serve until age thirty-one.[3] Eve, who was "verry old," may have gone to live with the Lynch family, but nothing indicates that she was freed. Moses had consumption, and what happened to him after 1818 remains unknown. As for the youngest, Margaret indicated that "the smaller children should be given to their parents if they were willing to accept them." And the parents surely did: John Lynch took Sam (age five), Bill (age three), and Henny (age two). Richard Garrett took Sampson (age six) and Margaret (age four). Richard's daughter Sukey, who was not freed but sold to a new owner, "accepted" her daughter Becky (age four). The children were relatively fortunate. Of the manumissions registered in the Baltimore court between 1790 and 1830, fewer than a third of people age eighteen and under were immediately freed.[4] No record remains of the parents purchasing the children, but no legal record was entered at the time to certify their release. Decades later, in the early 1840s, Brice tied up a few of these loose ends. He testified in court on behalf of Margaret and Bill to register their freed status. Due to uncertainty surrounding the status of Eve, Moses, and the six children, it is unknown whether Margaret can be credited with their freedom, despite singling them out.

Brice freed seven adults soon after Margaret's death: Richard Garrett and his wife, Dolly; John Lynch and his wife, Henny; and Jacob, Jerry, and Nat.[5] Four of the manumissions aligned with a 1796 law. It specified that enslaved persons under forty-five years old and able to support themselves could be freed.[6] Margaret's estate papers list Jerry, Nat, Jacob, and Dolly as

being forty-four years old, just shy of the legal cutoff age. While they actually could have been forty-four years old, Dolly's changing rate of age over
the remainder of her life might indicate that Brice estimated or assigned
their ages in order to free them. Dolly was forty-four years old in 1817, seventy in 1840, according to her certificate of freedom, and eighty-plus at the
time of her death, which occurred sometime between the 1850 and 1860
censuses (fig. 6.1). At each point, her age wobbles by a few critical years—
enough to raise the possibility that she was older than forty-four in 1817. A
fifth manumission aligned with an eighteenth-century tradition of freeing
enslaved persons at age thirty-one. John Lynch was thirty-one years old in
1818, when he was freed. On the other hand, why—or how—Brice freed
Richard Garrett or Henny Lynch is unknown. Richard, age fifty, may have
stayed on at Mount Clare to continue working as a gardener. Henny, age
forty, went to live with John Lynch, but the terms of her freedom are unknown. No evidence remains that Margaret made arrangements with any
members of the enslaved community for them to purchase their freedom.

The remaining thirty-four people at Mount Clare and The Caves were
sold under terms of delayed manumission. Brice sold twenty-nine people
over ten days between April 1817 and February 1818. Brice stipulated freedom for most females at age twenty-eight but a few at age twenty-five. The
ages for males ranged from twenty-eight to thirty-six years old. Females
between ages seven and twenty and males between ages seven and twenty-
two brought the highest prices. Their value resulted from their age, health,
and number of years left before manumission. Each male sold for three
hundred dollars, mothers with children for one hundred twenty or one
hundred seventy-five dollars, and females without children for two hundred or two hundred twenty dollars.[7] The one exception was Jacob Hall.
He was sold for one hundred dollars to Eleanor Dall, the only woman to
purchase an enslaved person from Margaret's estate. Some individuals were
sold with only a few years left in slavery, like Jacob Hall, whose freedom
was set for 1819, or Suckey from Mount Clare, in 1823. Manumitted children had the longest wait for emancipation. Six-year-old Nelson was to
wait twenty-two years—until 1839. Two-year-old Matilda was to be freed
in 1840 after twenty-three years. Five infants or small children were sold
with their mothers, but Brice assigned a year of freedom to only one child.

Margaret did not specify that children born of freedwomen would

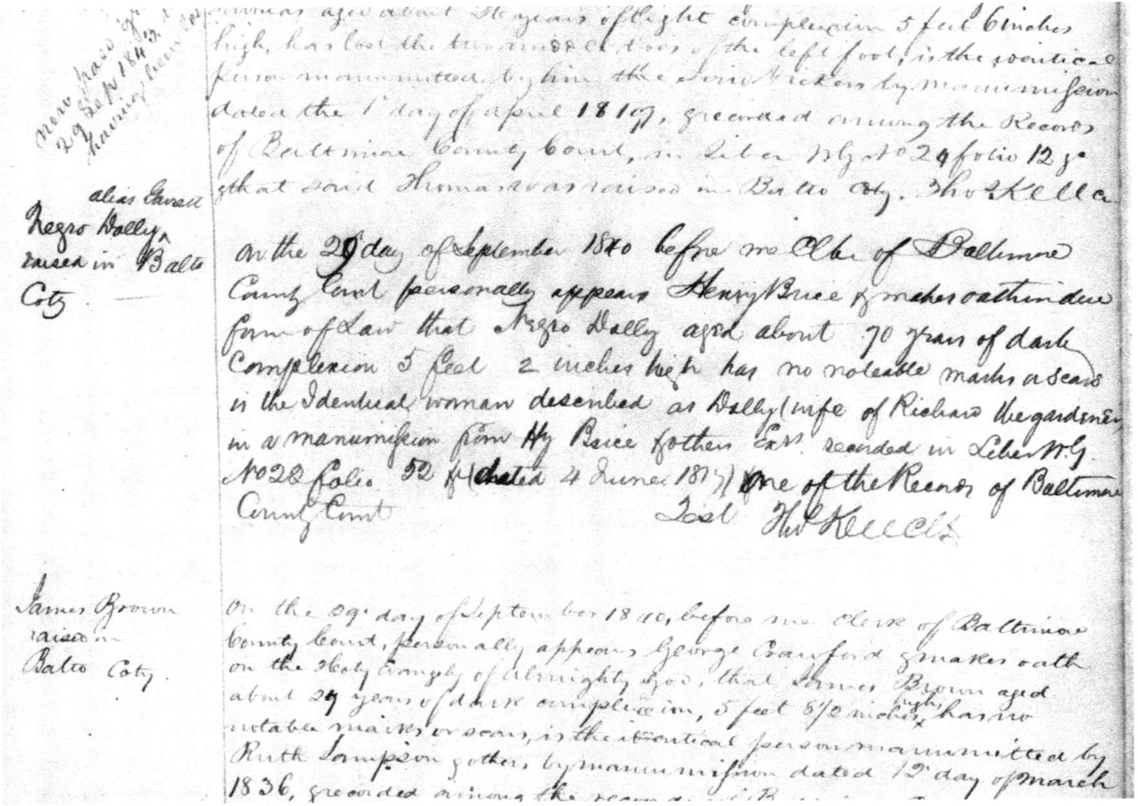

Negro Dolly alias Garrett raised in Balto Coty

On the 29 day of September 1840 before me Clerk of Baltimore County Court personally appears Henry Bruce & makes oath in due form of Law that Negro Dolly aged about 70 years of dark Complexion 5 feet 2 inches high has no noteable marks or scars is the Identical woman described as Dolly (wife of Richard the gardener) in a manumission from Hy Bruce & others Exrs recorded in Liber W.G. No 28 folio 52 &c (dated 4 June 1817) one of the Records of Baltimore County Court

Test Thos Kell Clk

Figure 6.1. Certificate of Freedom for Negro Dolly alias Garrett, September 29, 1840. Baltimore County Court. By permission of the Maryland State Archives.

themselves be free. A Maryland law passed in 1810 stipulated that the off-spring of a female slave remained enslaved after the mother's manumission, unless the manumitter stipulated a term of service, an age of release, or other contingency for the child.[8] Margaret did specify for children to be taken by their parents when possible; furthermore, it did not make sense to sell a toddler independently of the child's caregiver. Mothers and children sold together included Kitty and her two-year-old son, Nelson; Maria and her three-year-old son, Robert; Mary and her infant son, Daniel, and four-year-old son, Jerry; and Suckey from The Caves and her two-year-old daughter, Matilda. Of the children, Brice noted a year of freedom only for Matilda. Brice, however, appeared in court in 1841 to testify that Maria's son Robert had been overlooked and should be free. The four children not assigned an end date were legally enslaved for life, as were any additional offspring from their mothers. The question of why Margaret and Brice treated the children differently remains unanswered.

The sales broke apart families and dissolved the enslaved communities at Mount Clare and The Caves. For example, four members of the Garrett family were freed, but the other nine were divided among seven different owners. Parents Richard and Dolly were freed and given their two smallest children. Their daughter Sukey was given her four-year-old daughter and then sold to Edward Coale, but her six-year-old son was sold to William Gibson. Census records for the Richard Garrett family in 1820 suggest that Sukey and her four-year-old may have lived with her parents. Of Richard and Dolly's four sons ages nine to seventeen, one was also sold to Gibson, along with his cousin. The other three went to three different owners, one of whom lived in Annapolis. Kitty and her son were sold to Henry Payson. The division of families was not limited to the Garrett family. Six of John and Henny Lynch's children were divided among three owners. All four Harden family members were sold to different owners.

The manumission of enslaved blacks from The Caves had a side note by way of George Lindenberger, who purchased six enslaved blacks from Margaret's estate. They joined a group of people already enslaved by Lindenberger. When Lindenberger died in 1820, he passed the persons he purchased from Margaret's estate to his wife, Eliza, but shortened the terms left in their enslavement by two to eight years (Table 6.1). Brice set the age of freedom at twenty-eight years old for Jerry, James, Sam, Harry, and

Table 6.1. Terms of manumission, 1817 to 1820, by George Lindenberger

Name	Year to Be Freed, 1817 Terms	Age, 1817 Inventory	Year to Be Freed, 1820 Terms	Years to Serve	Age, 1820 Inventory	Term Difference	Year of Freedom Papers
Jerry	1825	20	1823	3	25	-2	
Jim (James Harden)	1833	12	1828	8	17	-5	1844
Sam	1835	10	1830	10	15	-5	
Harry	1825	22	1823	3	25	-2	1829
Frederick	1832	13	1827	7	18	-5	
Paul (Polly Ireland)	1833	9	May be "Alley" 1825/39	5	39	-8	1839

Frederick, and twenty-five years old for Polly. In his will, Lindenberger stipulated for "Negroes under twenty five years of age to serve till they respectively attain the age of twenty five years, and then to be free, also all my other Negroes for the term of three years after my decease, and then to be free."[9] For example, James was twelve years old in 1817 and Brice set his year of freedom at 1833, when he was twenty-eight. Lindenberg's will enabled him to be free in 1823, rather than 1825. The other persons enslaved on Lindenberger's estate, however, met different fortunes. Three individuals—Hetty or Kitty (age thirty), Sambo (age five), and Abraham (age four)—were enslaved for life. One person, Levi (no age listed), was to be freed on January 1, 1821, a few days after the inventory of Lindenberger's estate. Two others also had terms left in slavery: Jane, age ten, for six years, and Davy, age three, for eighteen years. No one was auctioned in 1821 with other parts of Lindenberger's property, meaning that they all remained enslaved by his wife, Eliza.[10] Only three individuals registered their freedom in court; those who did appeared somewhere between six and sixteen years after the year in which they were to be freed.

Even though James Carroll, the next resident of Mount Clare, brought in a new group of enslaved persons, some of the earlier residents may have stayed as tenant farmers or workers. His son, James Jr., may have purchased Samuel Harden in order to help his father manage Mount Clare. The 30-year-old man on James's 1818 tax assessment may be Samuel. James

Carroll's 1820 census includes thirty-six slaves, as well as four free males ages fourteen to twenty-six, one free male age twenty-six to forty-five, two free males age forty-five and older, and three free females age forty-five and older.[11] It is tempting to assign names of freedpersons to those slots, perhaps as tenant farmers: Richard and Jerry; Dolly, Henny, and Eve. Considering, however, that the Garretts and Lynches appeared separately on the 1820 census, they may not have been living on Mount Clare as free people.

Who was freed and when, or who was sold and under what terms, show that Margaret's executors freed individuals who would have been difficult to sell and kept in slavery many who were not. Brice and Tilghman ultimately determined the terms they "deemed best" on the basis of legal parameters, age, salability, and kin networks. Of the forty-nine people she enslaved in 1817, Margaret's estate papers and Baltimore court records document the freedom of only twenty-seven by the 1830s. Under her executor's watch, nine adults and six children were freed between 1817 and 1820. Thirty-four people went to new owners under terms of delayed manumission. No evidence has been found, however, that they were freed on time or that thirteen of them were ever freed. It is possible that they were sold again. Six people documented as free in Margaret's estate papers did not register a certificate of freedom in the Baltimore court. Thus, Brice saw that the terms spelled out in Margaret's last will and testament were carried out, often belatedly, for some—but not all—blacks, until his death in 1842.

Registering Freedom

Only twenty-one of the forty-nine blacks manumitted by Margaret registered in court; only one person did so in the same year in which he was freed. The others registered up to thirty-seven years after the year in which they were freed. Why did the people formerly enslaved by the Carrolls not register as soon as possible? Perhaps they did not know their years of freedom or did not hold copies of Margaret's will as proof of manumission but depended on Brice to intervene with new slaveholders and bring them to court. Brice, in fact, testified on behalf of all but one of the people manumitted in 1817. Brice, a slaveholder himself, had a track record of ensuring the freedom of enslaved people that he, or others whose estates he executed, manumitted when the new owner failed to release them.[12] Equally likely, however, was that the twenty-eight people who did not register either could not or did not know to go to court. Perhaps they had died: one estimate of slave mortality calculated that more than a third of enslaved persons were fifty years old and older by 1850. By 1860, the proportion had increased to half of all enslaved persons.[13]

Another explanation is that blacks sold from Mount Clare or The Caves were sold again, and their new enslavers forgot or ignored their manumission dates. The issue received legal attention around the time of Margaret's death. In 1817, the Maryland Assembly tightened its restrictions on the sale of enslaved persons entitled to freedom under delayed manumission either out of state or to persons who were not Maryland residents. The penalty for selling enslaved blacks under these circumstances was a jail sentence of up to two years. The law, however, included provisions to enable sellers to sell them outside the state. Sellers were required to register a bill of sale with identifying features of the enslaved person, as well as documentation that the purchaser acknowledged the individual's remaining term until freedom.[14]

Perhaps the people formerly enslaved at Mount Clare were scofflaws, meaning that they violated the law because it was too difficult to comply with, or that it was not necessary for them to take the law seriously to get by in Baltimore. Freedpersons, at least in Baltimore, failed to register because they did not need freedom papers in everyday life. The size and reach of the free and enslaved population throughout the region engendered a less stringent racial atmosphere than in rural areas. Racial control measures, such as checks for official freedom papers, were not enforced. Baltimore officials and courts repeatedly turned away cases testing the requirement to hold freedom papers. With no enforcement of the law, ex-slaves and others in Baltimore did not see registration with the court or freedom papers as necessary.[15] Another way of looking at the court and the law in general was that they were tools of dominant white power, or places unfriendly to blacks. From this perspective, a visit to the courthouse by a black person meant taking a chance that he or she would be treated unfairly. If the courthouse did not have a history of acknowledging blacks as equal members of society, the freedpersons from Mount Clare and The Caves may not have felt confident that the courts would help them.

Of the fraction of freed blacks who did register with the court, what drove them to do so? One explanation may come from comparing when blacks registered with events in Maryland and Brice's life. Eight people registered in 1832. Three of them were freed in 1795, a decade before Margaret's death: Fanny Cooper, Nell Williams, and Henny.[16] (According to court papers, the Henny freed in 1795 was twenty-four years old in 1817, and thus not John Lynch's wife.) Also in 1832, Brice testified for Milley Harden, Samuel and William Coney, Sukey, and Hetty/Kitty.[17] Three people registered in 1840; two per year in 1830 and 1841; and one per year in 1818, 1821, 1829, and 1839. Another registered in 1844, after Brice's death in 1842. Brice's death may have had the effect of locking a number of persons into slavery by eliminating their advocate. Statistically speaking, Brice appeared to push registration at times when whites took particular action to prevent blacks' integration into society, particularly in 1832.

White opposition stymied free blacks' efforts to enjoy the benefits of society. After the American Revolution, whites perceived a muddled hierarchical order and felt threatened by the increasing number of free blacks in society and the workforce. Social conservatives saw an opportunity to maintain their moral authority by pushing against blacks' freedom. They rallied other whites by characterizing free blacks as morally lax, dangerous, and a drain on society. The irony was that Marylanders who supported slavery were rattled by blacks' ability to find work as hired-out slaves or independent workers—in other words, to make their way in the free workforce despite slavery. Organizations such as the American Colonization Society (organized in 1817) were a conservative white response to the perceived threat of free blacks. The Maryland State Colonization Society met in early 1831 to address the perceived problem of free and manumitted blacks. Nicholas Brice, brother of Henry Brice, presided over the meeting of prominent whites. They voted to establish a colony on the African coast for free blacks.[18] In the process, they masked the effort to exorcise the black threat to conservative white control through a missionary, fundamentally Christian action.[19] Its task was made more urgent in whites' minds by Nat Turner's rebellion in August 1831. Turner led a group of enslaved persons in Southampton County, Virginia, where they murdered sixty whites. Turner's rebellion inspired a movement in Maryland to regulate the freedom of free blacks through their movements and by preventing future manumissions.[20]

A series of acts passed by the Maryland Assembly beginning in 1831 limited the freedom of freedpersons in Maryland. An act passed in March 1832 assigned the removal of freedpersons from Maryland to Liberia to a board of managers consisting of members of the society. The act required each county to compile a census of its free African American population so the board of managers could identify individuals to return to Africa. The law provided for the limited residence of blacks in the state and their forcible expulsion at the end of a specified period of time. Free blacks were subject to arrest if they refused to leave the state. A provision in the act, however, allowed the state's orphan court or Baltimore city court to grant a permit on an annual basis to any ex-slave to remain in the county if he or she could produce testimony of his or her exceptional good conduct and character. Drawing on earlier acts, the law allowed a manumitted person to remain in the state, but it was the responsibility of the manumitter to ensure that the former slave did not become a burden to society.[21] Another act, passed in June 1832, restricted the liberty of blacks in Maryland and sought to prevent more free or enslaved blacks from settling in the state. While the laws appear to have applied specifically to newly freed persons, they engendered the need to document those freed before 1831. These events—and the sentiments driving them—may have inspired Brice and freedpersons to register officially with the court.

Overall, freedpersons from Mount Clare and The Caves lived in a region that tolerated manumission and freedom relatively well for Maryland. By 1830, according to Stephen Whitman, "four-fifths of Baltimore's blacks were legally free, the largest group of free people of color in any U.S. city." The proportion of free blacks in Baltimore contrasted starkly with rural Maryland, where one quarter of the black population was free.[22] For comparative purposes, in 1840 enslaved persons constituted 90 percent of Charleston's black population, 79 percent of Richmond's, 55 percent of New Orleans's, and 79 percent of Washington, DC's.[23]

Life after the Carrolls

Freedpersons from Mount Clare lived during a time of explosive growth in Baltimore. Shipyards, mills, forges, furnaces, hotels, and other kinds of businesses grew. Blacks in the Baltimore region shaped an environment beneficial to themselves through support of demographic and economic growth, renegotiation of urban labor arrangements, shaping of urban social structures, and influence over occupation and ownership of urban land. The everyday struggles of people like the low-wage black workers of Baltimore became the foundation for the American working class. The communal effort of blacks as a group and in families pushed them out of slavery, but still they were not on equal footing with others in America. The development of black families amid a larger struggle for political independence and self-definition during the Revolutionary era enabled black society and culture to emerge. Families not only passed names and occupations from one generation to the next but also established social stability and family integrity, which proved fundamental to black cultural responses to domination.

Employment offered, in turn, opportunities for family life, skill specialization and diversification, and community development. Men in Baltimore found work in maritime trades, as brick makers, shoemakers, tailors, and artisans, while women took domestic employment as housekeepers, washerwomen, seamstresses, and cooks. The two adults' combined incomes were equally important in the survival of free black households.

Baltimore County and Maryland in general had slightly more male than female enslaved blacks of all ages. The disparity resulted from the import of females into Maryland and the export of males into the Lower South. On the other hand, females greatly outnumbered males in Baltimore City itself; in 1830, the ratio was almost 2:1.[24]

Individuals who transitioned from enslaved to free mixed in Baltimore with blacks who had relocated there from other regions. The combination of changing status and exposure to others' experiences may have helped Americanize blacks in Baltimore. Acculturation accelerated in freedom for persons who came to northern cities from plantations. Arguably, however, freedpersons used markers of citizenship modeled and understood by whites to integrate themselves into society in ways shaped by the African American experience. The roots of class formation in the antebellum era relate to the ways in which slavery and racial identity influenced the definition of class identity for all Americans. Former slaves, over the course of generations of freedpersons, extricated themselves from white households to live in nuclear families in ethnically clustered neighborhoods.

Freedpersons organized for racial uplift in churches, schools, abolitionist societies, and mutual aid societies.

Life in Freedom for Persons Freed by Margaret Carroll

Freedom did not mean equality: none of the people enslaved by Margaret reached a position in society in which they could enjoy the privileges that her white elite status had conferred upon her. Some of the people she enslaved carried their work specialties into jobs as freedpersons. Others did physical labor in a range of positions. Work also tended to be divided along gendered lines. Women conducted domestic tasks in homes or shops, while men worked a broader range of positions. While slavery no longer defined their status, racism did help dictate where they could insert themselves in free society. Few personal details remain of the lives of the people formerly enslaved at Mount Clare and The Caves in freedom, but those that do show a pattern of what life was like for first-generation freedpersons in Baltimore. The following sections outline what happened to the people formerly enslaved on the Carroll properties to demonstrate the lasting effects of racism after enslavement (Table 6.2).

The Garrett Family

Thirteen members of the Garrett family lived at Mount Clare in 1817. Richard, who was fifty years old in 1817, had worked as a gardener in the famous ornamental gardens, orchards, and orangery. He continued working as a gardener in the 1820s. Richard lived with Dolly and four of his children or grandchildren on Pennsylvania Avenue, west of Montgomery.[25] Richard passed away between the 1830 and 1840 censuses at about sixty-seven years old. Dolly was about seventy when she registered her freedom on September 29, 1840. She was described as having a dark complexion, measuring five feet two inches tall, and having no noticeable marks or scars.[26] Dolly was about eighty years old when she passed away, between 1850 and 1860. At the time, she lived with her youngest daughter, Margaret.

On April 13, 1830, William and Henry registered their freedom papers. They were supposed to be freed in 1828 and 1830, respectively. Only their heights were noted—five feet three inches and five feet seven inches.[27] No

Table 6.2. Families and manumission

Name	Age in 1817	Purchaser or Parent	Year/Age to Be Freed	Date Freedom Documented	Description at Freedom
GARRETT FAMILY AT MOUNT CLARE					
Sukey	23	Edward J. Coale	1822/1823, age 29	May 29, 1832, may refer to Sukey at The Caves	age 39, dark complexion, 4'10¾" tall, no notable marks/scars
Nelson	6	William Gibson	1839, age 28		
Betsy/Beckey	4	to Sukey	n.d.		
Hetty/Kitty	20/26	Henry Payson	1825, age 28/34	May 29, 1832	age 37, dark complexion, 5'3¾" tall, small mole on left side of nose
James	2		n.d.		
Henry	17	Jno. McClellan	1828, age 28	April 13, 1830	5'3½" tall
William	15	Wm. Smith	1830, age 28	April 13, 1830	5'7 ½" tall
Tom/Thomas	11	Charles Ross, Annapolis	age 31	September 29, 1840	age 36, dark complexion, 5'5 ½" tall, small scar on right side of mouth, crooked left middle finger
Richard	9	William Gibson	1836, age 28		
Sampson	6	to Richard	n.d.		
Margaret	5/4	to Richard	n.d.	April 14, 1840	age 27, dark complexion, 5'3" tall, scar on right side of head

(continued)

Table 6.2—*Continued*

Name	Age in 1817	Purchaser or Parent	Year/Age to Be Freed	Date Freedom Documented	Description at Freedom
Richard	50			September 29, 1840	age 70, dark complexion, 5'2" tall, no noticeable marks/scars
Dolly	44		n.d.		
Lynch Family at Mount Clare					
John Lynch	31		n.d.	December 14, 1821	bright black, age 35
Henny	40				
Maria	21	Edward J. Coale	1824, age 28		
Robert (Hall)	3		n.d.	March 1, 1841	age 27, dark complexion, 5'5 ½" tall, two scars on left cheek, four scars on forehead
George	13	John Short	1832, age 28		
John	11	Nicholas Brice	1834, age 28		
Ned	7	Nicholas Brice	1838, age 28		
Harriet	6	Nicholas Brice	n.d.		
Jim/Sam	5	to John Lynch	n.d.		
Bill/William	2/3	to John Lynch	n.d.	March 1, 1841	age 27, 5'5" tall, light complexion, scar on right eyebrow
Henny	2	to John Lynch			

Name	Age	Owner	Date, age	Date	Notes
Old Eve	very old				
JERRY'S FAMILY AT MOUNT CLARE					
Sam	12	Nicholas Brice	1833, age 28		
Jerry	44				
Archibald	13	George Roberts	1832, age 28		
MARY'S FAMILY AT MOUNT CLARE AND THE CAVES					
Mary	27/26	James L. Hawkins	1820, age 29		
Daniel	?		n.d.		
Jerry (Larson)	5/4	James L. Hawkins	1844, age 31		
SUCKEY'S FAMILY AT THE CAVES					
Suckey	22	Nathaniel G. Maxwell	1823, age 28		Sukey at Mount Clare?
Matilda	2		1840, age 25		
HARDEN FAMILY AT MOUNT CLARE AND THE CAVES					
Ephraem	23/30	Ashton Alexander	1824, age 30/37		
Sam	36/30	James Carroll, Jr.	1823, age 42/36		
Milley	17	Henry Brice	1825, age 25	March 29, 1832	age 31, 5'3¼" tall, light complexion, large scar on right arm above elbow

(continued)

Table 6.2—*Continued*

Name	Age in 1817	Purchaser or Parent	Year/Age to Be Freed	Date Freedom Documented	Description at Freedom
Jim/James	12	George Lindenberger	1833, age 28	June 4, 1844	age 40, light complexion, 5'9" tall, scar on right cheek
Henry			August 8, 1815	April 8, 1818	age 42, light, 5'9 ½" tall
OTHER INDIVIDUALS AT MOUNT CLARE OR THE CAVES					
Jacob Hall	29/28	Eleanor Dall	1819, age 31		
Sam/Samuel	25	Alexander Robinson	1822, age 30	May 4, 1832	age 43, dark complexion, 5'4¾" tall, no notable marks
Nat	44				
Moses					
William Coney	23/25	Frederick Jakes	1824, age 30/32	May 4, 1832	age 34, dark complexion, 5'7¾" tall, scar under left eye
Jacob	44				
Harry (Davis)	22/23	James L. Hawkins	1825, age 30	May 29, 1829	a "bright black," age 31, 5'7" tall, large scar and stiffness of middle finger on right hand (may be Harry Graham)
Jerry	20	George Lindenberger	1825, age 28		

Name		Owner		Date	Description
Sam	10	George Lindenberger	1835, age 28		
Harry (Graham)	22/23	George Lindenberger	1825, age 28	May 29, 1829	a "bright black," age 31, 5'7" tall, large scar and stiffness of middle finger on the right hand (may be Harry Davis)
Frederick	13	George Lindenberger	1832, age 28		
Poll/Paul/Polly (Ireland)	9	George Lindenberger	1833, age 25	May 27, 1839	age 26, 5'3" tall, scar on left eye bone, raised in Baltimore
Fanny Cooper			1795, born 1804	1832	age 28, dark complexion, 5'1½" tall, no notable marks/scars
Nell Williams			1795, age 16	1832	age 53, light complexion, 5'2½" tall, small scar on back of left hand near the wrist
Henny			1795, age 2	1832	age 39, light complexion, 5'2½" tall, scar on under-lip, under the right corner of mouth

Note: This table compares information from Margaret Tilghman Carroll's estate papers with manumission papers recorded in the Baltimore County Court. For citations, see endnotes 26–44.

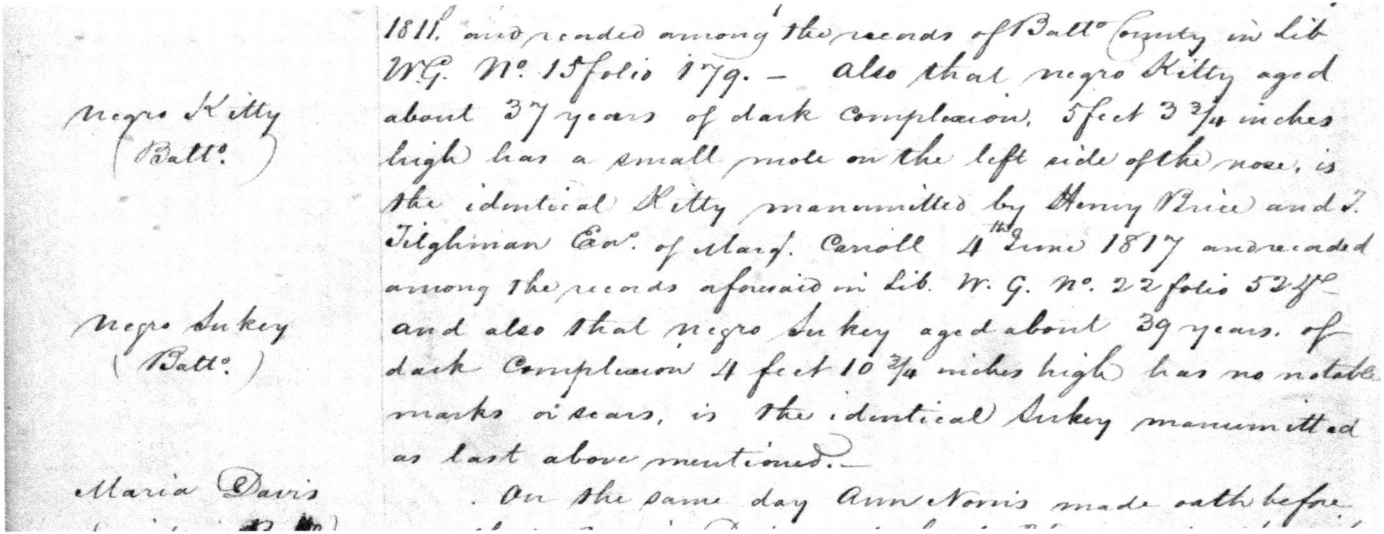

Negro Kitty
(Balt°.)

Negro Sukey
(Balt°.)

Maria Davis

1811, and recorded among the records of Balt° County in Lib
W.G. N°. 15 folio 179. — also that negro Kitty aged
about 37 years of dark Complexion, 5 feet 3 3/4 inches
high has a small mole on the left side of the nose, is
the identical Kitty manumitted by Henry Brice and T.
Tilghman Esq. of Mary. Carroll 4th June 1817 and recorded
among the records aforesaid in Lib. W. G. N°. 22 folio 52 &c.
and also that negro Sukey aged about 39 years. of
dark Complexion 4 feet 10 3/4 inches high has no notable
marks or scars, is the identical Sukey manumitted
as last above mentioned. —
On the same day Ann Norris made oath before

Figure 6.2. Certificate of Freedom for Negro Sukey and Negro Kitty, May 29, 1832, Baltimore County Court.
By permission of the Maryland State Archives.

further information has been found for Henry. William was a sawyer who lived at 8 Salisbury Alley in 1845.[28] He had a family; his son worked as a coachman. William and his wife, Caroline, both passed away between 1870 and 1880.

Sukey and Hetty/Kitty both registered in court on May 29, 1832. Sukey was supposed to be freed in 1822 or 1823 and Hetty/Kitty in 1825. Sukey was thirty-nine years old in 1832, had a dark complexion, was four feet ten and three-quarter inches tall, and had no notable marks or scars.[29] According to census records, she was a washerwoman and barber. No further information has been found about her children, Nelson and Beckey. Sukey died between 1870 and 1880. Hetty/Kitty was thirty-seven years old, had a dark complexion, was five feet three and three-quarter inches tall, and had a small mole on left side of her nose.[30] No further information about her or her son James's lives has been recovered.

Thomas Garrett, who had been sent to Annapolis, was freed in 1840. John H. Ing testified on behalf of Thomas, because "[Thomas] ought to have been manumitted in the year eighteen hundred and seventeen, with others, but [was] omitted." Thomas was about thirty-six years old. He had a dark complexion and was five feet five and a half inches tall with a small scar on the right side of his mouth and a crooked middle finger on his left hand.[31] He was a laborer who lived at "Howard Street extended." Census records indicate that he was a stonemason and his wife, Livinia, kept house. Their four sons were porters in stores; they also had two daughters.

Richard and Sampson did not register their freedom in court. Although Richard's occupation is unknown, he died between 1870 and 1880. His daughter worked in a packinghouse. Sampson worked as a farmer, and his wife, Elizabeth, kept house. Their two sons were identified as laborers in census records.

Margaret registered in the court in 1840, even though Brice had not stipulated a year of freedom for her in 1817. She was twenty-seven years old, had a dark complexion, was five feet three inches tall, and had a scar on the right side of her head.[32] Margaret married William Bordley (or Boardley), who was a brick maker. They lived at 1 North Amity Street in 1845.[33] Margaret and William had five children.

The Lynch Family

Little information is available on the Lynch family. The family may have been long enslaved by the Carrolls. A mulatto man named Jack Lynch escaped from Charles Carroll in 1780, the first Lynch noted in the Carroll records.

John Lynch arranged with Nicholas Brice to hold his children for a period of time, as suggested by the 1820 census. John Lynch worked in agriculture by 1820. His household included himself, Henny (one female age twenty-six to forty-five); John, Ned, Sam, and Bill (four males under age fourteen); Harriet and Henny (two females under age fourteen); and Eve (one female over forty-five).[34] No further information has been recovered on Maria, George, Ned, Harriett, Jem/Sam, or Henny. John received his freedom papers in 1821. He was described as a "bright black" man who was thirty-five years old.[35] In 1829, the city directory indicated that a John Lynch lived on German Street, east of Sharp.

By 1830, both Henny and Eve had passed away. John's household included four males age twenty-four to thirty-six, John (one male age thirty-six to fifty-five), one female under age ten, and perhaps John's daughter Henny (one female age ten to twenty-four). In 1833, Henny worked as a washerwoman.[36]

Of John and Henny's children, only Bill registered with the court. Brice testified for Bill (alias William Lynch) and his nephew Robert (alias Robert Hall) on March 1, 1841. Bill was about twenty-seven, five feet five inches tall, light complected, and had a scar on his right eyebrow.[37] Robert was about twenty-seven, dark complected, five feet five and a half inches tall, and had two scars on his left cheek and four scars on his forehead.[38] They were the last two persons freed by Brice. Although Jacob was to be free in 1819, he did not register in court, and if and when he was freed remains unclear.[39]

The 1845 city directory indicates that John Lynch was a laborer who lived at 48 Centre Street. After 1845, the family disappeared from census records, but John and/or his offspring may continue to appear in city directories.

Others

Some of the people formerly enslaved by Margaret Carroll did not have apparent family connections and may not have had the same kind of kinship supports that the Garretts, Lynches, and Hardens had.

Harry Davis and Harry Graham received their freedom papers on May 29, 1829, four years after their 1825 manumission date. Harry Davis was described as a "dark black man." Harry Graham was "bright black," about thirty-one years old, five feet seven inches tall, and had a large scar and stiffness of the middle finger on the right hand.[40]

Polly (alias Polly Ireland) registered on May 27, 1839, even though she was freed in 1833. Polly was described as being about twenty-six years old, five feet three inches tall, and having a scar on her left eye bone.[41]

None appear in city directories to indicate their vocations or locations in freedom.

The Harden Family

Free blacks with the last name Harden or Hardin lived in Baltimore by the late nineteenth century. They may have been related to the Hardens enslaved by the Carrolls. Abraham Hardin or Harding and another free person lived in Baltimore Town in 1790. By 1810, Belsy (Betsy?) Harden and another free person resided in Baltimore Ward 1 and a Mrs. (or possibly Wm.) Harden and seven others lived in Baltimore Western Precincts 3.

Henry Harden was manumitted on August 18, 1815, and recorded his freedom in court on April 8, 1818, at age forty-two (fig. 6.2). His complexion was light and he stood five feet nine and a half inches tall.[42] The city directory for 1822–1823 identified a Henry Harden as a minister of the Gospel who lived on Pearl Street on the west side, south of Lexington.[43] Henry last appeared in city directories in 1824. Henry will be discussed further in the next section of this chapter.

Milley (or Milly) was slated to be free in 1825, but she registered with the court on March 29, 1832. She was about thirty-one years old, five feet three and a quarter inches tall, with a light complexion and a large scar on her right arm above the elbow.[44] There was a Nelly Harden who was a laundress and lived on St. Mary's Street, west of Pennsylvania Avenue in 1827. Although the recorded names are slightly different, they may be the

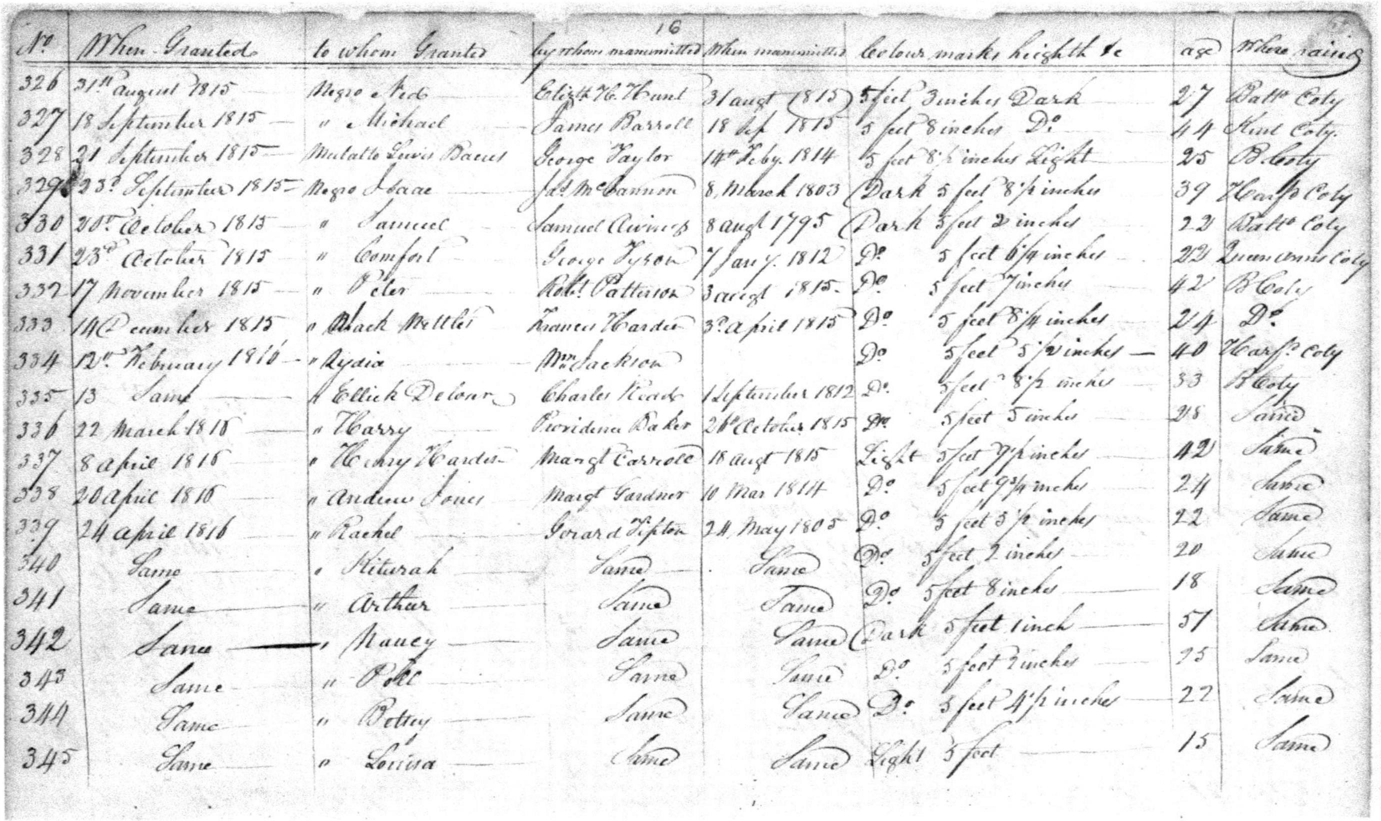

Figure 6.3. Certificate of Freedom for Henry Harden, April 8, 1815, Baltimore County Court. By permission of the Maryland State Archives.

same person. It is also tempting to associate Nelly Harden with the "Nell" manumitted by Margaret in 1795.

James Harden was to be free in 1833 by Margaret and in 1828 by George Lindenberger. His freedom papers in 1844 identified him as being forty years old, with a light complexion, five feet nine inches tall, and having a scar on his right cheek.[45] In 1833, James Harden was a bootblack who lived under 9 South Calvert Street, according to the city directory. Two James Hardens lived in Baltimore. In 1835–36 and 1847–48, city directories indicate that one James was a waiter who lived at 9 South Calvert Street at Ensor, opposite the Catholic church. The other James Harden worked as a sawyer and lived at 17 State Street Court. By 1860, James Harden the waiter was fifty-nine years old, about five years' difference in age from James's recorded age in 1817, suggesting that they might be the same James. Census records suggest that he died by 1870.

No freedom papers remain for other Hardens, if they ever existed. Sam was supposed to be free in 1823 and Ephraem in 1824. There was a Samuel Harden, a laborer, living on Saratoga Street on the south side east of Pearl in 1822–23. He moved to 27 Tyson Street by 1847, according to the directory. By 1864, he and possibly his son, Samuel S. Harden, were whitewashers living at 67 Arch Street.

Henry Harden

The "what next" of life in freedom is especially important because it reveals special events and people. Henry Harden, who was freed by Margaret in 1815, was among the early leaders of the African Methodist Episcopal Church (AME) in Baltimore. Harden's story proves that elite white men were not the only "great men" of Mount Clare. The stories of great men in the AME church show that blacks challenged white privilege and empowered both free and enslaved persons, despite societal pressure against them. Such actions enabled blacks to oppose racism through racial uplift. Although Harden's role in the AME church had been preserved in church histories and biographies, the connection had been lost with events in his life prior to his church work. The connection is important in telling the history of Mount Clare, because it exemplifies the work of blacks while enslaved or free who were inspired by inequality to lead social movements toward racial uplift and freedom.

Beginning in the 1730s, an evangelical movement called the Great Awakening swept across the American colonies. Characterized by powerful preaching and espousing equality among all Christians, evangelicalism departed from the ritual and ceremony of the Anglican church then dominant in Maryland. When the Methodists arrived in Maryland, the Anglican church—of which Margaret Carroll was a member—was controlled by white landholding slaveholders. It limited blacks' involvement and investment in church and spiritual matters because of their race. Since the church questioned the legality of holding baptized persons as slaves, it had not sanctioned the religious instruction and baptism of blacks. Methodists, on the other hand, established integrated churches and welcomed blacks to preach.[46]

Blacks encouraged white Methodists from the beginning. Robert Strawbridge, an Irishman, delivered the first Methodist sermon in the New World in Baltimore in June 1765. Caleb Hyland, a black man, arranged for Strawbridge to speak in front of his bootblacking shop and provided a table for the podium. Notably, Hyland's shop was later the meeting site for the early African Methodist Episcopal Church.[47] Early Methodist preachers, such as Rev. Jacob Gruber, observed that blacks "were treated [by whites] as if they had no souls." He argued that blacks had human feelings and that it was degrading to humanity to see human souls mixed with animals at auction, such as at slave sales. Gruber also said that he would not be surprised if enslaved blacks cut their masters' throats and poisoned their children.[48] For enslaved and free blacks, the Methodists' ideas were welcome, and they gravitated to the church. The Great Awakening inspired a deeply personal spirituality among enslaved blacks that channeled into Methodist practice. Listeners found revelation in their need of salvation by Jesus Christ, as well as guidance for spiritual conviction and a new standard of personal morality. In turn, evangelicalism gave birth to a religious and cultural movement among blacks. It offered an ethos around which they might organize themselves, exercise control, assert independence, and resist white authority.

Blacks and whites participated in Methodist Episcopal services in Baltimore at the Lovely Lane and Strawberry Alley meetinghouses. The spirit of equality and fellowship began to splinter, however, in the early 1780s. During this time, rules to excommunicate slaveholders from the Methodist Episcopal Church were ignored, and then tabled. They were finally withdrawn in 1787. In 1784, black members were displeased when existing black preachers were not ordained at the General Conference of Methodists. Starting in 1785, white parishioners restricted blacks to pews in the gallery and prohibited them from communing with whites at the altar.[49] Richard Allen, the leader of the AME church in the late eighteenth century, condemned the hypocrisy of white Methodists and refused to allow Christianity to be identified as a white religion. African customs and beliefs filtered through and meshed with biblical teachings as blacks met to dance, sing, and listen to preachers.[50]

In 1787, an independent prayer group of blacks began to meet in Caleb Hyland's bootblacking cellar and then at each other's homes. Harden was among its members. They rented a building at Fish Street (now Saratoga) near Gay Street in 1797 and it was consecrated "Bethel." Harden led the Bethel Church.[51] The group had consulted with Bishop Francis Asbury about the possibility of acquiring property and creating an "African, yet Methodist Church." The bishop, however, was concerned about blacks having such self-determination. He rejected the plan.[52] From a white perspective, his concern had merit, considering that black churches provided institutions for upending white control over blacks. Black churches and preachers, for example, were aiding blacks' escapes from slavery along what became known as the Underground Railroad.

Harden in the late eighteenth century remained enslaved to Margaret but still played an active role in the church. David Smith, who later joined Harden and others in the development of the AME church, witnessed his preaching. Alexander Murray, another early leader of black Methodists, persuaded Smith to join a watch meeting late one Saturday night. Smith described it as follows: "As we drew near the house and heard the sound of preaching, my hard heart was softened, and tears flowed down my cheeks as I entered into the door. Henry Harden was then preaching, and as he was illustrating on his subject he exclaimed that 'Jesus was a balm to cure the wound that sin had made' if we would only acknowledge ourselves sinners in his sight."[53] Harden may by then have approached Margaret about his freedom. Rev. Smith later wrote that Harden was among several men and women whose owners were persuaded to release them: "When such men became religious as they did, their owners became very much interested in me and did what they could to assist me, for religious reformation made this class of men and women better servants, and by their good behavior many of them became free. Stephen Hill, Henry Harden, Leben Lee, and many others were set free by their owners on account of their good behavior and industry."[54] In November 1814, Harden was still not free but lived on Raybourg and New Alley (now Arch Street). Church leaders met there to discuss purchasing the building on Fish Street.[55] At last, Margaret manumitted Harden on August 18, 1815.[56] He did not register in court until 1818. Brice testified on Harden's behalf, which suggests that Brice knew him prior to Margaret's death and that they knew how to get in touch after she died.

While Harden could be a leader for developing the black Methodist church, the role and opportunity was not available to him in white Methodism. The group created by Harden and others formed the foundation for the first two black churches in Baltimore: Sharp Street and Bethel.[57] The churches were symbols of free black Baltimoreans and, as a result, became targets for violence. In 1812, a mob moved to set fire to the Sharp Street church. Church members inside the building deflected the violence with threats of their own.[58] In 1816, black Methodists organized themselves and took a stand on the future of their worship and autonomy. Daniel Coker wanted black Methodists to separate from the white church, a move emboldened by the separation of black Methodists in Philadelphia into one self-governing body. He envisioned black Methodists in Philadelphia and Baltimore joining together. The black Methodist membership in Baltimore, however, was divided on what to do. Some felt that aligning with the white Methodist Episcopal Church had some advantages. They opposed Coker and the separatists, opting instead to remain within the governance of the Methodist Episcopal Church. They retained the African Methodist Episcopal Society name but were also known as the Sharp Street AME Church, due to its location at Sharp and Pratt Streets. The separatist group, of which Henry Harden was a part, followed Coker's vision and joined Richard Allen and Absalom Jones to create the African Methodist Bethel Church.[59]

Being a freeman enabled Harden to travel across state lines to perform his responsibilities with the church. He traveled to Philadelphia for the convention on April 9–11, 1816, that formally organized the AME Church. Harden represented Baltimore with Rev. Coker, Rev. Richard Williams,

Edward Williamson, Stephen Hill, and Nicholas Gilliard.[60] The convention marked a formal separation from the white Methodist church but also a division among black Methodists. During the convention, the participants elected Rev. Coker to be bishop; he declined, but Rev. Richard Allen accepted. Bishop Allen appointed Harden to succeed Coker as preacher-in-charge at Bethel in April 1817. He also assumed responsibility for Bearhill, Frederick Road, Mt. Gilboa, Sculltown, and Fells Point.[61] In May 1817, William Carman leased a plot of land, bounded by Fish and Gay, for $360 per year to Bethel. The church was not permitted to bury the dead on the land.[62]

On April 8, 1816, trustees of Bethel entered the constitution of the African Methodist Bethel Church of the City of Baltimore into the court records. The constitution specified requirements for trustees: five in number, descendants of Africans, free, and having membership for one year in the society. They were to be chosen every Easter Monday by male members at least twenty-one years old who were eligible to vote. The trustees held property in trust for the congregation. They were not permitted to dispose of Bethel Church or its lot of ground without consent of two-thirds of male members and church congregants twenty-one years of age or older. Article III specified that "The spiritual concerns of this church shall be regulated by a convention of coloured ministers and lay members, chosen by the male members of this and other African churches, which may at any time hereafter associate with this church." Daniel Coker, Jacob Gilliard Sr., George Douglass, Stephen E. Hill, and Don C. Hall signed the constitution.[63] Trustees entered a charter of incorporation of the African Methodist Bethel Church on April 3, 1820, to clarify parts of the 1816 constitution. It specified qualifications for trustees as being freemen, descendants of Africans, and older than twenty-five years of age, with two years in the church. Eight trustees were to be elected every fourth year on Easter Monday through a vote by free members of the congregation age twenty-five and older. The elder Henry Harden was the officiating minister who signed the incorporation with his trustees in office and male class leaders. The conditions of the constitution codified the leadership as being Africanist and male.

The AME church supported teaching and literacy, in part through the publication of books and other literature. In 1817, leaders of the AME church established the AME Book Concern, America's first black-owned publishing enterprise, which was based in Philadelphia until 1835. It published for 135 years. The first publications included *The Book of Discipline* (1817), the governing laws of the church; *The Hymn-Book* (1818), the songs sung during church services; and *The Doctrines and Discipline of the African Methodist Episcopal Church* (1819), a revision of the *Book of Discipline*.[64] Book stewards were appointed to print and sell the books. Don Carlos Hall, a layman, was elected book steward for the conference. Harden was appointed book steward for the circuit, which suggests that he was literate.[65]

The first AME church conference in Baltimore took place on April 7, 1818, at Stephen Williams' house under the presidency of Rev. Allen. Rev. Harden represented Baltimore with six other men. Harden, with Richard Williams and Charles Pierce, was nominated to attend the Philadelphia conference. In 1818, he once again attended the Philadelphia conference, which took place at Richard Allen's home, and he was elected and ordained as a church elder at the 1818 conference in Baltimore. Harden was appointed to the Harrisburg circuit by 1819, where he traveled on horseback from place to place to preach. Rev. Smith met up with Harden in Lancaster in 1820 and they traveled together to the Western School near West Chester. Harden preached there, and then they traveled to Philadelphia to attend the conference.[66] By 1822, the size of the church had increased such that its leaders decided to elect an assistant to the bishop. The vote was taken in Baltimore and Philadelphia. Henry Harden was one of three candidates. After the two votes, Henry Harden placed third with a total of thirteen votes against Morris Brown's sixteen votes and Jacob Matthew's twenty-four.

Harden twice appears in church records as promoting order and due process for the purpose of racial unity. At the 1819 Baltimore conference, a set of letters addressed to official members in Philadelphia were detained by the secretary for "some reasons" and handed to the bishop when he arrived in Baltimore. Whether or not the letters were shared with the conference is unknown, but the contents caused Harden to place a resolution before the conference, "that no minister or preacher belonging to the African Methodist Episcopal Conference, or any member, local or traveling, shall write any letter or letters or communications, verbally, or by any other way whatsoever, that will have the bearance of raising discord or hardness in the Connection," and another to the effect "that ways and means shall be entered into by the Conference to prevent any member or members of the Annual Conference of taking a part with any person or persons evading the Discipline of the said African Methodist Episcopal Church or Churches; or shall be found guilty of sowing discord, or raising schisms, tattling or tale-bearing, so that the Church or society may suffer injury by the strife of such person or persons, the Elder shall call him or them to trial; if found guilty, the Elder shall silence him or them until the setting of the Annual Conference, then the Elder shall deliver the charge to the Conference, in writing, and the Conference shall deal with the said offender according to Discipline." Harden placed a resolution at the 1819 conference in Baltimore to prohibit members from disloyalty or sowing discord against the AME church.[67] The resolution reflected his concern that white elders would learn the business of their meetings and act against the members. In 1821, he brought a motion to admit churches on the Eastern Shore of Maryland into the conference. He and Rev. David Smith, however, also put forth a motion against the churches so they could not complain about traveling preachers except in the case as a trial, and then only as witnesses.

Harden's role in establishing the African Methodist Church grew in 1820, when he was dispatched from the Philadelphia conference to lower Manhattan, New York. The move, however, was controversial. A former member of the Zion Church in New York, named William Lambert, obtained license from Bishop Allen in Philadelphia to preach. Upon returning to New York, the Asbury Church barred him from preaching. Lambert was determined to raise a church or congregation for Allen, so he obtained a schoolhouse on Mott Street, where, with the assistance of George White, he fitted a church. Once the building was under way, Harden arrived in the city to form a society with the assistance of Lambert and White, called Bethel Church. The preachers of Zion Church, however, were displeased about Bishop Allen and the Allenites moving into their domain to create a third society of African Methodists. They felt that Allen was taking advantage of the current unsettled state of the Methodist church in New York, which had been caused by a schism with the white church and nascent development of black parishes. They resolved not to preach for the Allenites or to permit them to preach for Zion. Nonetheless, the church on Mott Street was consecrated on July 23, 1820. Soon after, Bishop Allen visited. He sanctioned the work by Harden, Lambert, and White and soothed the concerns of the Zion and Asbury parishes.[68] The congregation at Bethel numbered twenty-nine people—mostly women—and Harden grew the church's membership on a weekly basis.[69] In August 1820, a parish in Brooklyn incorporated with Bethel, bringing about a hundred people. Harden attended the first conference for the New York district in 1822, where he was assigned supervision of a circuit in New Bedford, Massachusetts, led by a deacon named Charles Spicer.[70]

The 1822–1823 edition of the Baltimore directory places Henry Harden, "minister of the Gospel," on Pearl, west side of Lexington.[71] The 1827 edition indicates that he lived on "Hill, N side E Sharp."[72] Harden was "expelled" from the church in 1830[73] and withdrew in 1834.[74] If Harden was forty-two years old upon manumission in 1818, he was fifty-eight years old in 1834. He ceased to appear in Baltimore city directories starting in 1831. In 1849, a Henry Harden signed a petition regarding a dispute at Bethel, but it is not clear if he is the same Henry Harden who was expelled. No obituary or year of death has been recovered for Harden.

Henry Harden's story shows that great black men rose up from Mount Clare, but it also reveals the possibilities and limitations of blacks freed in antebellum Baltimore. Manumission was not clear-cut for the people enslaved at Mount Clare and The Caves, nor was it altogether a benevolent act. Blacks formerly enslaved at Mount Clare and The Caves needed to make profound adjustments after 1817. One of them was the adjustment to the promise of freedom at a future date, rather than freedom immediately upon Margaret's death. The date of freedom in Margaret's papers, the year actually freed, and the year of court registration were three separate dates for blacks at Mount Clare and The Caves. Fewer than half registered their freedom in court, and if they did it was oftentimes years later than when Margaret's executors specified their freedom was to begin. The others either lived free without registering in court or were never freed. Some individuals went to new owners and to new places, others kept families together, and others engaged with opportunities available in the city. Together, they demonstrate the complexity of the transition from slavery to freedom, from the life of individuals enslaved by a wealthy white widow to freedpersons entering newly charted waters of class and race as African Americans.

7

A Broader History

Perhaps the one common thread at Mount Clare between 1817, when Margaret Tilghman passed away, and 1987, when the museum became more professional, was the way in which the site addressed broader issues regarding race and inequality. The Mount Clare of 1987 would have been almost completely unrecognizable to its inhabitants of 1817. Many factors—changes in the property's ownership and the landscape's character, the unsustainability of slavery and the beginning of the Civil War, the creation of a recreational park and a historic house—added to or erased black history from the landscape. Events at Mount Clare and Carroll Park continued to show that not all members of society had the same rights or equal access to the benefits of society. By the early twentieth century, the lack of access to Mount Clare combined with the erasure of evidence about blacks and slavery to enable European American preservationist groups to claim the landscape as theirs alone.

A Turn from Slavery

Slavery continued at Mount Clare for another fifteen years after Margaret's death. James Maccubbin Carroll had inherited Mount Clare from his uncle, Charles Carroll the Barrister, but did not live there until after Margaret's death. After the people enslaved by Margaret were sold and moved away from the property, James brought a new community of enslaved and free blacks to Mount Clare in 1818. They joined a man whom he had been enslaving at the mill. By 1820, twenty-eight enslaved people and nine free blacks lived at Mount Clare.[1] By 1823, James enslaved twenty-one people. James tried to keep up Mount Clare as his aunt and uncle had, using enslaved persons to do it.[2] Just like Margaret and Charles, James

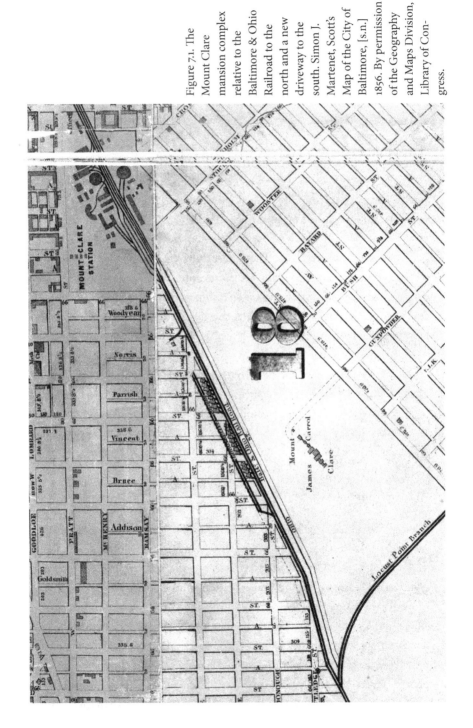

Figure 7.1. The Mount Clare mansion complex relative to the Baltimore & Ohio Railroad to the north and a new driveway to the south. Simon J. Martenet, Scott's Map of the City of Baltimore, [s.n.] 1856. By permission of the Geography and Maps Division, Library of Congress.

commissioned improvements to the mansion and a few outbuildings, including "the quarter," the kitchen, and the barn.[3] The layout of the main mansion complex remained the same as it had been during his aunt and uncle's ownership. He also hired a gardener.[4] Enslaved persons at Mount Clare thus followed the daily patterns of maintenance and personal life as those carried out by their predecessors.

During this time as well, Baltimore's urban area was pushing west and industry had taken hold of the region. James aligned Mount Clare with these trends by permitting significant reconfigurations of the property (fig. 7.1). He gave the newly formed Baltimore & Ohio Railroad a ten-acre parcel on the northeast corner for a depot in 1828. The railroad company purchased an additional fifteen acres from James in 1830 to expand the railroad complex.[5] Today the two parcels are part of the B&O Railroad Museum. The railway was sited across a high ridge on James's property, not far from the mansion and straight across the driveway from the north. James was forced to reorient the driveway to the mansion from the south. The reoriented landscape established permanent features, including the railway and the driveway, that are part of Mount Clare today, but that also make it more difficult to imagine the property as enslaved and free blacks saw it.

When James died in 1832, he still enslaved nineteen people. No account of sale was registered in court to indicate what happened to the people inventoried as part of his estate (Table 7.1).

The practice of slavery ended at Mount Clare with, or soon after, James Maccubbin Carroll's death—a turning point for black history at the property. James's son, James Jr., inherited Mount Clare. He may have lived there from 1832 to 1836. Farm records show that he twice hired Sam Harden, whom he purchased from Margaret's estate.[6] Beginning in 1836, James Jr. rented out the property to the first of a series of renters, none of whom appear to have been slaveholders. Although there is little information about the renters, archaeology at Mount Clare supports slavery's ending there in the 1830s. Artifacts began to accumulate across the property for the first time, because the gardens and orchards were no longer maintained or used for their original purposes. Places that had been kept clear, such as the bowling green or the forecourt, were now littered with debris. Without slavery or its symbolism, the showcase plantation style of Mount Clare fell away.

Table 7.1. Blacks on James Carroll's property, 1818–1832

	1818[a]	1820 (enslaved)[b]	1820 (free)	1823 (21 people)[c]	1832 (19 people)[d]
Males and females age 45 and over		5 males and 1 female	3 females		Richard, age 75; Lib, age 75; Priss, age 75; Old Priss, age 80; Charity, age 55
Males 26–45 years old	1 male, age 30, at the mill		2 males	Henry, age 35; Abram, age 35; Joseph, age 40; Anthony, age 40; Robert, age 35; Peter, age 35 (died 1829[e])	Henry, age 40 (at mill); Abraham, age 40; Charles Brown, age 28
Females 26–45 years old		4 females		Fanny, age 30; Rachel, age 20; Mary, age 20; Hannah, age 35	Fanny, age 44
Males and females 14–26 years old		5 males and 3 females	4 males	Charles, age 19; James, age 23	Bill, age 16
Males and females under 14 years old		7 males and 3 females		Joe, age 10; Lloyd, age 4; Elizabeth, age 6; Lydia, age 9; Alexander, age 4; James, age 2; Eliza Jane, age 8; Mary, age 2; Louisa, (6 mos.)	Joe, age 20; Lloyd, age 13; Betsy, age 16; Libby, age 18?; Tom, age 14; Trecy, age 10; Sophy, age 8; Becky, age 6; child of Fanny's at the breast
Total enslaved	1	28		21	19
Total free			9		

George Sugden rented Mount Clare starting in 1854, when the national debate about slavery was getting louder and louder. When the Civil War broke out in 1861 over slavery, it was only a matter of time before Mount Clare would become involved, due to its location near Baltimore at a hub along the B&O Railroad (fig. 7.2). Sugden, who was not a slaveholder, saw the Civil War come to his front door in 1861 while operating Mount Clare for a boardinghouse. It is said that officers stayed inside the mansion while federal troops camped in two places on the property (figs. 7.3 and 7.4). The solders' camp just northwest of the mansion was called Camp Carroll or Camp Chesebrough. Another camp was located near the Millington Mill, farther north.

The soldiers' actions helped to erase the physical evidence of black history on the property. The western wing was used as a jail and was in a state of ruin. Soldiers may have used the dependencies for fuel or housing, just as camps at other plantations did. Considering the impact of the two camps on his property, it is notable that James Jr. did not file a damages claim with the federal government after the war ended. Sugden, however, did file a claim. He was not entirely successful in recouping the claimed losses. The government compensated him for using a horse and wagon on three occasions in 1861 to transport deceased soldiers and commissary stores. It

---

Notes: This table accounts for the enslaved and free people on Mount Clare. In the columns for 1823 and 1832, several individuals appear in both lists. They are listed at the top of the cell for their age group.

a. Election District 1 (1818), p. 32. Assessors Field Book. Baltimore County Commissioners of the Tax, CR 68,893, CM1289-1. MSA.

b. Baltimore Ward 12. Fourth census of the United States, 1820. Washington, DC: NARA, 1820. Roll M33_42, p. 110.

c. Comparison of an undated list of slaves on James Carroll's property with his estate inventory from 1832 suggests that the undated list can reasonably be dated to 1823, when a tax assessment was taken for the county. n.d. 700 acres of land. Folder "n.d. James Carroll (1762–1832)," Box 9, MS 219, MdHS.

d. Baltimore County Register of Wills (Inventories), James Carroll, 1832, Liber 45, folio 118, MSA CM155-45, WK1075-1076-2.

e. "A Coroner's Inquest was held on Saturday afternoon near Booth's Gardens, West Baltimore Street over the body of Peter Moore, a coloured man of about 50 years of age, slave to James Carroll, of Mount Clare. Verdict of the jury: 'Death by Intemperance.'""Coroner's, Saturday." Baltimore Patriot [Baltimore, Md.], 28 July 1829, vol. 34, iss. 24, p. 2.

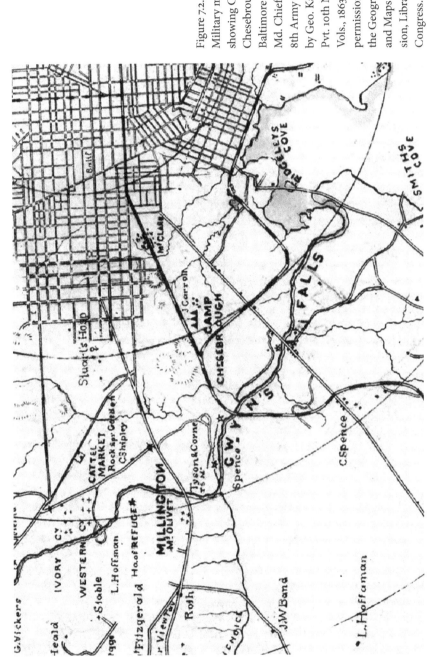

Figure 7.2. Military map showing Camp Chesebrough, Baltimore Co., Md. Chief Eng., 8th Army Corps, by Geo. Kaiser, Pvt. 10th N.Y. Vols., 1863. By permission of the Geography and Maps Division, Library of Congress.

Figure 7.3. E. Sachse and Co., Camp Carroll, Baltimore, Maryland, 1862. By permission of the Prints and Photographs Division, Library of Congress.

Figure 7.4. Detail of Sasche print of Camp Carroll, showing the mansion and dependencies.

1873

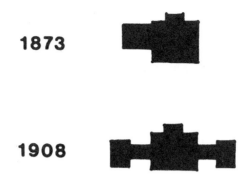

1908

Figure 7.5. The mansion in 1873 after the Schuetzens demolished the wings and in 1908 after Baltimore City commissioned new ones. By permission of Michael F. Trostel, FAIA, Trostel & Pearre, Architects.

denied him reimbursement for eight months' rent for storing commissary supplies for the Second Regiment of Maryland Volunteers, arguing that the regiment had stayed in tents.[7] Even so, by the end of the war, the mansion complex was in shambles.

After the end of the Civil War and legal slavery, Mount Clare went through another transition, when its first ethnic club moved in. James Jr. had been selling parcels of Mount Clare land to developers while Baltimore City grew west but had managed to keep the mansion area intact. It sat empty between 1867 and 1870. Then, in 1870, James Jr. rented fifteen acres of land plus the mansion to a German social club called the West Baltimore Schuetzen Association, for use as a clubhouse and recreational park.[8] The Schuetzens demolished the dilapidated dependencies in 1873 (fig. 7.5). They constructed a two-story kitchen to replace the east wing. The Schuetzens equipped the mansion with a shooting range, a ten-pin alley, a drinking hall, and a bandstand. Archaeologically recovered pig bones, beer bottles and glasses, and bullet casings attest to the Schuetzens' entertainments. The National Society of the Colonial Dames of America in the State of Maryland (the Maryland Society) chafed a century later at the "ignominy of [Mount Clare's] use as a public beer garden," in contrast to "what had once been the elegance and gentility of a gracious Colonial home."[9] No matter what the Schuetzens' intentions, their renovations at Mount Clare preserved the mansion complex best associated with elite whites in the past and modified it to suit their own purposes.

Preserving a Park and a Museum

The mayor and city council of Baltimore purchased the mansion and twenty acres from James Maccubbin Carroll Jr.'s heirs in 1890 to create a public park.[10] In 1917, the park entered into an agreement with the National Society of the Colonial Dames of America to manage Mount Clare as a museum. The park and the house became managed as separate but contiguous entities for the first time. It is important to note that organizations run by whites, such as the Schuetzens and the Maryland Society, both enjoyed the societal privilege of promoting white heritage and the legal and social power to do it in a way that blacks in society still could not.

It would be a mistake to think that black communities only started preserving their stories as a way to support racial uplift in a coordinated way after the Civil War. While both black and white historical organizations emphasized collecting documentary evidence, black organizations did not—or could not—take the place-based approach to historical interpretation that whites did. The Spanish and Dutch published a few narratives from enslaved persons in the 1500s. Places with large black communities developed newspapers and societies by the 1780s. The first African American literary and historical society was founded in Philadelphia in 1828. Abolitionist organizations published slave narratives starting in the 1830s, including those of Sojourner Truth and Frederick Douglass. In 1854, William Cooper Nell placed his own black ancestors alongside Washington and Jefferson as founders of the nation in his book *Colored Patriots of the American Revolution*. Solomon Brown was hired by the Smithsonian Institution in 1857 and became a leading preservationist in Washington, DC. In 1896, Frederick Douglass's wife and other community members established the first African American historic house at his home, Cedar Hill, in Washington, DC. The books and manuscripts about African literary achievements and the African diaspora collected by Dr. Jesse Moorland, Arthur Alonzo Schomburg, and Daniel Alexander Payne Murray became the basis for major collections at libraries, universities, and archives. Private libraries on black history were established, including the American Negro

Academy (1897) and the Negro Society for Historical Research (1902). In 1915, Carter G. Woodson founded the first national black history preservation organization: the Association for the Study of Negro Life and History. Whites also developed museums, libraries, and collections with the aim of preserving African or African American history, such as at the Hampton Institute.[11] Even societies like the Mount Vernon Ladies' Association and the Maryland Society preserved black history—albeit inadvertently—by saving historical records, sites, and artifacts. History, museums, and cultural institutions have a long history in African American life.

The fact that Mount Clare was taken up by a white women's organization betrays both the different interests of blacks and whites for preserving the past as well as the capacity of race-based social groups for racial uplift. Upper- and middle-class white women led the historic preservation movement in the late nineteenth century, ostensibly to enjoy remembering a different time, but ultimately promoting racial inequality. They focused on what was of the greatest interest to them: their ancestors, architecture, and decorative arts. In contrast, the agendas, concerns, and values of black women's organizations were materially and philosophically different from those of white women preservationists. Black women's organizations, for example, looked to the future rather than to the past. They joined and organized literary and intellectual societies, mutual aid societies, civic leagues, and civil rights organizations. They did not see their colonial past as something to celebrate; indeed, the black community was ambivalent about the degree to which slavery should be remembered. Black women rarely claimed former plantations as their heritage or sought to see such sites become museums, and few had the resources to devote to the maintenance of aging structures. Black women, instead, focused their resources on working within their community toward racial, moral, and intellectual uplift. Mount Clare enabled white women to celebrate the contributions of their white ancestors to the nation; black women placed their priorities for racial uplift closer to home and the community.

Preservation by white women in the nineteenth century took place within the colonial revival movement, in which preservationists focused on the nostalgic memory of a colonial past. Historic house museums promulgated the invention of an immutable American past by the European American middle class and bourgeois, who felt threatened by social instability. The founding mothers of historic house museums practiced what is today known as traditional or consensus history. Traditional history seeks to cull one true, official, and authoritative reality from all available information about the past. Its dependence on textual sources, such as government documents or business papers, supports a focus on politics and economics and moves to the forefront the people best represented in those sources. Women who participated in historical preservation valued their ancestral heritage and shared an interest in the archives, artifacts, and historic properties associated with it. Traditional history tends to represent best the roles of elites, whites, and men in the American past. It promotes social unity, the continuity of existing institutions, and loyalty to the status quo.

One of the first women's organizations for historic preservation was the Mount Vernon Ladies' Association. The association began work in 1853 to save George Washington's Mount Vernon. In addition, white women organized the Association for the Preservation of Virginia Antiquities in 1889, the Daughters of the American Revolution in 1890, the National Society of the Colonial Dames of America (NSCDA) in 1891, and the National Association of the Daughters of the Confederacy (now the United Daughters of the Confederacy [UDC]) in 1894, among others. The organizations sought to commemorate the sacrifices and contributions of their ancestors—all white men—to the nation. Patriotic organizations ignored African American and Native American history, other than to acknowledge that their ancestors owned slaves or fought indigenous peoples. They were just as reticent toward European immigrants. House museums found a niche by providing, as Pamela West put it, "a shared ancestral home and sacred heritage." They also, West argued, "confirmed that the rescue of 'sacred' historic houses was within the proper, domestically based 'sphere' of woman's activity."[12]

The Maryland Society of the NSCDA was part of the women's historic preservation movement. It was formed in 1891 to commemorate "the brilliant achievements of the founders of this great Republic, to the end that the women as well as the men of this land may be stimulated to better and nobler lives" by collecting "manuscripts, traditions, relics, and mementoes of bygone days for preservation."[13] The 1895 constitution stipulated that membership

...shall be composed entirely of women who are descended in their own right from some ancestor of worthy life who came to reside in an American Colony prior to 1750, which ancestor or some one of his descendants, being a lineal ascendant of the applicant, shall have rendered efficient service to his country during the Colonial period, either in the founding of a commonwealth, or of an institution which has survived and developed into importance, or who shall have held an important position in the Colonial government, and who by distinguished services shall have contributed to the founding of this great and powerful nation. Services rendered after 1783 not recognized.[14]

Women were required to be direct descendants of an ancestor who served and resided in the American colonies prior to 1750 and served the country in an official capacity before July 4, 1776. More specifically, a woman was eligible to join the Maryland Society if her ancestor was a provincial officer; a member of assemblies, conventions, and committees; part of the judiciary; or involved in military or naval contingents. Such positions were unavailable to blacks—and many whites, including women—in the colonial era, which made membership in the Maryland Society racially exclusive. African American women today are eligible to be members of the Maryland Society if they meet the standard for all applicants, including proof of lineage.

The Maryland Society was typical of organizations in historic house preservation, particularly in the way that traditional history combined with colonial revivalism to erase blacks. The Maryland Society focused on renovating and furnishing Mount Clare upon becoming its steward in 1917. At the time, Baltimore's population had expanded greatly due to immigration from abroad and population shifts within America. Alvin Brunson calculated that 90 percent of African Americans in Baltimore lived along Pennsylvania Avenue by 1920, which is near Carroll Park but not adjacent to it.[15] The Maryland Society incorporated Mount Clare into projects with immigrants, but whether or not African Americans were included or permitted inside Mount Clare is not clear from available records.

The approach of the Maryland Society to the Carrolls' history was typical at the time of the colonial revival movement. History museums appealed to northeastern Americans of English descent at a time when they felt that their culture was being threatened by immigrants. Stuart Hobbs writes that "Colonial revivalists used architectural and decorative forms from the eighteenth and early nineteenth centuries to create a mythologized past characterized by honest artisan labor and graceful living among beautiful objects."[16] Such was the case at Mount Clare, where Maryland Society members created a myth about the Carrolls while furnishing and restoring the house within a rapidly changing urban context. In the early 1920s, Mount Clare's board president, Emilie McKim Reed, expressed her satisfaction at a clean house lit with electric lights and her wish that they could "make the little room on the first floor into a library and next make the old dining room beautiful."[17] In correspondence members were thanked for their donations of furnishings, yet urged to be patient as they waited to see them arranged in the house. The Committee on Americanization (later Patriotic Service) started with the care of immigrants who stopped on their way west over the Baltimore & Ohio Railroad. Sioussat wrote in 1920 that

> Mount Clare continues to be a joy—and serves many ends not usually attained by an old Colonial mansion—as the population outside of Carroll Park hill—its beautiful terraces made long ago by the Barrister consists of great rarities of foreign form—and we like to see how the house and its relics attracts them and how they wander in and out of its historic walls with a sense of inclusion in its ownership which is the best ground work for their Americanization.[18]

The project continued into 1929, as Sioussat wrote,

> Mount Clare is more beautiful than ever—its doors are open to the pilgrims who come in increasing numbers to enjoy its charms, while its gate bears today the legend of our estate properly inscribed thereon. It has retained its stateliness in the midst of the foreign population and proves both inspiration and education to them.[19]

For women preservationist-reformers through the first third of the twentieth century, uncritical patriotism provided a guiding framework to address the rapid social changes occurring in urban areas.

While ignoring black history, the Maryland Society layered its agenda over Mount Clare, even when it had little to do with the history of the place.

The Maryland Society emphasized that its members' patriotic work in the twentieth century was a continuation of their ancestors' efforts. Members of the Maryland Society were active in war efforts and local causes. They hung framed coats-of-arms of Maryland families and arms of Maryland in the office. The names of Colonial Dames of Maryland who volunteered during World War I covered the south wall of the breakfast room, "thus linking the patriots of [17]'76 with those of 1914–1919."[20] The commemorative nature of Mount Clare extended to the yard. The historical division gathered names of men who served in the war for a tablet on the grounds in recognition of their service.[21] The tablet joined two other memorials. One was erected in 1914 by the National Star-Spangled Banner Centennial Commission to commemorate Charles Carroll and his Revolution-era associates. Residents of the neighborhood erected the other in 1918 to recognize local men who died during World War I. The effect was that the erasure of black history enabled the Maryland Society to appropriate Mount Clare for its own heritage needs. No history of the world wars or bicentennial existed at Mount Clare until the Maryland Society put it there.

Colonial revivalists created a usable past with which to address their concerns without challenging the system. The result was ultimately an inaccurate caricature of the Carrolls. Historian and genealogist Annie Leakin Sioussat codified the approach in her historical sketch of Mount Clare, which was published by the Maryland Society in 1926. No evidence of slavery is presented, even though her sources contained it. Sioussat depicted Mount Clare as an oasis amid the swift destruction wrought by modern life. She began the history with a romanticized discussion of the "red men" who traveled through the region before focusing on Charles Carroll and his plantation. Charles was characterized as a hardworking patriot: "a strong patriotic example for those who come after, of the days when purity of life and political probity were the ideals and guiding principles inherited from the earlier days." Charles's home in Annapolis, she wrote, had "long lost its identity and only the mansion of Mount Clare remains to the best of uses as his memorial and a shrine in which may be found, not articles collected here and there, presumably of the period, but the veritable furnishings and worldly gear, silver, etc., remain in the place for which they were purchased from London."[22] Sioussat did not discuss slaves or slavery, but instead documented the refurbished interior, architectural features, and landscaped setting at Mount Clare, of which the Colonial Dames were quite proud. Sioussat's history reflected the Maryland Society's lack of interest in the full story of the Carrolls and the development of Mount Clare.

Developing Carroll Park

The establishment of Carroll Park marked another chapter in black history at Mount Clare. The city hired Frederick Law Olmsted in 1903 to redesign Carroll Park and other Baltimore parks. The wings today flanking the mansion were constructed in 1908 for bathhouses and locker rooms. Olmsted despised slavery and believed in the equality of all races, but he believed that equal rights were to be earned through proper education and having a productive role in society. He envisioned his urban parks as a way to improve equality in society as well as individual morality and the mind. The Olmsted plans for Carroll Park, including baseball fields, outdoor gymnasiums for men and women, basketball courts, and a wading pool, were complete by 1915. The Olmsted features became central players in ongoing racial divisions at Carroll Park, when ball fields, golf courses, pools, and other areas became segregated. The tension between Olmsted's beliefs and the way in which the park's Olmsted features structured segregationist policy became another aspect of black history in Carroll Park.

Racist practices in the recreational areas of Carroll Park reflected the segregation of history at the Mount Clare Museum House and throughout the city. In 1923, Baltimore Parks and Recreation developed a municipal golf course to the west of Monroe Street on 102 acres, formerly of Mount Clare. All the golf courses in Baltimore were "white only" until the public protests of the Monumental Golf Club of Baltimore, an African American organization, forced them to change. The park board granted African Americans access to Carroll Park beginning on September 1, 1934. Wells writes that the park board did not believe "that an increased African American presence in the area would adversely impact the white neighborhoods of southwestern Baltimore in any significant way," due to the industrial character of the landscape surrounding the golf course.[23] White residents of southwestern Baltimore, however, successfully persuaded the mayor to ask the park board to reverse its decision.

African American golfers were given exclusive use of the Carroll Park golf course in 1936. On May 6, 1942, the Board of Parks and Recreation removed ordinances that prohibited blacks from golfing anywhere but Carroll Park. White golfers protested, and the ordinances were reinstated in June. Court cases brought by African Americans in 1942 and 1947 successfully argued that the Fourteenth Amendment guaranteed their right to equal access and facilities on Baltimore's golf courses.[24] The Fourteenth Amendment to the U.S. Constitution (proposed 1866, ratified 1868) provided equal rights for all people but allowed segregation to persist by leaving the determination of the method of equality up to the states. Full racial integration of all Baltimore golf courses took place in 1951.[25] Descendants of enslaved blacks organized the fight for desegregation, such as Juanita Jackson Mitchell (an enslaved daughter of Charles Carroll, father of Charles Carroll of Carrollton), members of the NAACP, and golfers, who, unlike their enslaved forebears, had the disposable income to afford golf. Unlike their forebears, twentieth-century African Americans had gained traction as members of society to bring court cases and defend their rights as equal citizens.

The park board's policies incited racial violence in Carroll Park. Anyone could use the eastern portion of Carroll Park surrounding the Mount Clare Museum House, but the park board's segregationist policies restricted its uses by blacks. The wading pool was white-only. Only one ethnic group could use a ball field at a time. Park officers were instructed to break up any interracial games. In October 1940, a nineteen-year-old African American man died from a stabbing wound that he received during a gang fight between whites and blacks. Some whites believed that they had, writes Wells, a "natural dominance over the park." In the 1940s, gangs from the poor, white neighborhood to the north of Carroll Park between Wilkens Avenue and Lombard Street were particularly intent on driving out blacks. Prompted by Brown v. Board of Education (1954), which challenged segregation in public places, the park board opened all its parks to all races. Whites in the surrounding neighborhoods were disgusted.[26]

No information is currently available about the Maryland Society's reaction to segregation in Carroll Park. The women who set to furnishing and keeping up the house did not engage with the movement for racial equality in the landscape surrounding Mount Clare. Nonetheless, the bowling green at the Mount Clare Museum House offers one place at which to discuss the differences between then and now. Enslaved blacks under the Carrolls' tenure tended the lawn and stood by as the Carrolls entertained guests with bowling games. The ability of African Americans 150 years later to play the game, and agitate for rights on the basis of their status, marked fundamental shifts in American society.

Continuing Focus on the Carrolls

Perhaps the main difference driving the pace of change at Carroll Park, as opposed to Mount Clare, was who wanted to use these places. The Mount Clare Museum House was not the lightning rod for racial equality and social benefits like the recreational park was. It, instead, continued to be a place for white women's use, a place at which they could control the memory of the past and exclude multiple perspectives. Women's patriotic organizations gained continued ideological vigor from World War I and II, even as war diverted resources from historic preservation to the wartime economy and support effort. After the wars, suburban expansion and federal urban renewal policies—which were themselves rooted in racism—instigated the destruction of old city sections. The loss of historic structures and the histories they represented—namely those of white, elite personages—instilled concern in preservationists. Even so, places representative of another time, such as Mount Clare, did manage to survive demolition.

Perhaps one reason Mount Clare survived was because of its dominant white colonial narrative, as well as the power of the Maryland Society. Few African American museums existed before the 1950s and 1960s—the era of the civil rights, black power, and black consciousness movements—when more than ninety African American museums were established in the United States. Community leaders versed in civil rights developed the new museums under the aegis of truth-telling to create positive myths and institutions. During this time, social history grew out of representation politics to contest traditional constructions of the past. Historians became interested in conflict, diversity, and multiple perspectives. Curators realized that they did not have sufficient artifactual evidence to support social history exhibits and, as a result, would have to look at their collections in new ways. Although traditional history persisted in the interpretation of places like Mount Clare, broader trends in museum practices placed pressure on the Maryland Society to change.

The civil rights era meant that African Americans became better represented in American cultural institutions. More African Americans entered the museum profession. Museum administrators realized that minorities were a part of American culture and they expected to see something of themselves during museum visits. Bigger institutions funded by federal money or endowments had greater resources than private societies to improve the representation of African Americans in historical projects. Large museums implemented exhibits devoted to African American history but did not necessarily integrate black and white history. The Smithsonian Institution established the Anacostia Neighborhood Museum in 1967 and staged black history–oriented exhibits at the National Portrait Gallery and the National Museum of American History. Colonial Williamsburg factored the eighteenth-century African American population into its interpretative programs beginning in the late 1970s.[27] Before then, a visit to Colonial Williamsburg reinforced the idea that blacks participated minimally in colonial society. Development of black history has continued at Colonial Williamsburg, including a reenacted slave auction in 1994 and tours and exhibits up to the present. In addition, descendant families have pushed back against dominant white narratives through contributions of oral history or DNA evidence to claim plantations as their heritage. Homecomings have taken place at Somerset Place Historic Site in Crenshaw, South Carolina; Monticello, Virginia; Montpelier in Montpelier Station, Virginia; and the Levi Jordan Plantation in Texas. The tables in this book are designed to aid the ancestors of the Garrett, Lynch, Harden, Bordley, and Hall families with research into their families' enslaved ancestors and assert their ancestors' significance at Mount Clare.

Shifts in the broader field of museums were slow to affect the interpretation of Mount Clare. Stewards of Carroll Park continued to focus on the Carrolls into the 1970s and 1980s and, in the process, avoid slavery and blacks. A 1971 publication by the Maryland Society stated, "The history of Mount Clare was a happy one for nearly a hundred years. The Georgian mansion . . . offered beauty and serenity to the family who lived there in an atmosphere of elegance and plenty."[28] Michael Trostel's history of Mount Clare, published in 1981, was commissioned by the Maryland Society to focus on the Carrolls and the house itself. Trostel's book enabled the Maryland Society to interpret the Carrolls and the mansion more fully than ever before. It was a missed opportunity for the Maryland Society to be able to commission an in-depth look at the history of the plantation and its inhabitants.

Docent training manuals from 1978 through 1987 instructed the Mount Clare docents to focus on architecture, decorative furnishings, and the "great men" of the Carroll family. No information was provided about the enslaved blacks living there, despite evidence about them in the same records used to build the histories of the Carrolls. Docents were also informed to mention the painter Charles Willson Peale and Revolutionary heroes such as George Washington, even though they each spent only a few days on the property, if that. Docents received room-by-room descriptions of the furnishings, including the date of manufacture, the origin, and which Carroll family member owned each item. They were encouraged to identify only those items belonging to Carroll family members. They learned about "typical" eighteenth-century dress, meaning the fashionable garb worn by Margaret Carroll and other wealthy women. Some Colonial Dames as docents wore reproduction dresses during group tours. Starting in the mid-1980s, the manuals gave docents more information about the Baltimore Iron Works. The information focused on who owned the business, rather than who worked it. In addition, a 1987 docent manual stated, "Mount Clare was the scene of gracious entertaining on the part of the Carroll family, and it is our privilege to extend that graciousness to our twentieth-century guests. Long after most of the factual details have faded, the memory of a warm welcome will persist if we are properly interpreting Charles and Margaret Carroll's lives at Mount Clare."[29] The manual states relevance as a goal but does not specify why Mount Clare was relevant, or to whom.[30]

Between 1817 and 1987, slavery ended at Mount Clare, African Americans were agitating for equal rights and access, and black history was gaining prominence at institutions across the nation. But there was still resistance to interpreting the truth at Mount Clare and making the historic house museum a place where all members of society could learn about their heritage. As a result, the Maryland Society was struggling with its relevance amid a nation more aware of social justice and equal rights.

8

Conclusion

In the first chapter, I mentioned that I see racist actions at Carroll Park where the Maryland Society or Carroll Park Foundation may not. Racism and racialized activities have not ended in United States, but many people are sensitive to being labeled racist, because their beliefs about themselves do not match up with the historical implications of the term. We—meaning, people of all colors and all backgrounds—are conscious of not wanting to seem or be racist when other people tell us we are.

A visit to Mount Clare or Carroll Park today reveals nothing overtly discriminatory: no exclusionary signage, no restricted water fountains, no separate entrances. And yet, neither the Maryland Society nor the Carroll Park Foundation provides a permanent exhibit or tour on black history. Thus, there is the lingering hum of racism, because the focus has been so clearly on the white elite class. The majority population who lived on Mount Clare was enslaved blacks, but their stories have been muted in favor of the Carrolls or famous whites who visited once or twice, such as George and Martha Washington, or even the stories of the Maryland Society. The minority population of white elites continues to receive the interpretive emphasis, and that sends a message. Even so, Mount Clare has something to teach about blacks in American life for the entire history of the nation. If social justice is about fair and equal access to all benefits of society, then the caretakers and interpreters of Mount Clare have a responsibility to facilitate all visitors' ability to make personal connections with the past.

Although the Maryland Society has not been publicly called racist, lineage-based women's historic preservation societies do have a reputation for discrimination and exclusion of black history. The Daughters of the

American Revolution and the United States Daughters of the Confederacy have been publicly accused of racism. In 1939, the DAR refused permission to Marian Anderson, an African-American contralto, to sing to an integrated audience at Constitution Hall in Washington, DC. The venue had a "white performers only" policy. The first African American woman invited to join the DAR was invited in 1977. In 1985, Lena Lorraine Santos Ferguson and her two sponsors claimed that the DAR denied her membership on the basis of her race. Ferguson told a *Washington Post* reporter that "The reason I kept pursuing it is I wanted to prove that if this organization stands for what it says it stands for—honoring people who served in the revolution—I should be able to join."[1] As a result of such public shaming, the DAR now forbids discrimination on the basis of race. Organizations like the DAR racialized nationalism, in effect determining who could justly benefit from being a member of society.

More recently, these organizations have worked to dispel public perceptions of their racism. Essie Mae Washington-Williams, the biracial daughter of former U.S. Senator Strom Thurmond, applied for membership in the USDC based on her father's lineage. Washington-Williams explained that she did not see the organization as explicitly racist, as popular sentiment makes it out to be. She saw, instead, an opportunity for encouraging dialogue as both a white and a black person.[2] In 2011, the USDC named Mattie Clyburn Rice the second African American "real daughter" to join the organization, meaning that she descended from a soldier who served the Confederacy. Two of Rice's daughters have also joined the USDC.[3] The contrasting view is that Clyburn was a slave, not an enrolled soldier, who applied for a pension after the rules changed in the 1920s. The argument is that the USDC is using Clyburn to support the myth that blacks served as Confederate soldiers. Recent analysis has identified the USDC as part of the neo-Confederacy movement.

The Maryland Society has not been publicly accused of racism, but the habit of thought of excluding blacks from the interpretation of Mount Clare does raise questions about the underlying reasons why. In addition, the Carroll Park Foundation has erected barriers to accessing the archaeological collection, which has been in serious need of rehousing, completion of cataloguing, and stabilization since the first collection assessment in the early 1990s. The assessments began to weave together archaeology at Mount Clare since the 1970s, but the result has not been integrated into the site's interpretation.[4] The racial tones of women's patriotic organizations are part of their institutional histories and, as a result, are part of the history of Mount Clare.

Civil Rights and African American Museums

Interpretation at Mount Clare and in the surrounding landscape has become more inclusive in the past several years by the Maryland Society and the Carroll Park Foundation. It may be due to pressure from outside and inside to be relevant to a broader segment of society. Images over the twentieth century show little change in the furnishing of Mount Clare, demonstrating continuing interest in decorative arts (figs. 8.1 and 8.2). They also betray little change in interpretation at Mount Clare, considering that the house tour had not changed in order to communicate the ways in which enslaved people interacted with the people, spaces, and objects within the rooms.

Figure 8.1. Dining room at Mount Clare, 1958. By permission of the Historic American Buildings Survey, Library of Congress.

Figure 8.2. Living room at Mount Clare, 1958. By permission of the Historic American Buildings Survey, Library of Congress.

In the mid-1980s, the Maryland Society learned that Mount Clare would be affected by a long-term plan to overhaul the interpretation of the historic easement area in which it sits. Mount Clare had become more visible than ever before due to development at Inner Harbor. The restoration of Fells Point and Federal Hill turned developers toward southwest Baltimore. Plus, archaeological excavations brought press to the site. The Maryland Society felt pressure to demonstrate its competency as custodian of the house. A letter to the editor of the Maryland Society's newsletter in 1989 called for the organization to keep up with the times. The writer urged the Maryland Society to recognize the current trends among museums, such as the broadened interpretations of furnished houses, museums as businesses with standards of management, and that museums are open to all rather than a privileged few. The writer bemoaned the sense that the Maryland Society was hoarding the museum.[5]

Since then, and as of this writing, African American history appears in various degrees at Mount Clare. Depending on the docent, a visitor may hear about enslaved and free blacks, or, more colloquially, "servants." One emphasis lies on freedom, as evidenced by newspaper advertisements seeking the return of escaped slaves. Framed advertisements for the return of runaways appear on the walls of the room where visitors are introduced to the site's history. The advertisements supported the successful application of the Mount Clare site to the National Underground Railroad: Network to Freedom register that is maintained by the National Park Service.[6] An update to the museum's website in the spring of 2007 includes substantial material on African American history in the region and at Mount Clare.[7] The content demonstrates a major shift in the Colonial Dames' knowledge about African American history but raises questions about why it does not manifest more fully in docents' tours. Unlike the Carrolls, no furnished or reconstructed areas depict African American life. Future interpretive goals include a better kitchen exhibit, demonstrations of indentured servant life and of enslaved persons, and the effects of slavery on the landscape. Although (as the museum's website shows) strides are being made to present a more inclusive view of Mount Clare's past, the fact remains that onsite interpretation concentrates on the Carrolls, the standing Georgian house, and the antiques inside it.

Docents at Mount Clare rarely discuss slavery or the black population, which disenfranchises visiting African Americans from accessing their heritage. African Americans expect to see something of themselves at historic sites, but their ancestors are not necessarily well developed in site interpretations. Interpretive programs at Colonial Williamsburg, for example, tended to frame black history around positive views of white enslavers and to reduce blacks to their monetary value. A 2002 survey of museum plantations and sites in the American South found that only black-run sites and a handful of white-run sites adequately addressed slavery. The majority ignored or trivialized slavery and black labor, preferring instead to focus on owners and interior decoration. Jennifer L. Eichstedt and Stephen Small see these places as racialized rather than racist, meaning that even well-meaning people can perpetuate racially oppressive systems by using language that neutralizes the charged atmosphere of race-based slavery.[8] E. Arnold Modlin concluded from his analysis of southern historic house tours that docents continue to marginalize slavery by deflecting the discussion of slavery, trivializing it, or segregating facts and artifacts to remote locations.[9] Antoinette Jackson's use of ethnographic techniques connects past and present black groups through integrating culturally appropriate knowledge and techniques of relating to historic places.[10] Focusing on the agency of enslaved blacks provides a way for heritage sites to expand their interpretations and establish places that matter to contemporary descendants.

Based on my experiences of the docent tours at Mount Clare, a wide range of comfort levels with the subject matter of blacks and slavery is evident. All the tours focus on the lives and accomplishments of Dr. Carroll, Charles Carroll the Barrister and Margaret, James, and James Jr. Expected to impart the grandeur of an elite family's fabulous life, the docents' tours obfuscated the ways in which enslaved blacks were woven throughout the Carrolls' existence. The effect is a failure to acknowledge that the Carrolls' experiences cannot be generalized to include all people who lived at Mount Clare. In 2012, however, the Baltimore & Ohio Railroad Museum assumed the daily operation of Mount Clare, including its educational programs. The Carroll Park Foundation has retained stewardship of the archaeological collections and the Maryland Society maintains the decorative arts collections inside the house. Since the administrative shift, the Mount Clare Museum House has worked to integrate black history into the interpretive programs in a more inclusive way. The Carroll Park Foundation, however, has not updated its website since 2008 and the organization appears to have no regular black history programming. Its work in recent years has been geared toward rehousing the archaeological collection and maintaining a replanted orchard.

Historic plantations have a responsibility to present truthful and well-rounded information to visitors. African Americans trust museums, but not as much as white Americans. Roy Rosenzweig and David Thelan found that on a scale of 1 to 10 in a national sample of four ethnic groups, museums (8.4) ranked higher than family accounts (8.0) as trustworthy sources of information about the past. African Americans, however, ranked family accounts higher than museums, whereas white Americans ranked museums higher. Museums ranked highest in trustworthiness across all age, gender, education, and income categories.[11] Though African Americans trust museums more than many other sources, studies of interpretation at historic plantations demonstrate that they have little reason to. Why, indeed, should African Americans trust the Maryland Society and the Carroll Park Foundation to tell the truth about their ancestors' contributions to American culture?

Slavery constituted a form of cultural trauma that shaped African American identities, such that the dramatic loss of identity led to new collective identities at times of crisis. The deconstruction and construction of identity constitutes part of the way in which contemporary visitors can learn about the making of American culture. The interpretation of history as racially integrated is furthermore important because it confronts visitors' stereotypes, preconceived notions, and discomfort. Such presentations emphasize that the development of the United States has not been easy or completely dictated by whites. Presenting a rounder, more nuanced view of slavery and blacks at Mount Clare explores the complexity of the black experience and makes the landscape of greater relevance to contemporary groups.

The tendency of historic preservation to layer history on physical remnants of the past presents a major opportunity for Mount Clare to discuss both black history and its erasure over time. The preservation of the plantation supplies an ideological symbol, a tourist destination, a mnemonic device, and a theater of memory. Old messages are not erased, but added to, so that the past can be interpreted in different ways. For example, the history of women in the preservation of Mount Clare is part of the story to tell. Historic structures preserved by women should have women's preservation efforts as part of their story of significance. In a similar way, a national story for preservation exists, but it is not necessarily the most important story when compared with local practices. The history of women's preservation in the Chesapeake region provides important context for the erasure of black history from Carroll Park. Women preservationists have controlled the racialization of historic sites and the ways in which Americans remember or think about the past. Race is central to the ways in which Americans remember or forget. One place to discuss the issue is in front of a Maryland Society member's reproduction of Charles Willson Peale's landscape of Mount Clare. The reproduction is displayed in an upstairs bedroom, with a laminated detail of Peale's painting nearby. Comparison of the two shows that the artist of the reproduction changed the groom's skin color from brown to white and erased the house beyond the mansion, which may have housed blacks or an overseer. It is an opportunity to acknowledge that the stewards of Carroll Park are trying to change its traditional interpretation and be more inclusive.

The erasure of black history from historic sites is common, even today. Museums tend to be conservative because they fear that visitors will shy away from difficult history. But avoiding the interpretation of conflict is tantamount to condoning the actions of the past. Emphasis on positive or light elements of the Carrolls' lives, such as furniture or parties, constructs a particular and one-dimensional view of whites at Mount Clare. Slavery is, comparatively, a stain on the memory of a family that the Maryland Society wishes to venerate. But avoiding difficult history or conflict also means that visitors to Mount Clare do not learn about empowering or positive elements of the site's black history, such as success in their struggles for freedom and equality. Slavery constituted a form of cultural trauma that shaped African American identities, such that the dramatic loss of identity led to new collective identities at times of crisis. The memory of the trauma is a form of history that shapes African American identity in changing or generational ways over time. The deconstruction and construction of identity constitutes part of the way that contemporary visitors can learn about the making of American culture. The interpretation of history as racially integrated is furthermore important because it confronts visitors' stereotypes, preconceived notions, and discomfort. Such presentations emphasize that the development of America has not been easy or completely dictated by whites. Presenting a rounder, more nuanced view of slavery and blacks at Mount Clare explores the complexity of the black experience and makes the landscape of greater relevance to contemporary groups.

Blacks' experiences in the history of Mount Clare are muted in the present. Women's preservation by hereditary organizations has a tradition in historic house museums of avoiding difficult history. Their focus, instead, has been on architecture and material things, as well as an image of the past that is gracious and civilized. Passing along such an image, however, perpetuates in the present the racialized practices of the past to disenfranchise blacks from claiming a place as theirs. Problems in the interpretation of black history are not unique to Mount Clare; indeed, a pattern exists whereby black heritage is erased or not included. A theme among historic plantations is discomfort with topics that challenge white supremacy, such as enslaved persons' agency, activism, and power. The result is unequal access to heritage and a lack of support for social justice. Such work would demonstrate the extent of racist practices as an impediment to social justice, meaning that social attitudes seek excuses for individuals' behaviors within the individual, rather than examining systemic themes—many based in history—that can be misinterpreted. Although physical traces of black history have eroded from the landscape since the 1830s, site stewards today have a responsibility to stop the process from going any further.

NOTES

Foreword

1. Starn, "A Historian's Brief Guide to New Museum Studies," 68, 71.
2. Burton and Scott, "Management Museums."
3. Ross, "Interpreting the New Museology," 84.

Chapter 1. Introduction

1. A note on terminology: The specific geographic or tribal origins of the people enslaved at Mount Clare remain uncertain. Their homelands might have been located on the African continent or in the West Indies, Brazil, or interstitial locations along slave trade routes to America. I acknowledge the ambiguity by using the term "black" instead of African or African American. I emphasize that slavery was imposed upon blacks, not chosen, through the use of the term "enslaved," rather than "slave," and "enslaver" instead of "master," "mistress," "slaveholder," or "slaveowner." I employ the term "servant" only for hired or indentured persons of European descent.

Several men named Charles Carroll lived in the Maryland colony in the eighteenth century. They are believed to have been cousins or distant cousins who descended from kings in Ireland, and all moved in similar social, business, and political circles. The men adopted monikers to identify each from the other. Personal papers, business records, and government documents inconsistently apply the monikers. I focus on Dr. Charles Carroll (1691–1755) and Charles Carroll the Barrister (1723–83). Others included Charles Carroll the Settler (1660/1–1720), Charles Carroll of Annapolis (1702–82), Charles Carroll of Carrollton (1737–1832), and Charles Carroll of Homewood (1775–1825). "Charles Carroll Esq." is used in records to identify any one of the men.

2. Sandercock, "Introduction: Framing Insurgent Historiographies for Planning."
3. Nieves, "Memories of Africville," 82.
4. Mullins, "Racializing the Commonplace Landscape," 70.

5. Three societies in the United States call themselves "Colonial Dames." All are women-only organizations that rely on genealogical connections with the colonial era for membership. The Mount Clare Museum House is associated with the National Society of the Colonial Dames in America (NSCDA). The NSCDA was founded in 1891 and is currently headquartered at the Dumbarton House in Washington, DC. The Colonial Dames of America (CDA) was founded in 1890. It is headquartered in the Mount Vernon Hotel Museum and Gardens in New York, New York. The CDA has a chapter in Baltimore, Maryland. The National Society of Colonial Dames XVII Century has its headquarters in Washington, DC. It is specifically interested in seventeenth-century genealogy and history.

6. Letter Book of Charles Carroll, 1716–31, p. 106, MS 208, MdHS.

7. Sidbury, *Becoming African in America*, 6; Breen and Innes, "*Myne Owne Ground*"; Davis, *Inhuman Bondage*, 51.

8. Lopez, *White by Law*; Smedley, *Race in North America*.

9. Wheeler, *The Complexion of Race*, 2–7; Frederickson, *The Black Image in the White Mind*, 2; Davis, *Inhuman Bondage*, 53.

10. Omi and Winant, *Racial Formation in the U.S.*, vii and 55.

11. Vaughn, "Preface," *Roots of American Racism*, ix.

12. Horton and Horton, *In Hope of Liberty*; Nash, "Forging Freedom"; Berlin, *Generations in Captivity*.

13. Hall, *Slavery and African Ethnicities in the Americas*.

14. Sioussat, "*Mount Clare*" *Carroll Park, Baltimore*.

15. Trostel, *Mount Clare*, ix.

16. W. S. Holt, "Charles Carroll, Barrister: The Man"; Giffen, "'Mount Clare,' Baltimore"; NSCDA, *Adventurers, Cavaliers, Patriots* and *Mount Clare*.

17. Tamplin, "Chatelaine of Mount Clare," 95–103.

18. Mount Clare Museum House, Slavery (Mount Clare Museum House, 2007), Online: http://www.mountclare.org/history/slavery.html (accessed October 9, 2009).

19. Carroll Park Foundation, Carroll's Hundred (Carroll Park Foundation, 2008), Online: http://www.carrollshundred.org/index.html (accessed October 9, 2009).

20. Gurman, *The Importance of Being Relevant*, Introduction.

21. Moyer, *Museum Practicum*.

Chapter 2. Slavery and Iron at Georgia

1. Cassimere Jr., *Origins and Early Development of Slavery in Maryland*, 3–7, 10–11, 27, 29, 101–3, 133, 143–44.

2. Breen and Innes, "*Myne Owne Ground*," 3–6, 10, 18.

3. Wax, "Black Immigrants," 32–33, 35–36, 38.

4. Walsh, *From Calabar to Carter's Grove*, 134–35, 145.

5. Libby, *African Ironmaking Culture*.

6. Walsh, *From Calabar to Carter's Grove*, 102.

7. Ignatiev, *How the Irish Became White*, 41.

8. Papenfuse et al., *A Biographical Dictionary*, vol. 1, 193–94; Harley, "Dr. Charles Carroll," 93.

9. Liber B. W. No. 1, Accounts and Debts, *MHM* 18: 204.

10. Dr. CC to Thomas Catton, April 5, 1747, p. 161 and Dr. CC to Mary Wolsen, 18th 9or 1749, p. 237, Letter Book 1742–52, MS 208, MdHS.

11. "Run Away," *Maryland Gazette* [Annapolis], September 6, 1745.

12. Baltimore County Court (Land Records) John Townsend to Charles Carroll, Chyurgeon, October 14, 1730, Liber IS L, folio 23, MSA CE 66–16. Conversion to 2008 dollars: £81 = $15,727. Nye, *Pounds to Dollars*.

13. Mssrs. Charles and Daniel Carroll et al., 1731, Letter Book of Charles Carroll, 1716–31, p. 13–14, MS 208, MdHS. Charles Carroll and his son Daniel enslaved a woman named Coffee at the ironworks. List of Taxables Returned Belonging to the Baltimore Company, 1733, Folder "1733–34, Employee Records: Baltimore Company," Box 6, MS 219, MdHS. Conversion to 2008 dollars: £81 = $18,921. Nye, *Pounds to Dollars*.

14. Land Office (Certificates, Patented, BA) Blacks, Patented Certificate 1886, July 11, 1732, MSA S1190-26, MdHR 40,004-1876/1950. Georgia consisted of: a resurvey of eight tracts of land in Baltimore, including Black Walnut Neck (1664, Hugh Hensey), Howard's Chance (1668, John Howard), Milhaven (1695 to John Mercer), James's Park (1700, James Carroll), Monmouth Green (1702, John Bale), Gill's Outlet (1717, John Gill), Barley Hills (1728, Charles Carroll), Discovery (1729, Charles Carroll and Co.), Land Certificates 1658–1766, p. 23, MS 210, MdHS.

15. Thomas Clagett to Blacks, September 26, 1730, in Archives of Maryland, *Provincial Court Land Records 1724–1731*, vol. 697, p. 461; Baltimore County Circuit Court (Patent Record), Charles Carroll, Caves, 1770 acres, 1738, Patent Record EI 5, p. 359, MSA 1582; Baltimore County Circuit Court (Patented Certificates) Dr. CC, Carrolls Island, 334 acres, 1746, Patented Certificate 942, MSA S1190-13, MdHR 40,004-901/975.

16. Lewis, *Coal, Iron, and Slaves*, 23, and "Slavery on Chesapeake Iron Plantations Before the American Revolution," 243.

17. Baltimore Company, Agreement of Copartnership, October 1, 1731, MS 208, MdHS.

18. Johnson, "Genesis of the Baltimore Ironworks," 162, and "Baltimore Company Seeks English Markets," 40–41, 162.

19. Mssrs. Charles and Daniel Carroll et al., 1731, vol. 1716–31, p. 14, MS 208, MdHS.

20. "Things to be performed by Dr. Carroll if agreed with as manager," n.d., Folder "[1730s] Baltimore Company," Box 6, MS 219, MdHS.

21. Charles Carroll [Esq.?] to Clement Plumsted, February 18, 1730, p. 7 and Clement Plumsted to Charles Carroll of Annapolis, April 20, 1731, vol. 1, p. 8, MS 65, MdHS; Johnson, "Genesis of the Baltimore Ironworks," 165.

22. Robbins, *Principio Company*, 127–29; Johnson, "Baltimore Company Seeks English Markets," 32; Lewis, *Coal, Iron, and Slaves*, 227.

23. Dr. Carroll's math is incorrect. He provides a total of twenty-six, but the itemized lists do not add up to that number. The inconsistency is preserved here. "Cost of a Furnace 24 by 26 foot square," Folder "1730s? Financial Records: Baltimore Company," Box 8, MS 219, MdHS.

24. "Estimate of Charges and Profit on the Works," Folder "1730s, Financial Records, Baltimore Iron Company," Box 8, MS 219, MdHS. Elements of this and other documents date the discussion to the mid- to late 1720s. Conversions to 2008 dollars: £30 = $6,262, £15 = $3,131, £20 = $4,175. Nye, *Pounds to Dollars*.

25. Carlson, "William Parks, Colonial Printer, to Dr. Charles Carroll," 409.

26. Lewis, *Coal, Iron, and Slaves*, 8.

27. Johnson, *Establishment of the Baltimore Company*, 110.

28. Minute Book, Baltimore Company, p. 5, Folder "1732–75, Minutes: Baltimore Company," Box 6, MS 219, MdHS; When Each of the Co. Sent Their Negroes or Servants to the Workes on Patapscoe, Folder "1733, Employee Records: Baltimore Company," MS 219, MdHS. Conversions to 2008 dollars: £20 = $4,175. Nye, *Pounds to Dollars*.

29. Baltimore Iron Works, List of persons employed, April 30, 1734, Box 6, MS 219, MdHS; Lewis, *Coal, Iron, and Slaves*, 23.

30. Daniel Dulany Esq. to Negros to be put into the work of agreement and their work hereafter stated to July 31, 1733; 1731 Dr. Charles Carroll to Negros to be put into the work of agreement and their work hereafter stated to July 31, 1733, Folder "1733, Employee records: Baltimore Company," Box 6, MS 219, MdHS.

31. Blacks, Account of time worked by negroes, July 31, 1733, Box 6, MS 219, MdHS.

32. Daniel and Charles Carroll of Annapolis's personal inventory indicates which of the total belonged to them: Bush or Bath or Bash, Long Harry, Caine, Dick, Poplar Jones, Boy Jack, Betty, Coffee, and Hannah. List of Taxables Returned Belonging to the Baltimore Company, 1733, Folder "1733–34, Employee Records: Baltimore Company"; Chas and Danl Negroes at the Iron Works, Folder "1733, Employee records: Baltimore Company," and Account of taxables at the works, 1733, Box 6, MS 219, MdHS. The discrepancy between 1733 and 1734 may relate to when the fiscal year fell.

33. Account of persons employed at the Baltimore Iron Works, April 30, 1734;

A List of Taxables, 1733, Folder "1733–34, Employee records: Baltimore County" and Account of Persons Employed at the Baltimore Iron Works, continued, 1734, Box 6, MS 219, MdHS.

34. Copy of List, 1736, vol. 3, p. 54, MS 65, MdHS.

35. Baltimore County Court (Tax List) Patapsco Upper Hundred, 1737, M1560-22, MSA CM918-9. The tax list counted all enslaved persons over age sixteen.

36. At the Furnace, n.d., Folder "n.d. Employee Records: Baltimore Company," Box 6, MS 219, MdHS.

37. Baltimore County (Tax Lists) Upper Hundred of Patapsco, 1737, MSA CM918-9, M1560-22.

38. Moses Maccubbins appears on Baltimore Iron Works registers in the expectation of supplying cords of wood in 1736. Account, 1736, vol. 3, p. 36 and Copy of List, 1736, p. 54, vol. 3, MS 65, MdHS; Dr. Cha. Carroll Company Account, 1741, Folder "1741 January–July, Financial Records: Baltimore Company" and "Amount of Cordwood in Stock and Expected, 1737/1738, Folder "1738, Financial Records: Baltimore Company," Box 8, MS 219, MdHS.

39. Baltimore County (Tax Lists) Back River Upper Hundred 1737, MSA CM918-2, M1560-16.

40. Stephen Onion to Charles Carroll Esq., July 16, 1737. Folder "1737 June–July, Correspondence: [Baltimore Company?]" Box 6, MS 219, MdHS; Dr. Carroll's Account with the Baltimore Company 1745 to 1747, Folder "1748, Financial Records: Baltimore Company," Box 8, MS 219, MdHS; Dr. Carroll Baltimore Company Account 1741/42, "Folder 1742 October–December, "Financial Records: Baltimore Company," Box 8, MS 219, MdHS.

41. Charles Carroll of Carrollton to the Baltimore Company, with replies, October 28, 1767, MSA M 4214-4715; Richard Croxall to Charles Carroll and Company, April 27, 1768, MSA M 4214-4723; Account and receipt, December 1735 to April 7, 1736, MSA 4215-4885.

42. Johnson, "Genesis of the Baltimore Ironworks," 174–77.

43. Johnson, "Genesis of the Baltimore Ironworks," 157, n. 2; Advertisement, "To Be Sold," Virginia Gazette, Ad Date: May 31, 1770. Conversions to 2008 dollars: (1752) £400 = $77,379, £10,000 = 1,934,476; (1783) £7,000 = $1,139,824. Nye, Pounds to Dollars.

44. Edwards-Ingram, "African American Medicine and the Social Relations of Slavery," 34–41; Fett, Working Cures, 4–5 and chapter 3.

45. Dr. Carroll's Acct as Phisick, 1733, Folder "1733 January–July, Financial Records: Baltimore Company," Box 8, MS 219, MdHS.

46. Burnston, "The Cemetery at Catoctin Furnace, MD: The Invisible People," 19–31; Kelley and Angel, "The Workers of Catoctin Furnace," 2–17.

47. Dent et al., *Archaeological Excavations at the Carroll Family Tomb in Saint Anne's Church Yard.*

48. Minute Book, Baltimore Company, p. 5, Folder "1732–75, Minutes: Baltimore Company," and When Each of the Co. Sent Their Negroes or Servants to the Workes on Patapscoe, Folder "1733, Employee Records: Baltimore Company," Box 6, MS 219, MdHS. Conversions to 2008 dollars: £20 = $4,175. Nye, *Pounds to Dollars.*

49. C. Daniell to Charles Carroll Esq., October 25, 1734, vol. 2, p. 15, MS 65, MdHS.

50. Hazzard had worked at the ironworks for two years. He was enslaved to Benjamin Tasker. Coffee was a New Negro. C. Daniell to Charles Carroll Esq., December 6, 1734, p. 26, and Stephen Onion to Charles Carroll Esq., December 16, 1734, p. 29, vol. 2, MS 65, MdHS.

51. Alexander Lawson to Charles Carroll Esq., March 21, 1737, vol. 3, p. 82, MS 65, MdHS.

52. Stephen Onion to Charles Carroll Esq., August 7, 1737, Folder "1737 August Correspondence: [Baltimore Company]," Box 6, MS 219, MdHS.

53. Lewis, *Coal, Iron, and Slaves,* 82.

54. Pennington, *A Text Book of the Origin and History* and *The Fugitive Blacksmith,* 8.

55. Dr. CC to Charles Carroll, Esq., November 9, 1732, vol. 1, p. 33, MS 65, MdHS.

56. Stephen Onion to Charles Carroll Esq., July 1, 1734, vol. 1, p. 87, MS 65, MdHS.

57. Advertisement, "Eighteen Pistoles Reward," *Pennsylvania Gazette,* September 12, 1754.

58. See *Maryland Gazette:* John Plat or Platt (convict, ran from Carroll's Quarter near Baltimore Iron Works on Patapsco, November 16, 1752, no. 393, and November 30, 1752, no. 395), Edward Lee or Edward Mortimer (ran from Baltimore Iron Works station at Gorsuch Point, July 19, 1734, no. 71), Mary Rider (convict, April 19, 1749, no. 208), Samuel Milburn and William Blayden (convicts, June 26, 1751, no. 322). Abstracted in Green, *The Maryland Gazette, 1727–1761.* Also, William Jones (servant, July 9, 1743, *Pennsylvania Gazette*); John Roberts to Blacks, May 4, 1747, Folder "1747 May–December, Correspondence: [Baltimore Company]," Box 7, MS 219, MdHS; Accounts, Chas Carroll of Carrollton and Benjamin Tasker, 1748–50, Folder "1750, Financial Records: Baltimore Company," Box 8, MS 219, MdHS.

59. Richard Croxall to Charles Carroll Esq., May 16, 1748, Folder "1748 January-May Correspondence: [Baltimore Company]," Box 7, MS 219, MdHS.

60. Stephen Onion to Charles Carroll Esq., July 1, 1734, vol. 1, p. 87, MS 65, MdHS.

61. Stephen Onion to Charles Carroll Esq., March 23, 1734, vol. 1, p. 75, MS 65, MdHS; Advertisement, Baltimore County (Maryland), *The Pennsylvania Gazette*, November 30, 1752; Advertisement, "Baltimore, February 24, 1764," *Pennsylvania Gazette*, March 8, 1764.

62. Advertisement, "Baltimore, February 24, 1764," *Pennsylvania Gazette*, March 8, 1764.

63. Invoice, November 7, 1737, Folder "1737 September–December, Correspondence: [Baltimore Company]," Box 6, MS 219; Letter Books of Dr. Charles Carroll, MS 201, MdHS.

64. Lewis, *Coal, Iron, and Slaves*, 159 and 163, and "Slavery on Chesapeake Iron Plantations," 246.

65. Inventory of Store Goods and Stock, 1736, Folder "1736 Baltimore Company Inventory of Store Goods," Box 12, MS 219, MdHS.

66. William Hammond to Charles Carroll of Carrollton, March 15, 1771, MSA M 4218-5008 Item No. [4741]; Replies of Charles Carroll of Carrollton, March 17, 1771, Charles Carroll, Barrister, and Walter Dulany, appended, MdHS, MS 2243. Film No.: MSA M 4214-4742 Item No. [4742]. I found no record of a court case to prosecute the men.

67. Dr. CC to CCB, February 2, 1753, Letter Books 1752–55 and 1755–69, p. 60–64, MS 208, MdHS.

68. It was near Kingsbury furnace on the west side of a branch of the Back River. Johnson, *Establishment of the Baltimore Company*, 280.

69. Dr. CC to William Black, September 1, 1746, Letter Book 1748–52, pp. 127–32; Dr. CC to William Black, December 4, 1746, Letter Book 1748–52, p. 136, MS 208, MdHS.

70. Dr. CC to Daniel Dulany and Company, January 25, 1750, Letter Book 1748–52, p. 293, and Dr. CC to Daniel Dulany and Company, January 26, 1750, Letter Book 1748–52, p. 295, MS 208, MdHS; Indenture, Dr. CC to Daniel Dulany and Company, January 30, 1750, Box 3, MS 219, MdHS.

71. "Cost of a Furnace 24 by 26 foot square," Folder "1730s? Financial Records: Baltimore Company," Box 8, MS 219, MdHS.

72. Trostel uses the dimensions of the basement to support his assertion. My research, however, indicates that it is just as possible that the memo applies to Dr. Carroll's own forays into ironworks on Carrolls Island (patented 1746) or in western Maryland. Trostel, *Mount Clare*, 6–7, 20–22.

73. Dr. CC to CCB, February 2, 1753, Letter Book, vol. 2, pp. 60–64, MS 208, MdHS.

74. Dr. CC to CCB, May 15, 1753, Letter Book, vol. 2, pp. 82–83, MS 208, MdHS.

75. Dr. CC to John Henry Carroll, September 15, 1753, in Archives of Maryland, *Provincial Court Records 1749–1756*, vol. 701, p. 400.

76. Dr. CC to Daniel Dulany and Company, January 25, 1750, Letter Book 1748–52, p. 293, and Dr. CC to Daniel Dulany and Company, January 26, 1750, Letter Book 1748–52, p. 295, MS 208, MdHS; Indenture, Dr. CC to Daniel Dulany and Company, January 30, 1750, Box 3, MS 219, MdHS; Johnson, *Establishment of the Baltimore Company*, 238–41. The location of the two mills and outbuildings are mapped on a plat dating to 1826; see Baltimore County Court (Ejectment) Nicholas Carroll et al. vs. James Carroll, March/September 1826, MSA C2042-165. In 1750, Dr. Carroll laid out a higher and drier route.

77. Dr. CC to CCB, February 2, 1753, Letter Books 1752–55 and 1755–69, p. 60–64, MS 208, MdHS.

78. Proposal to erect a furnace, Dr. CC, February 14, 1753, Letter Books 1752–55 and 1755–69, pp. 68–74, MS 208, MdHS.

79. Winter, "Antietam Furnace," 207–8.

80. Dr. CC to CCB, April 17, 1749, in Archives of Maryland, *Provincial Land Records 1744–1749*, vol. 700, p. 568.

81. Dr. CC to Mssrs. Cheston and Sedgley, June 30, 1753, pp. 87–88; Dr. CC to CCB, October 4, 1753, pp. 107–8; Dr. CC to CCB, July 9, 1754, pp. 129–30; Dr. CC to Mssrs. John Newbury and Co., August 29, 1754, pp. 130–31, Letter Book, vol. 2, MS 208, MdHS.

82. Dr. CC to William Black, August 18, 1751, MS 208.1, MdHS.

83. "Your overseers Richard and Patrick promise to have all your tobacco ready for Judd and to do all they can for you." Dr. CC to CCB, July 24, 1752, MS 208.1, MdHS. Four hogsheads of tobacco were shipped to England in 1751 from Charles's quarter, seven in 1752 and fourteen in 1753. Dr. CC to CCB, September 12, 1754, Letter Book, vol. 2, pp. 134–35, MS 208, MdHS; Dr. CC to CCB, February 2, 1753, Letter Books 1752–55 and 1755–69, pp. 60–64, MS 208, MdHS.

84. Dr. CC to CCB, May 8, 1754. Letter Book 1752–55, MS 208, MdHS. Conversions to 2008 dollars: £2000 = $378,088, £10,000 = $1,890,439, £5,000 = $945,220, £818 = $ 154,638, £4,000 = $756,176. Nye, *Pounds to Dollars*.

85. Land, "Economic Base and Social Structure," 653.

86. Prerogative Court (Wills) [Dr.] Charles Carroll of Annapolis, September 14, 1754, Liber WB29, folio 503, SR4423-2, MSA SM-43. Dr. Carroll directed his executors not to enter a probate or account of sale into the public record. No final calculation of slaveholding can be determined. Charles's sister, Mary (Carroll) Maccubbin inherited slaves, livestock, and land from her uncle Richard Bennett in 1749. Bennett stipulated that they should go to her younger brother, John Henry,

if she died. Prerogative Court (Wills), Richard Bennett, 1749, Liber 28, folio 466, SR 4422-2, MSA SM16-41.

87. Lewis, *Coal, Iron, and Slaves*, 23.

Chapter 3. The Creation of Mount Clare

1. Talbot County Register of Wills (Wills, Original) Margaret Ward, 1746, Box 25, Folder 10, MSA C1926-31, MdHR 9053-25-1/36; Talbot County Register of Wills (Inventories) Margaret Ward, 1747, Liber JB and JG4, folio 51, CM1029-5, MSA WK594-595-2.

2. Talbot County Register of Wills (Wills) Matthew Tilghman, 1787, Liber JB4, folio 125, WK 569-570-4, MSA CM1041-4. Ann Tilghman died in 1794. She indicated that her slave Matt ("son of Francis Jones") should be freed within six months of her death. Talbot County Register of Wills (Wills) Ann Tilghman, 1794, Liber JB4, folio 315, WK 569-570-4, MSA CM1041-4.

3. CCB to William Anderson, [—] September 1760, MHM 32: 367–68, and continued in MHM 33: 187–88.

4. CCB to William Anderson, October 4, 1764, p. 285, and CCB to William Anderson, November 10, 1764, p. 292, Letter Book 1755–69, MS 208, MdHS.

5. CCB to William Anderson, November 17, 1765, Letter Book 1755–69, p. 303, MS 208, MdHS.

6. See, for example, CCB to William Anderson, October 29, 1766, MHM 36: 32.

7. Vlach, *Back of the Big House*, 154–55, and "Not Mansions . . . But Good Enough," 93–96, 114.

8. Minute Book, The Baltimore Company, pp. 19–23, MS 219, MdHS.

9. CCB to William Anderson, February 24, 1767, MHM 37: 60; CCB to William Anderson, September 10, 1767, MHM 37: 416. Conversions to 2008 dollars: £20 = $2,934, £200 = $29,433. Nye, *Pounds to Dollars*.

10. Charles Carroll of Annapolis to Walter Dulany with replies appended, August 29, 1767, MSA 4214–4708. Robbins, *Maryland's Iron Industry During the Revolutionary War Era*, 130.

11. Norman, "An Example of Inference in Historical Archaeology"; and Charles Carroll the Barrister to William Anderson, [—] September 1760, MHM 32: 367–68, and continued in MHM 33: 187–88.

12. Baumgarten, *What Clothes Reveal*, 132; White and White, "Slave Clothing and African-American Culture"; Schwartz, "Men's Clothing and the Negro," 86–89.

13. Douglass, *Life and Times*, 67.

14. CCB to William Anderson, [—] September 1760, MHM 32: 367–68, and continued in MHM 33: 187–88; CCB to William Anderson, September 2, 1763,

MHM 33: 378–80; CCB to William Anderson, October 29, 1766, MHM 36: 338–41.

15. Invoice, August 6, 1767, Letter Book, vol. 2, p. 534, MS 208, MdHS; CCB to William Anderson, Summer 1768, transcribed in Trostel, *Mount Clare*, 43–46.

16. Trostel, *Mount Clare*, 21, 35, 49; Logan and Seidel, *Mount Clare's Kitchen*, Figure A-3.

17. CCB to William and James Anderson, July 21, 1768, Letter Book, vol. 2, p. 346 and 356, MS 208, MdHS.

18. Margaret Tilghman Carroll, Account Book, 1815–21, MS 2751, MdHS.

19. Logan and Seidel, *Mount Clare's Kitchen*, 25, 34–35.

20. Logan, *Archaeology at Charles Carroll's House and Garden and of His African-American Slaves*, 2; Galke, "Did the Gods of Africa Die?"

21. Cochran, "Hoodoo's Fire"; Harmon and Neuwirth, *Archaeological Investigations at the James Brice House.*

22. Gomez, *Exchanging Our Country Marks*, 150.

23. Fennell, "Conjuring Boundaries."

24. Leone et al., "Spirit Management among Americans of African Descent."

25. Gomez, *Exchanging Our Country Marks*, 288.

26. Roylance, "Crystal's Past."

27. Twitty, *Fighting Old Nep*, 13, 20.

28. CCB to William Anderson, September 2, 1763, MHM 33, 378–80. The same four spices were ordered at least once every year in the years thereafter.

29. Margaret Tilghman Carroll, 1742–1817, Account Book, 1815–21, MS 2751, MdHS.

30. Logan and Seidel, *Mount Clare's Kitchen*, 21.

31. Allen, *Threads of Bondage*, 115–16, 118.

32. Holt, *Mount Clare Kitchen Floral and Faunal Analysis*, Table 3.

33. Donahue, *Eighteenth Century Chesapeake Clothing*, 51–54.

34. William Henry Darlington (Brandywine Guards, Co. A, 1st Pa. Reserves), July 24, 1861, [West Chester] *West Chester Village Record.*

35. Ball, *Fifty Years in Chains*, 138–39.

36. Buonocore, *Within Her Garden Wall*, i–ii, 109.

37. Entry for July 25, 1774, Account Book (1767–86), MCMH. Conversion to 2008 dollars: £25 = $3,367. Nye, *Pounds to Dollars.*

38. See, for example, Ambler, "Diary of M. Ambler, 1770"; George Washington to Margaret Carroll, September 16, 1789, Image 39; George Washington to Margaret Carroll, November 22, 1789, Image 63; and George Washington to Margaret Carroll, October 14, 1789, Image 53, Letter Book 17, Series 2, George Washington Papers 1741–99, Library of Congress.

39. Kryder-Reid, "As Is the Gardener," 136.

40. Beiswanger, "The Temple in the Garden."

41. Yentsch, *A Chesapeake Family and Their Slaves*, 113–30.

42. Blair et al., *Draft: Phase II Archaeological Testing*, 157.

43. Pogue, *Archaeological Investigations*, 33.

44. Goodwin, "Flowerpots of Mount Vernon's Upper Garden 44FX762/43."

45. John Kille, personal communication, 2009.

46. Ferguson, *Uncommon Ground*, xxxv, 27–28, 44–46; Singleton and Bograd, "Looking for the Colono in Colonoware," 4–6, 8–9.

47. Hogendorn, *The Shell Money of the Slave Trade*, 1–4.

48. Dr. Charles Carroll to Samuel Hyde, September 9, 1734, MHM 24: 63.

49. Invoice, August 6, 1767, Letter Book, vol. 2, p. 534, MS 208, MdHS; CCB to William Anderson, Summer 1768, transcribed in Trostel, *Mount Clare*, 43–46.

50. Flanagan, *The Sweets of Independence*, 50.

51. White and White, "Slave Clothing and African-American Culture," 166; Allen, *Threads of Bondage*, 143–44, 154–55, 167–70.

52. CCB to William Anderson, October 6, 1764, MHM 34: 187; CCB to William Anderson, October 29, 1766, MHM 36: 338–41.

53. CCB to Sedgley Hilhouse and Randolph, January 28, 1768, MHM 38: 182.

54. CCB to William Anderson, October 29, 1766, Letter Book, vol. 2, p. 315, MS 208, MdHS.

55. Carroll, *Families of Dr. Charles Carroll*, 30.

56. Ball, *Slavery in the United States*, 138–39, 142, 167–68; Vlach, *Back of the Big House*, 64–65.

57. Charles Carroll the Barrister to William Anderson, April 2, 1765, MHM 34, 202; Holt, *Mount Clare Kitchen Floral and Faunal Analysis*.

58. Genovese, *Roll, Jordan, Roll*, 535–40.

59. Ball notes in his description of the layout of one southern plantation that the corn crib and potato house was located near the overseer's house. Ball, *Slavery in the United States*, 119–20, 139–40.

60. The overseer's house is shown in Peale's 1775 painting. The smokehouse and cornhouse are listed on the 1798 assessment.

61. Charles Carroll the Barrister to William and James Anderson, MHM 37: 65–68.

62. Weld, *American Slavery As It Is*, 32.

63. Olmsted, *A Journey into the Seaboard Slave States*, 693–94.

64. Dunaway, *The African-American Family in Slavery and Emancipation*, 104; Weld, *American Slavery As It Is*, 98.

65. Quoted in Twitty, *Fighting Old Nep*, 21.

66. Thompson, *Life of John Thompson*, 17, 44, 75.

67. Ball, *Slavery in the United States*, 26.

68. Weld, *American Slavery As It Is*, 31.

69. Franklin, "The Archaeological Dimensions of Soul Food," 89, 97–99.

70. CCB to William Anderson, November 17, 1765, 70–71, and CCB to William Anderson, October 29, 1766, 338–41 in MHM 36; CCB to William Anderson, November 3, 1766, MHM 36: 333–34.

71. CCB to William Anderson, July 27, 1767, MHM 37: 65–68.

72. Account Book (1767–86), MCMH.

73. Douglass, *Narrative of the Life of Frederick Douglass*, 15–16.

74. Rawick, *The American Slave*, 57; Douglass, *Life and Times of Frederick Douglass*, 21.

Chapter 4. Slavery and Revolution

1. McDermott, *Charles Carroll of Carrollton*, 94.

2. Maryland State Papers (Scharf Collection) Charles Wallace to Charles Carroll (Barrister), November 29, 1770, MSA S1005-134-17528 MdHR 19,999-120-024. Maryland State Papers (Scharf Collection) John Morton Jordan to Charles Carroll (Barrister), February 10, 1771, MSA S1005-134-17506 MdHR 19,999-120-003. Maryland State Papers (Scharf Collection) Charles Wallace to Charles Carroll (Barrister), November 24, 1771, MSA S1005-134-17505 MdHR 19,999-120-002. The account included the order on September 26, 1769, for four bunches of garnets, one set silk mitts, and one backgammon table; on September 30, four sets of gauze thread stockings; on October 19, six tablecloths and one necklace; on October 23, three dozen porter; on November 8, two sets Norway doe gloves; on November 22, two hairpins and one Marquisett; on December 11, one black satin bonnet; on December 12, one cap 39/6 and ditto 17; on March 10, 1770, four fig blue and one hank silk, six dozen shirt buttons. The total due was £22.0.1. Also: Chancery Court (Chancery Papers, Exhibits) Wallace, Davidson & Johnson, Order Book November 21, 1773–November 16, 1775, April 1774, no page, MdHR 1520, MSA S528-28.

3. Baltimore County Court (Tax List), Charles Carroll (Barrister), Middlesex Hundred, 1773, M1560-9, MSA CM918-21.

4. Baltimore County Court (Tax List), Charles Carroll (Barrister), Back River Upper Hundred, 1773, M1560-2, MSA CM918-14.

5. Account Book (1767–86), MCMH. Conversions to 2008 dollars: £10 = $1,628, £13 = $2,117. Nye, *Pounds to Dollars*.

6. Account Book (1767–86), MCMH. Conversions to 2008 dollars: £0.35.0 = $47, £25 = $3,368, £20 = $2.694, £100 = $15,298, £75 = $11,473, £0.20.0 = $32, £0.15.0 = $24. Nye, *Pounds to Dollars*.

7. Maryland State Papers (Federal Direct Tax) Baltimore County, Middlesex

Hundred, Nos. 2833–3147: Particular List of Dwelling Houses, Particular List of Lands, Lots, Buildings, and Wharves, M3469-7, MSA SM56-29.

8. Maryland State Papers (Federal Direct Tax) Baltimore County, Back River and Middle River Upper Hundreds, Nos. 999–1499: Particular List of Dwelling Houses; Particular List of Lands, Lots, Buildings, and Wharves; Particular List of Slaves, M 3469-2, MSA SM56-2.

9. Annapolis, December 15, *The Pennsylvania Gazette*, December 21, 1774.

10. Maryland State Papers (Maryland State Papers, Index) Benjamin Rumsey to Governor, August 25, 1777, MSA S 989-327, MdHR 4561-69; William Paca to Governor, September 26, 1777, MSA S 989-354, MdHR 4562-01; Thomas Stone to Governor, December 9, 1777, MSA S 989-339, MdHR 4561-81; George Cook, November 1783, Deposition, MSA 0990-6-127 MdHR 4644-02.

11. Papenfuse et al., *A Biographical Dictionary of the Maryland Legislature*, 195–97.

12. Maryland's Declaration of Independence, July 3, 1776, MSA SC 4560-1.

13. Annapolis, December 15, *The Pennsylvania Gazette*, December 21, 1774.

14. MacLeod, *Slavery, Race, and the American Revolution*, 8.

15. Joshua Johnson to the firm, June 4, 1771, p. 1. "Joshua Johnson's Letter Book: 1771," Joshua Johnson's Letter Book 1771–74: Letters from a merchant in London to his partners in Maryland (1979), pp. 1–23. Online: http://www.british-history. ac.uk/report.aspx?compid=38787 (accessed: July 7, 2008).

16. *Maryland Gazette*, September 17, 1772.

17. Chancery Court (Chancery Papers, Exhibits), Joshua Johnson to Charles Carroll Esq. Barrister, Wallace, Davidson, and Johnson Letter Book 1, August 19, 1772, p. 96, MSA SM 79-37. Also see Joshua Johnson to Lloyd Tilghman, August 19, 1772, p. 96–97.

18. Charles Wallace per Capt. Wallace, August 19, 1772, p. 46. Joshua Johnson's Letter Book: 1772 (July–Dec), Joshua Johnson's Letter Book 1771–74: Letters from a merchant in London to his partners in Maryland (1979), pp. 40–56. Online: http://www.british-history.ac.uk/report.aspx?compid=38789 (accessed: June 20, 2008).

19. Chancery Court (Chancery Papers, Exhibits), Joshua Johnson to Charles Carroll Esq. Barrister, Wallace, Davidson, and Johnson Letter Book 1, 10 April 1773, p. 155, MSA SM79-37.

20. Horton and Horton, *In Hope of Liberty*, 55–60.

21. Runaway Advertisement, *Maryland Journal and Baltimore Advertiser*, Press date: August 19, 1777, Ad Date: August 15, 1777. Conversions to 2008 dollars: £5 = $732. Nye, *Pounds to Dollars*.

22. Runaway Advertisement, *Maryland Journal and Baltimore Advertiser*, Press date: July 11, 1780, Ad date: July 10, 1780. Conversions to 2008 dollars: $400 =

$6,480. *Six Ways to Compute the Relative Value of a U.S. Dollar Amount, 1774 to Present*. Online: http://www.measuringworth.com/uscompare/ (accessed December 20, 2009).

23. Windley, *Runaway Slave Advertisements*, xiv; Bradley, *Slavery, Propaganda, and the American Revolution*, 25–44.

24. Pennington, *Fugitive Blacksmith*, 5; Thompson, *Life of John Thompson*, 76.

25. *Federal Gazette* [Baltimore, MD, published as *Federal Gazette & Baltimore Daily Advertiser*], June 15, 1799, vol. X, iss. 1744, p. 4.

26. Charles Carroll of Carrollton to Gentleman, December 8, 1773, Folder "1773 Correspondence: Baltimore Company," Box 6, MS 219, MdHS.

27. Minute Book, January 24, 1731, Box 6, MS 219, MdHS; Clement Brooke to Gentlemen, February 4, 1774. Folder "1774 Correspondence: Baltimore Company," Box 7, MS 219, MdHS.

28. Clement Brooke to Charles Carroll and Company, April 10, 1775, with replies, MSA M 4214-4751.

29. Clement Brooke to The Baltimore Company, August 7, 1783, MS 1228, MdHS.

30. CCB to Clement Brooke, May 1769, Miscellaneous Correspondence, NYPL.

31. Lewis, *Coal, Iron, and Slaves*, 150.

32. Clement Brooke to Gentlemen. April 10, 1775, Folder "1775 Correspondence: Baltimore Company," Box 7, MS 219, MdHS.

33. George Gordon to Council of Safety, July 3, 1776, MSA S 1004-6-662 MdHR 6636-6-18E Location: 1/7/3/27. Conversions to 2008 dollars: £4.12 = $601. Nye, *Pounds to Dollars*.

34. Lewis, *Coal, Iron, and Slaves*, 22.

35. Nicholas Carroll to Margaret Carroll, Articles of Agreement, July 6, 1792, p. 83, Baltimore County Court Chattel Records 1791–94, Baltimore County Court, MS 2865.1, MdHS.

36. Advertisement, "To Be Sold," The Pennsylvania Gazette, Ad Date: February 27, 1785, Post Date: March 9, 1785. Slaves were also sold with the property as per *The Pennsylvania Gazette*, July 5, 1770. Vertical files, Mount Clare Museum House. To Be Sold, February 26, 1785. *Maryland Gazette* [Annapolis, MD], March 10, 1785.

37. Bezis-Selfa, *Forging America*, 141–42.

38. Trostel, *Mount Clare*, 67.

39. Baltimore County Register of Wills (Wills), Charles Carroll, 1783, Liber WB3, folio 503. CR72,241-1, MSA CM188-3.

40. Middlesex Hundred. Baltimore County, Assessment Record, 1783. General Assembly House of Delegates. M 871, SM59, MSA.

41. According to the 1783 assessment, Fairbrother enslaved three children under eight years old, one male or female nine to fourteen, one male age fifteen to forty-five, and one female age fourteen to thirty-six. By the 1790 census, however, Fairbrother's household included no slaves or freedpersons. Annapolis Hundred. Assessment Record, 1783. General Assembly House of Delegates. M 871, SM59, MSA.

42. Francis Fairbrother to Margaret Carroll, November 3, 1783: "I received the box you sent by Lucy in vollunts boat containing the coffee pot and my books all safe."

43. Carroll, *Families of Dr. Charles Carroll*, 26.

Chapter 5. White Widowhood

1. Dornan, "Masterful Women," 387.

2. Wood, "Broken Reeds and Competent Farmers," 43, 50.

3. Tamplin, "Chatelaine of Mount Clare," 95–103.

4. Charles Carroll of Carrollton to CCB, December 3, 1771, MSA M 4193-497 Item No. 497.

5. Margaret Carroll to Mrs. Ellicott, March 30, 1802, Henry Maynadier Fitzhugh Family Collection, 1698–1902. M11760, MSA SC 4688-13.

6. Newsletter, *The Clarion*, September 1984. Folder "Colonial Dames, Clarion Newsletters 1978–1986." Eliza Coale Funk Papers, circa 1758–2004. Box 4 of 7. Series III: Eliza Coale Funk: Activities and Organizations, MS3065, MdHS.

7. Tamplin, "Chatelaine of Mount Clare," 95–103.

8. Moreno, *Mistress of Mount Clare*.

9. Whitman, *The Price of Freedom*, 9–11.

10. The men in between Hammond and Carroll were Charles Ridgeley (117), James Franklin (84), Annias Divas (74), and James Gittings and Phillip Chamberlain (55 apeice). Nicholas Carroll's census information for The Caves was listed under Christopher Turnpaugh, the overseer. The women were Eleanor Croxall [incorrectly listed as Croxtell] and Susannah Buchannan. Department of Commerce, *Heads of Families of the First Census*, Baltimore City and Baltimore County.

11. Eleanor Croxall in Soldiers Delight Hundred enslaved twenty-seven people, twelve between ages twelve and fifty. Her "sundry tracts" included one frame dwelling house (62 by 18 with piazza, 62 by 8), one frame kitchen (54 by 16), one stone milk house (12 by 12, one story), one frame milk house (one story, 12 by 12), one frame smoke house (16 by 16, one story), one frame negros quarter (one story, 18 by 18), and one log negroe quarter (one story, 20 by 18). The assessor assessed her house at $500. Also a carriage house, barns, houses, corn houses, etc., all worth $4,337.50. Maryland State Papers (Federal Direct Tax) Baltimore County, Back River and Middle River Upper Hundreds, Nos. 999–1499: Particular List of

Dwelling Houses; Particular List of Lands, Lots Buildings, and Wharves; Particular List of Slaves, 1798, M 3469-2, MSA SM56-2. Conversions to 2008 currency: $15,467.52 = $279,370. *Seven Ways to Compute the Relative Value of a U.S. Dollar Amount. Online:* http://www.measuringworth.com/uscompare/, accessed May 23, 2014.

12. Baltimore County Commissioners of the Tax (Assessed Persons List) Margaret Carroll, 1804, CR 39,605-10, MSA CM 1204-1.

13. Baltimore, May 18. *The Pennsylvania Packet and Daily Advertiser* [Philadelphia, Pa.], May 25, 1790, Issue 3530, p. 3.

14. Baltimore County Register of Wills (Accounts of Sale), Margaret Tilghman Carroll, Liber WB 6, folio 441, MSA CM 125-6, CR 9513-1.

15. Breen and White, "'A Pretty Considerable Distillery.'"

16. Changes to the Mount Clare Mill occurred by 1819: Policy #6033, October 1, 1819. Box 3, Record of Policies E, Baltimore Equitable Society Insurance Records. MS 3020, MdHS.

17. Advertisement, *Federal Intelligencer* [Baltimore, MD], vol. III: 433, published March 24, 1795); Advertisement, *Federal Gazette & Baltimore Daily Advertiser* [Baltimore, MD], September 22, 1797, vol. 7, iss. 1208, p. 4.

18. Blassingame, *The Slave Community,* 159.

19. Fogel and Engerman, *Time on the Cross,* 115–16.

20. Maryland State Papers (Federal Direct Tax) Baltimore County, Back River and Middle River Upper Hundreds, Nos. 999–1499: Particular List of Dwelling Houses; Particular List of Lands, Lots Buildings, and Wharves; Particular List of Slaves, 1798, M 3469-2, MSA SM56-2.

21. Maryland State Papers (Federal Direct Tax) Baltimore County, Middlesex Hundred, Nos. 2833–3147: Particular List of Dwelling Houses, Particular List of Lands, Lots, Buildings, and Wharves; Particular List of Slaves, 1798. Maryland State Papers. M3469-7. MSA SM56-7.

22. Vlach, "Not Mansions . . . But Good Enough," 114.

23. Carson, *Ambitious Appetites,* 40–48, 61, 129.

24. Baumgartner-Wagner, *Archaeology at Mount Clare,* 14.

25. Carson, *Ambitious Appetites,* 28–29.

26. Collins, reprinted in Olmsted, *A Journey into the Seaboard Slave States,* 694.

27. Ottley, *Black Odyssey,* 127, 266.

28. Author unknown, *Journal of Trip from Annapolis to The Caves,* MS 1873, MdHS. Transcribed in Carroll, *Families of Dr. Charles Carroll.*

29. Allen, *Threads of Bondage,* 118.

30. Baltimore County Register of Wills (Inventories), Margaret Tilghman Carroll, Liber 30, folio 539, MSA CM 155-30, WK 1068-1069-1.

31. Margaret Tilghman Carroll, 1742–1817. Account Book, 1815–21, MS 2751, MdHS.

32. *Federal Gazette & Baltimore Daily Advertiser* [Baltimore, MD], June 15, 1799, vol. X, iss. 1744, p. 4.

33. White and White, "Slave Clothing and African-American Culture in the Eighteenth and Nineteenth Centuries," 148; Schwartz, "Men's Clothing and the Negro."

34. Anne Arundel County Register of Wills (Testamentary Papers), Nicholas Carroll, 1812, Acc. 4767-105-1/55, MSA C149-123. Two people on Nicholas's inventory—Abraham (or Abram) and Fanny—may have been purchased by James Carroll, as they are listed on a tax statement in 1832. The Carrolls Island population was probably sold. The enslaved population listed in 1812 and 1817 at The Caves does not appear to overlap. Nicholas C. Carroll, son of Nicholas Carroll, enslaved forty-five people at The Caves in 1813. They managed thirteen horses, seventy black cattle, forty-eight hogs, and fifty-eight sheep. James Carroll kept enslaved persons near the old forge and grist mill and on the property called Mud Bank. Baltimore County Commissioners of the Tax (Assessment Record) Margaret Carroll or James Carroll, District 1, 1813, p. 5, C277-4, MdHR 12,502. Baltimore County Commissioners of the Tax (Assessment Record), Nicholas Carroll, 1813, District 7, p. 163, C277-4, MdHR 12,502. See Appendix B.

35. Reamy and Reamy, *Records of St. Paul's Parish*, vol. 2, 29.

36. Schwartz, *Born in Bondage*, 3–5; White, *Ar'n't I a Woman?*, 92.

37. Ball, *Slavery in the United States*, 196; Baltimore County Commissioner of the Tax (Assessment Record), Margaret Carroll, Middlesex and Patapsco Lower Hundreds, 1804, CR39,605-2, MSA CM1203-2.

38. Baltimore County Commissioners of the Tax (Assessment Record) Margaret Carroll, 1813, p. 5, MSA C277-4.

39. White, *Ar'n't I a Woman?*, 50–51.

40. King, *Stolen Childhood*.

41. Pennington, *The Fugitive Blacksmith*, 2.

42. White, *Ar'n't I a Woman?*, 98, 100–105.

43. Cassell, "Slaves of the Chesapeake Bay Area and the War of 1812," 152, 155.

44. Baltimore County Court (Certificates of Freedom), Henry Harden, April 8, 1818, p. 16, MSA C-290-1.

45. Dornan, "Masterful Women," 389–91.

46. Milly was hired out to F. Hollingsworth. Baltimore City Assessor (Tax Records), Margaret Carroll, 1800, RG 4, Series 2, p. 76; Baltimore City Assessor (Tax Records), Margaret Carroll, First District, 1808–10, RG 4, Series 2, p. 449; Baltimore City Assessor (Tax Records), Mrs. Carroll (widow), 1813, RG 4, Series 2, p. 73, Baltimore City Archives.

47. June 24, 1786: Negros Jack, Moses and Bobb to cash in full for 3 days work—0.7.6. Account Book (1767–86), MCMH.

48. George H. Sumwalt [?] appeared for Nell and Fanny. Nell was about 53 years old, light complexion, 5'2½" tall, with a small scar on the back of her left hand near the wrist. Fanny was about 28 years old, dark complexion, 5'1½" tall, no notable marks or scars. Baltzer Schaffer appeared for Henny, who was described as about 39 years old, light complexion, 5'2½" tall, and having a scar under the right corner of the mouth. Nell Williams, p. 59; Fanny Cooper, p. 215; Henny, p. 235. Baltimore County Court (Certificates of Freedom, 1830–32), MSA C-290-2.

49. Margaret Tilghman Carroll to Mary Ridout, October 22, 1795, Miscellaneous Manuscripts, NYPL.

50. Charles Carroll of Carrollton and others to Jacob Gilliard, June 26, 1792, p. 78; Charles Carroll and others to Negro Nat Rice and Others, Manumission, March 25, 1794, p. 305; and Charles Carroll and others to Negro Joe Jacobs and Others, Manumission, March 25, 1794, p. 306, Baltimore County Court Chattel Records 1791–94, Baltimore County Court, MS 2865.1, MdHS. Baltimore Company, Division of Stock [March 26] 1805, Vertical file, MdHS; Moreno, *Mistress of Mount Clare*, 57–58.

51. Douglass, *Narrative of the Life of Frederick Douglass*, 2.

52. Close, *Elderly Slaves of the Plantation South*; Pollard, "Aging and Slavery."

53. Anne Arundel County Register of Wills (Testamentary Papers), Nicholas Carroll, 1812, Box 105, Folder 36, MSA C149-123.

54. Close, *Elderly Slaves of the Plantation South*, 45, 50.

55. Carr, "Inheritance in the Colonial Chesapeake," 169–70.

56. Wallace, "*Fair Daughters of Africa*," 88–90.

57. Douglass, *My Bondage and My Freedom*, 115.

58. Phillips, *Freedom's Port*, 23, 27–28.

59. An Act to prevent disabled and superannuated Slaves being set free, or the Manumission of Slaves by any last Will or Testament, June 1752, Proceedings and Acts of the General Assembly, 1752–54. *Archives of Maryland*, vol. 70, p. 56.

60. An act relating to negroes, December 1796. Proceedings and Acts of the General Assembly, 1796, chapter 67, vol. 105, p. 249.

61. James Carroll, To the Worshipful Justices, Orphans Court, Anne Arundel County, August 20, 1813, Register of Wills, 1809–20 (Petitions and Orders), pp. 27–28, MSA, CR 63,126.

62. Morgan, "'To Get Quit of Negroes,'" 427.

63. Maryland Society for Promoting the Abolition of Slavery, and the Relief of Free Negroes, and Others, Unlawfully Held in Bondage. *Constitution of the Maryland Society for Promoting the Abolition of Slavery*.

64. Klein and Smith, "Racism in the Anglican and Episcopal Church of Maryland."

65. Beirne, *St. Paul's Parish*, 46–47.

66. United States of America, Bureau of the Census. Seventh Census of the United States, 1850, Washington, DC: National Archives and Records Administration, 1850, M432.

67. Whitman, *The Price of Freedom*, 105, 109.

68. Condon, *Manumission, Slavery and Family in the Post-Revolutionary Rural Chesapeake*, 114, 118.

Chapter 6. Manumission and Freedom

1. Only Henry Brice appears to have acted as executor. Samuel Cole and Richard Lewis inventoried Margaret's property. Baltimore County Register of Wills (Wills), Margaret Carroll, March 20, 1817, WB 10, p. 297, CR 72,244-2, MSA.

2. Moreno, *Mistress of Mount Clare*, 60–65.

3. Census records for 1820 list several white and free black heads of household under the name Charles Ross. Tom is not in the Anne Arundel County manumission records. Hynson, *Maryland Freedom Papers*, vol. 1.

4. Phillips, *Freedom's Port*, 44.

5. No manumissions by Dr. Carroll, Charles Carroll the Barrister, or Margaret were recorded among the land records of Baltimore or Anne Arundel counties. Other kinds of deed books or chattel records are lost for this period. Preserved records are: Chattel Records (Baltimore County Court, C298-2, MSA) 1763–73; Chattel Records (MS 2865, MdHS) 1773–88; Chattel Records (MS 2865.1, MdHS) 1791–94; Chattel Records (Baltimore County Court, C298-3, MSA) 1800–1801; Certificates of Freedom (Baltimore Register of Wills, CM280-1, MSA) 1805–30; Chattel Records (MS 2865, MdHS) 1811–12; Chattel Records (Baltimore County Court, C298-4, MSA) 1813–14; Certificates of Freedom (Baltimore County Court, CM 821-1 to -7, MSA) 1806–16, 1830–32, 1832–41, 1841–47, 1841–48, and 1848–51 (pp. 1–26 only); Miscellaneous Court Records (Baltimore County Court, CM 1, MSA) 1729–1851. In the miscellaneous court records, only freedpersons linked with the names Margaret Carroll or Henry Brice and Tench Tilghman could conclusively be identified as formerly enslaved at Mount Clare. None of the new owners, as per Margaret's estate account of sale, appeared in court to testify. The persons formerly enslaved at Mount Clare, however, may have been sold again and manumitted by those owners without acknowledgment of Margaret Carroll's will. The Maryland Colonization Society also recorded manumissions, but no manumissions for former Carroll slaves appear. Hynson, *Maryland Colonization Society Manumission Book 1832–1860*, vol. 3. Runaway dockets for Baltimore remain

from 1831 through 1864. None of the individuals documented appear to be from enslavers of individuals formerly at Georgia; then again, these records begin fourteen years after the dispersal of the enslaved community. Baltimore County Court (Runaway Docket) 1831–32, CR 79,169-1, MSA CM1351-1 and Baltimore County (Runaway Docket) 1832–36, CR 79,169-2, MSA CM1352-2.

6. An act relating to negroes, December 1796, Proceedings and Acts of the General Assembly, 1796, chapter 67, vol. 105, p. 249.

7. Conversions to 2008 currency: $300 = $5,011, $120 = $2,004, $175 = $2,293, $200 = $3,341, $220 = $3,675, $100 = $1,670. *Seven Ways to Compute the Relative Value, Online:* http://www.measuringworth.com/uscompare/, accessed May 23, 2014.

8. "An Act to ascertain and declare the condition of such Issue as may hereafter be born of Negro or Mulatto Female Slaves, during their servitude for Years, and for other purposes therein mentioned," Session Laws 1809, Chapter CLXXI, November, Laws of Maryland; "An act to ascertain and declare the condition of such Issue as may hereafter be born of Negro or Mulatto Female Slaves, during their servitude for Years, and for other purposes therein mentioned," Session Laws 1809, chapter CLXVIII, vol. 570, p. 118. Archives of Maryland.

9. Baltimore County (Wills), George Lindenberger, October 1820, Liber 11, folio 185, CR72,245-1, MSA CM188-11.

10. Baltimore County Register of Wills (Accounts of Sale), George Lindenberger, Liber WB 8, folio 217, CR 9513-3, MSA CM125-8.

11. James Carroll, U.S. Census 1820, Ward 12, Baltimore, Series M33, Reel 42, p. 276.

12. Baltimore Ward 11. Fourth census of the United States, 1820. Washington, DC: NARA, 1820. Roll M33_42, p. 433; Manumission, Henry Brice to Ned Hill, p. 266. Chattel Records, Baltimore County. C-298-3, MSA; Brice sold Ned Hill to Samuel Rideout of Annapolis to serve for seven years beginning January 1, 1797. Hill was sold to Thomas B. Randall of Baltimore but was never manumitted as Brice intended. Brice set the date of Hill's freedom as January 2, 1804. The document was signed August 19, 1800.

13. Close, *Elderly Slaves of the Plantation South*, 45, 50.

14. "An Act to prevent the unlawful exportation of Negroes and Mulattoes, and to alter and amend the Laws concerning Runaways," Ch. 112, Lib. TH., No. 6, fol. 1, 1817. Passed February 3, 1818. vol. 192, p. 2109. Archives of Maryland.

15. Phillips, *Freedom's Port*, 64–65.

16. Baltimore County Court (Certificates of Freedom, 1830–32), Nell Williams, p. 59; Fanny Cooper, p. 215; Henny, p. 235. MSA C 290-2, MdHR 40,131-2.

17. Baltimore County Court (Certificates of Freedom), Milly, alias Milly Harden, March 29, 1832, p. 50; Negro William and Negro Samuel, May 4, 1832, p.

96; Negro Kitty, May 29, 1832, p. 213, and Negro Sukey, May 29, 1832, p. 213, MSA C 290-2, MdHR 40,131-2.

18. Campbell, *Maryland in Africa*, 16–17.

19. Frederickson, *Black Image in the White Mind*, 6.

20. Campbell, *Maryland in Africa*, 35.

21. "An act relating to the People of Color in this state," passed March 12, 1832, *Session Laws, 1831*, chapter 281, vol. 213, p. 343. Archives of Maryland Online. An act passed the following year protected enslaved persons who received manumissions before 1831. "A supplement to an act, entitled, An act relating to People of Colour in this State," Passed March 22, 1832, *Session Laws, 1832*, chapter 296, vol. 547, p. 354. Archives of Maryland Online.

22. Whitman, *The Price of Freedom*, 1.

23. Wallace, "Fair Daughters of Africa," 87.

24. Wallace, "Fair Daughters of Africa," 24–29.

25. Jackson, *The Baltimore Directory*; Richd Garrett, 1820, Baltimore Ward 12, Baltimore, Maryland; 1820 United States Federal Census. Roll M33_42, p. 531. NARA; Rich'd Garrett, Baltimore Ward 12, Baltimore, Maryland. 1830, Baltimore Ward 12, Baltimore, Maryland. 1830 United States Federal Census, Roll 54, p. 455, NARA.

26. Baltimore County Court (Certificates of Freedom), Negro Dolly alias Garrett, September 29, 1840, p. 215, MSA C 290.

27. Baltimore County Court (Miscellaneous Court Papers), William Garrett and Henry Garrett, Case no. 366, April 13, 1830 MSA C 1-70.

28. Murphy, *Baltimore Directory for 1845*.

29. Baltimore County Court (Certificates of Freedom) Sukey, May 29, 1832, p. 213, MSA C 290-2, MdHR 40,131-2.

30. Baltimore County Court (Certificates of Freedom), Kitty, May 29, 1832, p. 213, MSA C 290-2, MdHR 40,131-2.

31. Baltimore County Court (Miscellaneous Court Papers), Thomas Garrett, Case no. 248, September 29, 1840, p. 216, MSA C1-90.

32. Baltimore County Court (Certificates of Freedom), Margaret alias Margaret Bordley, April 14, 1840, MSA C 90.

33. Murphy, *Baltimore Directory for 1845*. Baltimore Ward 16, Baltimore, MD. Seventh Census of the United States, 1850. Washington, DC: NARA, M432_286, p. 148.

34. John Lynch, 1820 Census, Ward 11, Series M33, Roll 42, p. 242, NARA.

35. Baltimore County Court (Miscellaneous Court Papers), John Lynch, Case no. 328, December 14, 1821. MSA C 1-53, MdHR 50,206-707/714.

36. Matchett, *Baltimore Director for 1833*.

37. Baltimore County Court (Certificates of Freedom), Bill (son of Henny)

Lynch, alias William Lynch, and Robert Hall (son of Maria), March 1, 1841, p. 221, MSA C 290-3, MdHR 40,131-3.

38. Baltimore County Court (Miscellaneous Court Papers), Robert Hall, Case no. 272, March 1, 1841, MSA C 1-92, MdHR 50,206-1103/1111.

39. Three freedmen named Jacob Hall lived in Baltimore County in 1820. U.S. Census 1820, Baltimore, MD. Roll M33_41; pp. 201, 207.

40. Baltimore County Court (Miscellaneous Court Papers), Harry Davis and Harry Graham, Case no. 339, May 29, 1829, MSA C 1-68, MdHR 50,206-861/871.

41. Baltimore County Court (Certificates of Freedom), Negro Polly alias Polly Ireland, May 27, 1839, p. 136. MSA C 290-3, MdHR 40,131-3.

42. Baltimore County Court (Certificates of Freedom), Henry Harden, April 8, 1818, p. 16, MSA C-290-1.

43. Keenan, *Baltimore Directory for 1822 and 1823.*

44. Baltimore County Court (Certificates of Freedom), Milly, alias Milly Harden, March 29, 1832, p. 50, MSA C 290-2, MdHR 40,131-2.

45. Murphy, *Baltimore Directory for 1845*; Baltimore County Court (Certificates of Freedom), James Harden, June 4, 1844, p. 57, MSA C 290-5.

46. Thomas, "Sharp Street Memorial Methodist Episcopal Church," 2.

47. Melton, "African American Methodism in the M.E. Tradition," 2.

48. Martin, *Trial of the Rev. Jacob Gruber*, 31–33.

49. Handy, *Scraps of African Methodist History*, 13–14; Smith and Payne, *Biography of Rev. David Smith*, 18, 20, 26.

50. Raboteau, "The Slave Church in the Era of the American Revolution," 194, 196, 205–7, 209.

51. Handy, *Scraps of African Methodist History*, 1, 14.

52. Thomas, "Sharp Street Memorial Methodist Episcopal Church," 1.

53. Smith, *A Brief Account of the Awakening and Conversion of David Smith*, 7.

54. Smith and Payne, *Biography of Rev. David Smith*, 20.

55. Handy, *Scraps of African Methodist History*, 26; Melton, "African American Methodism in the M.E. Tradition," 11.

56. Baltimore County Court (Certificates of Freedom), Henry Harden, April 8, 1818, p. 16, MSA C-290-1.

57. Thomas, "Sharp Street Memorial Methodist Episcopal Church," 1.

58. Melton, "African American Methodism in the M.E. Tradition," 10.

59. Thomas, "Sharp Street Memorial Methodist Episcopal Church," 3.

60. Handy, *Scraps of African Methodist History*, 1; Smith and Payne, *Biography of Rev. David Smith*, 32.

61. Handy, *Scraps of African Methodist Episcopal History*, 26.

62. Bethel Church. *This Constitution or Incorporation, is an Extract from the Records of the State of Maryland.* Baltimore: Bethel Church. 1842. Baltimore City

Circuit Court (Equity Papers A, Miscellaneous) [T53-949-1] African Methodist Bethel Church vs. Joel Carmack et al. MSA SC 4239-13-1, pp. 487–89.

63. Ibid., pp. 483–85.

64. Joyce, "AME Book Concern."

65. Payne, *History of the African Methodist Episcopal Church*, 17, 20, 22.

66. Smith, *A Brief Account of the Awakening and Conversion of David Smith*, 11.

67. Payne, *History of the African Methodist Episcopal Church*, 28.

68. Rush, *A Short Account*, 33.

69. Handy, *Scraps of African Methodist History*, 63.

70. Payne, *History of the African Methodist Episcopal Church*, 36–37.

71. Keenan, *Baltimore Directory for 1822 and 1823*.

72. Matchett, *Baltimore Director for 1827*, 120

73. Porter, *Early Negro Writing*, 197.

74. Moore, *History of the A.M.E. Church in America*, 387.

Chapter 7. A Broader History

1. Baltimore Ward 12. Fourth census of the United States, 1820. Washington, DC: NARA, 1820. Roll M33_42, p. 110.

2. Election District 1 (1818), p. 32. Assessors Field Book. Baltimore County Commissioners of the Tax. CR 68,893 CM1289-1, MSA.

3. The quarter had 311 [measurement not recorded] of mason and 23 perches of quarry. Jacob Sedden to James Carroll Jr., Bill for work, February 2, 1822, Folder "1815–22, James Carroll, Jr. (1791–1873) Papers," Box 10, MS 219, MdHS.

4. James Carroll, Account Book, 1813–69, p. 97.

5. Baltimore County Court (Land Records), James Carroll to The Baltimore and Ohio Railroad Company, Liber WG208, folio 448, WK1186-1187-1, MSA CE66-258.

6. He also hired Jerry Johnson, but I could not determine if he was the same Jerry listed in Margaret's probate record. James Carroll, Account Book 1813–69, p. 82, MS 217, MdHS.

7. Register (for claim 19-923), Quartermaster Claims, Book 19, p. 233. Ent. 802. RG92. NARA-DC.

8. Baltimore City Superior Court (Land Records), James Carroll to West Baltimore Schuetzen Assoc., Liber GR448, folio 19, MSA CE 168-496, MdHR CR 4725-1.

9. National Society of the Colonial Dames of America in the State of Maryland, *Mount Clare: Home of Charles Carroll, Barrister*, 1, 16.

10. Baltimore City Superior Court (Land Records), Sally W. Carroll & c. to Mayor and City Council of Baltimore, November 8, 1890, Liber JB 1318, folio 1, MSA CR 5117-1, CR 5117-2.

11. Ruffins and Ruffins, "Recovering Yesterday."

12. West, *Domesticating History*, 3, 36.

13. Maryland Society of the Colonial Dames of America, *Constitution and by-Laws*, 5–6.

14. National Society of the Colonial Dames of America, *Constitution and Eligibility Lists*, 10–11.

15. Brunson, "The Avenue."

16. Hobbs, "Exhibiting Antimodernism," 54.

17. Letter, Emilie McKim Reed to Annie L. Sioussat, [no date]. Folder "ND Annie L. Sioussat Corr. Emilie McKim Reed." Leakin-Sioussat Papers, c.1650–c.1960, MS 1497, MdHS. The date of the letter is established by Reed's term, from about 1917 until the early 1920s.

18. Draft, Historians Report [1920]. Folder "Colonial Dames Historian Reports (ALS)," Box 22. Leakin-Sioussat Papers, c.1650–c.1960, MS 1497, MdHS.

19. Circular Letter of the Historian, March 1929. Folder "Colonial Dames Printed Material" Box 22. Leakin-Sioussat Papers, c.1650–c.1960, MS 1497, MdHS.

20. Sioussat, *Mount Clare*, 13.

21. Letter, Mrs. William Reed, Mrs. Edward Shoemaker, and Mrs. Benjamin W. Corcoran Jr. to Mrs. A. L. Sioussat, February 17, 1920. Folder "Annie L. Sioussat Corr. 1920 Jan–Jun," Box 11. Leakin-Sioussat Papers, c.1650–c.1960, MS 1497, Maryland Historical Society.

22. Sioussat, *Mount Clare*, 1, 13, 15.

23. Wells, *Historical Geography*, 10, 57–58.

24. Durkee v. Murphy, 181 Md. 259, 29 A.2d 253, 255; Law v. Mayor and City Council of Baltimore et al., Ciy. A. No. 3837, United States District Court for the District of Maryland, 78 F. Supp. 346; 1948 U.S. Dist; Baltimore Golf Unrestricted, Washington Post [Washington, DC], June 19, 1948, B2.

25. Wells, *Historical Geography*, 11.

26. Wells, *Historical Geography*, 11, 72, 74.

27. Ellis, "Interpreting the Whole House," 69.

28. National Society of the Colonial Dames of America in the State of Maryland, *Mount Clare*, 1.

29. National Society of the Colonial Dames of America in the State of Maryland, Inc. Mount Clare (1754) Docent Information Packet. September 1987. Eliza Coale Funk Papers, circa 1758–2004. Box 4 of 7. Series III: Eliza Coale Funk: Activities and Organizations, MS 3065, MdHS.

30. National Society of the Colonial Dames of America in the State of Maryland, Inc. Mount Clare (1754) Docent Information Packet. September 1978; National Society of the Colonial Dames of America in the State of Maryland, Inc.

Mount Clare (1754) Docent Information Packet. March 1984; National Society of the Colonial Dames of America in the State of Maryland, Inc. Mount Clare (1754) Docent Information Packet. September 1987. Eliza Coale Funk Papers, circa 1758–2004. Series III: Eliza Coale Funk: Activities and Organizations, MS 3065, MdHS.

Chapter 8. Conclusion

1. Kessler, "Sponsors Claim Race Is a Stumbling Block; Black Unable to Join Local DAR," *Washington Post*, March 12, 1984, A1.

2. Dewan and Hart, "Thurmond's Biracial Daughter Seeks to Join Confederate Group," *New York Times*, July 2, 2004, A13.

3. Jones, "After Years of Research, a Confederate Daughter Arises," *National Public Radio*, August 7, 2011. Online: http://www.npr.org/2011/08/07/138587202/after-years-of-research-confederate-daughter-arises.

4. Logan, *Review and Assessment, Report I*; *Review and Assessment Report II*; and *Review and Assessment, Report III*, 32.

5. Letter to the editor from Priscilla Lee Miles, *The Clarion*, April 1989.

6. Adams, *Mount Clare Museum House*.

7. Mount Clare: Slavery, Online: http://www.mountclare.org/history/slavery.html (accessed December 12, 2007).

8. Eichstedt and Small, *Representations of Slavery*, 12; Butler, Carter, and Dwyer, "Imagining Plantations."

9. Modlin Jr., "Tales Told on the Tour," 265–87.

10. Jackson, *Speaking for the Enslaved*.

11. Rosenzweig and Thelen, *The Presence of the Past*, 235, 245–47.

Bibliography

Adams, Carolyn. *Mount Clare Museum House: National Underground Railroad Network to Freedom Nomination*. National Park Service, December 2004. On file, Mount Clare Museum House.

Allen, Gloria Seaman. *Threads of Bondage: Chesapeake Slave Women and Plantation Cloth Production, 1750–1850*. Thesis (Ph.D.), George Washington University, 2000.

Ambler, Mary. "Diary of M. Ambler, 1770," *Virginia Magazine of History and Biography*, 45 (1937).

Archives of Maryland. *Provincial Land Records 1744–1749*. Annapolis: State of Maryland, N.d.

Ball, Charles. *Fifty Years in Chains, or, The Life of an American Slave*. New York: H. Dayton; Indianapolis: Asher & Co., 1859.

———. *Slavery in the United States: A Narrative of the Life and Adventures of Charles Ball, a Black Man, Who Lived Forty Years in Maryland, South Carolina and Georgia, as a Slave Under Various Masters, and was One Year in the Navy with Commodore Barney, During the Late War*. New York: John S. Taylor, 1837.

Baltimore Company Records, 1703–1737. 3 vols., MS 65. Maryland Historical Society.

Baumgarten, Linda. *What Clothes Reveal: The Language of Clothing in Colonial and Federal America*. Williamsburg and New Haven: Colonial Williamsburg Foundation and Yale University Press, 2002.

Baumgartner-Wagner, Norma A. *Archaeology at Mount Clare*. 1981. On file, Maryland Historical Trust.

———. *A Brief Summary of Excavations at Mount Clare Mansion*. On file, Maryland Historical Trust.

Beirne, Francis F. *St. Paul's Parish, Baltimore: A Chronicle of the Mother Church*. Baltimore: Horn-Shafer, 1967.

Beiswanger, William L. "The Temple in the Garden: Thomas Jefferson's Vision of the Monticello Landscape," in *British and American Gardens in the Eighteenth-*

202 · BIBLIOGRAPHY

Century, edited by Robert P. Maccubbin and Peter Martin, pp. 170–202. Williamsburg: Thomas Jefferson Memorial Foundation, 1983.
Berlin, Ira. Generations in Captivity: A History of African American Slaves. Cambridge: Harvard University Press, 2003.
Bezis-Selfa, John. Forging America: Ironworkers, Adventurers, and the Industrious Revolution. Ithaca, NY: Cornell University Press, 2003.
Blair, John E., Matthew D. Cochran, and Stephanie N. Duensing. Draft: Phase II Archaeological Testing on Wye Greenhouse (18TA314), Talbot County, Maryland, Archaeology in Annapolis, 2008. On file, University of Maryland, College Park.
Blassingame, John W. The Slave Community: Plantation Life in the Antebellum South. New York: Oxford University Press, 1972.
Bradley, Patricia. Slavery, Propaganda, and the American Revolution. University Press of Mississippi, 1999.
Breen, Eleanor E., and Esther C. White. "'A Pretty Considerable Distillery': George Washington's Whiskey Distillery," Quarterly Bulletin of the Archeological Society of Virginia, 61, no. 4 (2006): 209–20.
Breen, T. H., and Stephen Innes. "Myne Owne Ground": Race and Freedom on Virginia's Eastern Shore, 1640–1676. New York: Oxford University Press, 1980.
Brunson, Alvin. "The Avenue: The Legacy of Historic Pennsylvania Avenue," ChickenBones: A Journal, Online: http://www.nathanielturner.com/avenuein-baltimore.htm.
Buonocore, Susan C. "Within Her Garden Wall": The Meaning of Gardening for the Republican Woman, Rosalie Stier Calvert and the Gardens of Riversdale (1803–1821). Volumes in Historical Archaeology 35, edited by Stanley South. Columbia, S.C.: University of South Carolina, 1996.
Burnston, Sharon Ann. "The Cemetery at Catoctin Furnace, MD: The Invisible People." Maryland Archaeology 17, no. 2 (1981): 19–31.
Burton, Christine, and Carol Scott. "Management Museums: Challenges for the 21st Century." International Journal of Arts Management 5, no. 2 (2003): 56–68.
Butler, David, Perry L. Carter, and Owen J. Dwyer. "Imagining Plantations: Slavery, Dominant Narratives, and the Foreign Born." Southeast Geographer 48, no. 3 (2008): 288-302.
Campbell, Penelope. Maryland in Africa: The Maryland State Colonization Society, 1831–1857. Decatur: [s.n.], 1969. On file, Maryland Historical Society.
Carlson, Patricia Ann. "William Parks, Colonial Printer, to Dr. Charles Carroll." The Virginia Magazine of History and Biography 86, no. 4 (1978): 408–12.
Carr, Lois Green. "Inheritance in the Colonial Chesapeake," in Women in the Age of the American Revolution, eds. R. Hoffman and P. J. Albert. Charlottesville, VA: University Press of Virginia, 1989, pp. 155–208.
Carroll, Charles. "Extracts from Account and Letter Books of Dr. Charles Carroll

of Annapolis," *Maryland Historical Magazine* 18 (1923), 19 (1924), 20 (1925), 21 (1926), 22 (1927), 23 (1928), 24 (1929), 25 (1930), 26 (1931), 27 (1932).

———. Letter Book and Business Account 1716–1769. 3 vols. MS 208. Maryland Historical Society.

———. Letter Book 1731–1748. 1 vol. MS 208.1. Maryland Historical Society.

———. "Letters of Charles Carroll, Barrister," *Maryland Historical Magazine* 31 (1936), 32 (1937), 33 (1938), 34 (1939), 35 (1940), 36 (1941), 37 (1942).

———, 1737–1832. Papers 1749/50 to ca. 1896. MS 1225. Maryland Historical Society.

Carroll, Charles, 1691–1755, and Carroll, Charles, 1723–1783. Letter Books and Business Account, 1716–69. MS 208. Maryland Historical Society.

Carroll, Douglas. *Families of Dr. Charles Carroll (1691–1755) and Cornet Thomas Dewey (160?–1648)*. Brooklandville, MD: Douglass Carroll. On file, Maryland Historical Society.

Carroll Family, 1691–1755. Papers, 1730–1926. MS 1873. Maryland Historical Society.

———. Mill Account Book. 1803. Mount Clare Museum House.

Carroll, James. Account Books, 1813–1869, MS 217, 2 vols. Maryland Historical Society.

Carroll, Margaret Tilghman, 1742–1817. Account Book, 1815–1821, MS 2751. Maryland Historical Society.

Carroll-Maccubbin. Account Book, 1767–1786, Mount Clare Museum House.

———. Papers, MS 219. Maryland Historical Society.

Carson, Barbara G. *Ambitious Appetites: Dining, Behavior, and Patterns of Consumption in Federal Washington*. Washington, DC: American Institute of Architects Press, 1990.

Cassell, Frank. "Slaves of the Chesapeake Bay Area and the War of 1812." *Journal of Negro History* 57 (1972): 144–55.

Cassimere Jr., Ralph. *Origins and Early Development of Slavery in Maryland, 1633–1715*. Thesis (Ph.D.), Louisiana State University in New Orleans, 1971.

Close, Stacey K. *Elderly Slaves of the Plantation South*. New York and London: Garland Publishing, 1997.

Cochran, Matthew David. "Hoodoo's Fire: Interpreting Nineteenth Century African-American Material Culture at the Brice House, Annapolis, Maryland." *Maryland Archaeology* 35, no 1 (1999): 25–33.

Condon, John Joseph. *Manumission, Slavery and Family in the Post-Revolutionary Rural Chesapeake: Anne Arundel County, Maryland, 1781–1831*. Thesis (Ph.D.), University of Minnesota, 2001.

Davis, David Brion. *Inhuman Bondage: The Rise and Fall of Slavery in the New World*. New York: Oxford University Press, 2006.

Dent, Richard J., S. Elizabeth Ford, and Richard Hughes. *Archaeological Excavations at the Carroll Family Tomb in Saint Anne's Church Yard, Annapolis, Maryland.* November 10, 1984. On file, Carroll Park Foundation.

Donahue, Alice D. *Eighteenth Century Chesapeake Clothing: A Costume Plan for the National Colonial Farm.* Master's Thesis, University of Maryland, Baltimore County. 2008.

Dornan, Inge. "Masterful Women: Colonial Women Slaveholders in the Urban Low County." *Journal of American Studies* 39, no. 3 (2005): 383–402.

Douglass, Frederick. *My Bondage and My Freedom.* New York: Miller, Orton & Mulligan, 1855.

———. *Narrative of the Life of Frederick Douglass, an American Slave. Written by Himself.* Boston: Anti-Slavery Office, 1845.

———. *Life and Times of Frederick Douglass, Written by Himself.* Boston: De Wolfe & Fiske Co., 1892.

Dunaway, Wilma. *The African-American Family in Slavery and Emancipation.* Cambridge: Cambridge University Press, 2003.

Edwards-Ingram, Ywone. "African American Medicine and the Social Relations of Slavery." In *Race and the Archaeology of Identity,* edited by Charles E. Orser Jr., pp. 34–53. Salt Lake City: University of Utah Press, 2001.

Eichstedt, Jennifer L., and Stephen Small. *Representations of Slavery: Race and Ideology in Southern Plantation Museums.* Washington and London: Smithsonian Institution, 2002.

Ellis, Rex M. "Interpreting the Whole House." In *Interpreting Historic House Museums,* edited by Jessica Foy Donnelly, pp. 61–80. Walnut Creek, CA: AltaMira, 2002.

Fennell, Christopher. "Conjuring Boundaries: Inferring Past Identities from Religious Artifacts," *International Journal of Historical Archaeology* 4 (2000) no. 4: 281-313.

Ferguson, Leland. *Uncommon Ground.* Washington, DC: Smithsonian Institution Press, 1992.

Fett, Sharla M. *Working Cures: Healing, Health, and Power on Southern Slave Plantations.* Chapel Hill: University of North Carolina Press, 2002.

Flanagan, Charles M. *The Sweets of Independence: A Reading of the "James Carroll Daybook, 1714–21."* Thesis (Ph.D.), University of Maryland, 2005.

Fogel, Robert, and Stanley Engerman. *Time on the Cross: The Economics of American Negro Slavery.* Boston: Little and Brown, 1974.

Franklin, Maria. "The Archaeological Dimensions of Soul Food: Interpreting Race, Culture, and Afro-Virginian Identity." In *Race and the Archaeology of Identity,* edited by Charles E. Orser Jr., pp. 88–107. Salt Lake City: University of Utah Press, 2001.

Frederickson, George M. *The Black Image in the White Mind: The Debate on Afro-American Character and Destiny*. Middletown: Wesleyan University Press, 1971.

Galke, Laura J. "Did the Gods of Africa Die? A Re-Examination of a Carroll House Crystal Assemblage." *North American Archaeologist* 2000 21(1): 19–33.

Genovese, Eugene D. *Roll, Jordan, Roll: The World the Slaves Made*. New York: Pantheon Books, 1972 [1974].

Giffen, Lilian. "'Mount Clare,' Baltimore," *Maryland Historical Magazine* XLII: 29–34.

Gomez, Michael A. *Exchanging Our Country Marks: The Transformation of African Identities in the Colonial and Antebellum South*. Chapel Hill: University of North Carolina Press, 1998.

Goodwin, James. "Flowerpots of Mount Vernon's Upper Garden 44FX762/43," September 2005. On file, Mount Vernon Archaeology Department.

Gurman, Karen. *The Importance of Being Relevant: Understanding the Complex Connections Between Museum and Community*. Master's thesis, Department of Historic Preservation, University of Maryland, 2010.

Hall, Gwendolyn. *Slavery and African Ethnicities in the Americas: Restoring the Links*. Chapel Hill: University of North Carolina Press, 2005.

Handy, James A. *Scraps of African Methodist History*. Philadelphia: A.M.E. Book Concern, 1902.

Harley, R. Bruce. "Dr. Charles Carroll—Land Speculator, 1730–1755," *Maryland Historical Magazine* 56: 93–107.

Harmon, James, and Jessica Neuwirth. *Archaeological Investigations at the James Brice House (18AP38): A National Historic Landmark Site*. Annapolis, Maryland. Report prepared for the Historic Annapolis Foundation, 2000.

Hobbs, Stuart D. "Exhibiting Antimodernism: History, Memory, and the Aesthetized Past in Mid-Twentieth-Century America." *The Public Historian* 23, no. 3 (2001): 39–61.

Hogendorn, Jan S. *The Shell Money of the Slave Trade*. Cambridge: Cambridge University Press, 1986.

Hollyday, Henry I., 1725–1789. Papers, 1677–1905. MS 1317. Maryland Historical Society.

Holt, Cheryl. *Mount Clare Kitchen Floral and Faunal Analysis*, Baltimore: Analytical Services for Archaeologists, 1986.

Holt, William Stull. "Charles Carroll, Barrister: The Man." *Maryland Historical Magazine* 31 (1936): 112–26.

Hopkins III, Joseph W. *Phase II Investigations of a Proposed Parking Lot, Mount Clare Mansion, Carroll Park, Baltimore City, Maryland*. Prepared for Baltimore City Department of Parks and Recreation. Baltimore: Joseph Hopkins Associates, Inc. September 2003.

Horton, James O., and Lois E. Horton. *In Hope of Liberty: Culture, Community, and Protest Among Northern Free Blacks, 1700–1860*. New York: Oxford University Press, 1997.

Ignatiev, Noel. *How the Irish Became White*. New York and London: Routledge, 1996.

Hynson, Jerry M. *Maryland Freedom Papers, vol. 1, Anne Arundel County*, Westminster: Family Line Publications, 1996.

———. *Maryland Colonization Society Manumission Book 1832-1860*, vol. 3, Westminster: Willow Bend Books, 2001.

Jackson, Antoinette T. *Speaking for the Enslaved: Heritage Interpretation at Antebellum Plantation Sites*. Walnut Creek: Left Coast Press, 2012.

Jackson, Samuel. *The Baltimore Directory*. Baltimore: [s.n.], 1819.

Johnson, Keach. *The Establishment of the Baltimore Company: A Case-Study of the American Iron Industry in the Eighteenth Century*. Thesis (Ph.D.), State University of Iowa, 1949.

———. "The Genesis of the Baltimore Ironworks." *Journal of Southern History* 19, no. 2 (1953): 157–79.

———. "The Baltimore Iron Company Seeks English Markets: A Study of the Anglo-American Iron Trade, 1731–1755." *The William and Mary Quarterly* 16, no. 1 (1959): 37–60.

Joyce, Donald Franklin. "AME Book Concern," In *Black Book Publishers in the United States: A Historical Dictionary of the Presses, 1817–1990*, Westport, CT: Greenwood Press, 1991.

Keenan, C. *Baltimore Directory for 1822 and 1823*. Baltimore: C. Keenan, 1822.

Kelley, Jennifer Olsen, and J. Lawrence Angel. "The Workers of Catoctin Furnace." *Maryland Archeology* 19, no 1: 2–17.

King, Wilma. *Stolen Childhood: Slave Youth in Nineteenth-Century America*. Bloomington: Indiana University Press, 1995.

Klein, Mary, and Kingsley Smith. "Racism in the Anglican and Episcopal Church of Maryland." Presented at the Tri-History Conference (National Episcopal Historians and Archivists; the Historical Society of the Episcopal Church; Episcopal Women's History Project), June 24–27, 2007, Williamsburg, VA.

Kryder-Reid, Elizabeth. "'As Is the Gardener, So Is the Garden': The Archaeology of Landscape As Myth." In *Historical Archaeology of the Chesapeake*, pp. 131–48, edited by Barbara J. Little and Paul A. Shackel. Washington, D.C.: Smithsonian Press, 1994.

Land, Aubrey C. "Economic Base and Social Structure: The Northern Chesapeake in the Eighteenth Century." *The Journal of Economic History* 25 (1965) no. 4: 639–54.

Leone, Mark P., Gladys-Marie Fry, and Timothy Ruppel. "Spirit Management among Americans of African Descent." In *Race and the Archaeology of Identity*, edited by Charles E. Orser Jr., pp. 143–57. Salt Lake City: University of Utah Press, 2001.

Lewis, Ronald L. "Slavery on Chesapeake Iron Plantations Before the American Revolution." *The Journal of Negro History* 59, no. 3 (1974): 242–54.

———. *Coal, Iron, and Slaves*. Westport: Greenwood Press, 1979.

Libby, Jean. *African Ironmaking Culture Among African American Ironworkers in Western Maryland, 1760–1850*. Thesis (M.A.), San Francisco State University, 1991.

Logan, George C. *Review and Assessment of Archaeology at Carroll Park (18BC10), Report I: Status of Records, Objects, and Reports*. Carroll Park Restoration Foundation, Inc., 1992. On file, Carroll Park Foundation.

———. *Review and Assessment of Archaeology at Carroll Park (18BC10), Report II: Historical Overview of Previous Archaeological Investigations*. Carroll Park Restoration Foundation, Inc. On file, Carroll Park Foundation.

———. *Review and Assessment of Archaeology at Carroll Park (18BC10), Report III: Assessing Results of Previous Archaeological Investigations*. Carroll Park Restoration Foundation, Inc., 1993. On file, Carroll Park Foundation.

———. *Archaeology at Charles Carroll's House and Garden and of His African-American Slaves*. Historic Annapolis Foundation. N.d. On file, Carroll Park Foundation.

Logan, George, and John L. Seidel. *Mount Clare's Kitchen: 1986 Archaeological Research at Carroll Park (18BC10K)*. Baltimore: Carroll Park Restoration Foundation, Inc., April 1995. On file, Maryland Historical Trust.

———. *The 1984 Shovel Test Pit Survey of Mount Clare, in Carroll Park*. Baltimore: Carroll Park Restoration Foundation, Inc., April 1995. On file, Maryland Historical Trust.

Lopez, Ian Haney. *White by Law: The Legal Construction of Race*, 10th ed., New York: New York University Press, 2006.

MacLeod, Duncan J. *Slavery, Race, and the American Revolution*. Cambridge: Cambridge University Press, 1974.

Martin, David. *Trial of the Rev. Jacob Gruber, Minister in the Methodist Episcopal Church*, Fredericktown: David Martin, 1819.

Maryland Society of the Colonial Dames of America. *Constitution and by-Laws of the Maryland Society of the Colonial Dames of America*. Baltimore: Guggenheimer, Weil, and Co., 1892.

Matchett, R. J. *Baltimore Director for 1827*. Baltimore: R. J. Matchett, 1827.

———. *Baltimore Director for 1833*. Baltimore: R. J. Matchett, 1833.

———. *Baltimore Director for 1835–36*. Baltimore: R. J. Matchett, 1835.

Mauer, Karen. *The Maryland Gazette, 1727–1761: Genealogical and Historical Abstracts*. Galveston: Frontier Press, 1990.

Maynadier, Henry Fitzhugh Family Collection. 1769–1902. MS 2880. Maryland Historical Society.

McDermott, Scott. *Charles Carroll of Carrollton: Faithful Revolutionary*. New York: Scepter Publishers, 2002.

Melton, J. Gordon. "African American Methodism in the M.E. Tradition: The Case of Sharp Street (Baltimore)." *The North Star: A Journal of African American Religious History* 8, no. 2 (2005): 1–20.

Modlin Jr., E. Arnold. "Tales Told on the Tour: Mythic Representations of Slavery by Docents at North Carolina Plantation Museums." *Southeast Geographer* 48, no. 3 (2008): 265–87.

Moore, John Jamison. *History of the A.M.E. Church in America, Founded 1796 in the City of New York*. York, PA: Teachers' Journal Office, 1884.

Moreno, Kimberly Collins. *Mistress of Mount Clare: The Life of Margaret Tilghman Carroll 1742–1817*. Thesis (M.A.), University of Maryland, Baltimore County, 2004.

Morgan, Philip D. "'To Get Quit of Negroes': George Washington and Slavery." *Journal of American Studies* 39, no. 3 (2005): 403–29.

Moyer, Teresa S. *Museum Practicum: A Walking Tour of Mount Clare and Georgia in Carroll Park, Baltimore, Maryland*. College Park: Department of American Studies, University of Maryland, 2009. On file, University of Maryland.

Mullins, Paul R. "Racializing the Commonplace Landscape: An Archaeology of Urban Renewal Along the Color Line." *World Archaeology* 38 (2006): 60–71.

Murphy, John. *Baltimore Directory for 1845*. Baltimore: John Murphy, 1845.

Nash, Gary B. "Forging Freedom: The Emancipation Experience in the Northern Seaport Cities 1775–1820." In *Slavery and Freedom in the Age of the American Revolution*, edited by Ira Berlin and Ronald Hoffman, 3–48. Charlottesville, VA: University Press of Virginia, 1983.

National Society of the Colonial Dames of America. *Constitution and Eligibility Lists of the National Society of the Colonial Dames of America*. Baltimore: Guggenheimer, Weil, and Co., 1895.

National Society of the Colonial Dames of America in the State of Maryland, *Mount Clare: Home of Charles Carroll, Barrister*. Baltimore: National Society of the Colonial Dames of America in the State of Maryland, 1971.

National Society of the Colonial Dames of America in the State of Maryland, *Adventurers, Cavaliers, Patriots* and *Mount Clare: Home of Charles Carroll, Barrister*. Baltimore: National Society of the Colonial Dames of America in the State of Maryland, 1994.

Nieves, Angel. "Memories of Africville: Urban Renewal, Reparations, and the Africadian Diaspora." In *Black Geographies and the Politics of Place*, edited by Katherine McKittrick and Clyde Woods. Cambridge: South End Press, 2007.

Norman, J. Gary. "An Example of Inference in Historical Archaeology: Reviewing the Options at Mount Clare." Presented at the 53rd Annual Meeting of the Eastern States Archaeological Federation, November 2, 1986.

———. *Restoration Archaeology Report: Archaeological Investigations in the Forecourt at Mount Clare Mansion, Baltimore, Maryland, 18BC10H.* Baltimore: Baltimore Center for Urban Archaeology, 1986.

———. "Restoration Archaeology Report: Archaeological Investigations in the First Terrace at Mount Clare Mansion, Baltimore, Maryland, 18BC10G." In *Research Series No. 13.* Baltimore, MD: Baltimore Center for Urban Archaeology, 1987.

Nye, Eric. *Pounds Sterling to Dollars: Historical Conversion of Currency.* University of Wyoming: Department of English. Online: http://www.uwyo.edu/numimage/currency.htm (accessed December 20, 2009).

Olmsted, Frederick Law. *A Journey into the Seaboard Slave States.* London: Mason Brothers, 1861.

Omi, Michael, and Howard Winant. *Racial Formation in the U.S.* New York: Routledge, 2nd ed., 1994.

Ottley, Roi. *Black Odyssey.* New York: Charles Scribner's Sons, 1948.

Papenfuse, Edward C., Alan F. Day, David W. Jordan, and Gregory A. Stiverson. *A Biographical Dictionary of the Maryland Legislature, 1635–1789.* Vol. 1: A–H. Baltimore and London: Johns Hopkins University Press, 1979.

Payne, Daniel Alexander. *History of the African Methodist Episcopal Church.* Nashville: A.M.E. Sunday School Union, 1891.

Pennington, James W. C. *A Text Book of the Origin and History, &c. &c. of the Colored People.* Second ed. Original edition Hartford: L. Skinner, Printer, 1841. Detroit: Negro History Press, 1969.

———. *The Fugitive Blacksmith; Or, Events in the History of James W. C. Pennington, Pastor of a Presbyterian Church, New York, Formerly a Slave in the State of Maryland, United States.* 3rd ed., Reprinted from 1850 edition. Westport: Negro Universities Press, 1971.

Phillips, Christopher. *Freedom's Port: The African American Community of Baltimore, 1790–1860.* Urbana: University of Illinois Press, 1997.

Pogue, Dennis, et al. *Archaeological Investigations at the Mount Clare Orangery (18BC10B), Baltimore City, Maryland.* Mount Vernon: Mount Vernon Ladies' Association, 2000.

Pollard, Leslie J. "Aging and Slavery: A Gerontological Perspective," *The Journal of Negro History* 66, no. 3 (1981): 228-234.

Porter, Dorothy. *Early Negro Writing 1760-1837.* Boston: Beacon Press, 1995.

Raboteau, Albert J. "The Slave Church in the Era of the American Revolution," in Ira Berlin and Ronald Hoffman (eds.), *Slavery and Freedom in the Age of the American Revolution.* Charlottesville: University Press of Virginia, 1983.

Rawick, George P. *The American Slave: A Composite Autobiography*. Westport, CT: Greeenwood Publishing Co., 1972.

Reamy, Bill, and Martha Reamy. *Records of St. Paul's Parish*. Vols. 1 and 2. Westminster: Family Line Publications, 1988.

Robbins, Michael W. *The Principio Company: Iron-Making in Colonial Maryland, 1720–1781*. Thesis (Ph.D.), Colgate University, 1972.

———. *Maryland's Iron Industry During the Revolutionary War Era: A Report Prepared for the Maryland Bicentennial Commission*. Annapolis: The Commission, 1973.

Rosenzweig, Roy, and David P. Thelen. *The Presence of the Past: Popular Uses of History in American Life*. New York: Columbia University Press, 1998.

Ross, Max. "Interpreting the New Museology." *Museum and Society* 2, no. 2 (2004): 84–103.

Roylance, Frank D. "Crystal's Past Clearly Divides Archaeologists." *The Sun* [Baltimore, MD] November 19, 1994: 1B–2B.

Ruffins, Faith Davis, and Paul Ruffins, "Recovering Yesterday: An Overview of the Collection and Preservation of Black History," *Black Issues in Higher Education* 13, no. 25 (1997): 16.

Rush, Christopher. *A Short Account of the Rise and Progress of the African M.E. Church in America*. Christopher Rush and George Collins, 1866.

Sandercock, Leonie. "Introduction: Framing Insurgent Historiographies for Planning." In *Making the Invisible Visible*, edited by Leonie Sandercock, 1–36. Berkeley: University of California Press, 1998.

Schwartz, Jack. "Men's Clothing and the Negro." *Phylon* 24, no. 3 (1963): 221–31.

Schwartz, Marie Jenkins. *Born in Bondage: Growing Up Enslaved in the Antebellum South*. Cambridge: Harvard University Press, 2000.

Shackel, Paul A. and Barbara J. Little, eds. *Historical Archaeology of the Chesapeake*. Washington, DC: Smithsonian Institution Press, 1994.

Sidbury, James. *Becoming African in America: Race and Nation in the Early Black Atlantic*. New York: Oxford University Press, 2007.

Singleton, Theresa A., ed. *The Archaeology of Slavery and Plantation Life*. San Diego: Academic Press, 1985.

Singleton, Theresa A. and Mark Bograd. "Breaking Typological Barriers: Looking for the Colono in the Colonoware." In *Lines That Divide: Historical Archaeologies of Race, Class, and Gender*, edited by James A. Dell, Stephen A. Mrozowski, and Robert Paynter. Knoxville: University of Tennessee Press, 2000.

Sioussat, Annie Leakin. *"Mount Clare" Carroll Park, Baltimore: An Historical Sketch Issued under the Auspices of the Maryland Society of the Colonial Dames of America*. Baltimore: Maryland Society of the Colonial Dames of America, 1926.

Smedley, Audrey. *Race in North America*, 3rd ed., Boulder, CO: Westview Press, 2007.

Smith, David. *A Brief Account of the Awakening and Conversion of David Smith, Preacher of the Gospel, in the African Methodist Episcopal Church*, Washington, DC: D. Rapine, 1822.

Smith, David, and Daniel Alexander Payne. *Biography of Rev. David Smith of the A.M.E. Church; Being a Complete History, Embracing over Sixty Years' Labor in the Advancement of the Redeemer's Kingdom on Earth*. Including "The History of the Origin and Development of Wilberforce University. Xenia: Xenia Gazette Office, 1881.

Starn, Randolph. "A Historian's Brief Guide to New Museum Studies." *The American Historical Review* 110, no. 1 (2005): 68–98.

Still, William. *The Underground Railroad: A Record of Facts, Authentic Narrative, Letters, and C., Narrating the Hardships, Hair-Breadth Escapes and Death Struggles of the Slaves in Their Efforts of Freedom, as Related by Themselves and Others, or as Witnessed by the Author*. Philadelphia, PA: Porter and Coates, 1872.

Tamplin, Joanna Tilghman. "Chatelaine of Mount Clare." In *Behind the Maryland Scene: Women of Influence 1600–1800*, edited by the Southern Regional Committee National Society of the Colonial Dames of America in the State of Maryland, and Dame Guests from other Maryland Committees, 95–103. Baltimore: National Society of the Colonial Dames of America in the State of Maryland, Southern Maryland Regional Committee, 1977.

Thomas, Bettye C. "History of the Sharp Street Methodist Episcopal Church, 1787–1920." Sharp Street Memorial Church Collection, Maryland State Archives SC 4010.

Thompson, John. *Life of John Thompson*. Worcester, MA: John Thompson, 1856.

Trostel, Michael F. *Mount Clare: Being an Account of the Seat Built by Charles Carroll, Barrister, upon his Lands at Patapsco*. Baltimore: National Society of the Colonial Dames of America in the State of Maryland, 1981.

Tunbridge, J. E., and G. J. Ashworth. *Dissonant Heritage: The Management of the Past as a Resource in Conflict*. West Sussex: John Wiley and Sons, 1996.

Twitty, Michael. *Fighting Old Nep: The Foodways of Enslaved Afro-Marylanders 1634–1864*, Michael Twitty, 2006.

Vaughn, Alden T. *Roots of American Racism: Essays on the Colonial Experience*. New York: Oxford University Press, 1995.

Vlach, John Michael. *Back of the Big House: The Architecture of Plantation Slavery*. Chapel Hill and London: The University of North Carolina Press, 1993.

———. "Not Mansions . . . But Good Enough: Slave Quarters as Bi-Cultural Expression." In *Black and White Cultural Interaction in the Antebellum South*, edited by Ted Ownby, pp. 89–114. Jackson, MS: University Press of Mississippi, 1993.

Wallace, Barbara Elizabeth. *"Fair Daughters of Africa": African American Women in Baltimore, 1790–1860*. Thesis (Ph.D.), University of California–Los Angeles, 2001.

Walsh, Lorena S. *From Calabar to Carter's Grove: The History of a Virginia Slave Community*. Charlottesville, VA: University Press of Virginia, 1997.

Washington, George. Papers. Series 2, Letter Books, Library of Congress.

Watkins, James. *Narrative of the Life of James Watkins, Formerly a Slave in Maryland, U.S.; containing an account of his escape from slavery, with notices of the Fugitive slave law, the sentiments of American divines on the subject of slavery, and the labours of the fugitive in England, etc., etc.* 4th ed. Birmingham: W. Watton, Printers, 1853.

Wax, Darold D. "Black Immigrants: The Slave Trade in Colonial Maryland." *Maryland Historical Magazine* 73, no. 1 (1978): 30–45.

Weber, Carmen A. *Archaeology at Mount Clare*. On file, Maryland Historical Trust.

Weld, Theodore. *American Slavery As It Is: Testimony of a Thousand Witnesses*. New York: American Anti-Slavery Society, 1839.

Wells III, James E. *The Historical Geography of Racial and Ethnic Access Within Baltimore's Carroll Park: 1870–1954*. Thesis (M.A.), Ohio University, 2006.

West, Patricia. *Domesticating History: The Political Origins of America's House Museums*. Washington, DC: Smithsonian Institution, 1999.

Wheeler, Roxann. *The Complexion of Race: Categories of Difference in Eighteenth-Century British Culture*. Philadelphia: University of Pennsylvania Press, 2000.

White, Deborah Gray. *Ar'n't I a Woman?: Female Slaves in the Plantation South*. New York: W.W. Norton and Company, 1985/1999.

White, Shane, and Graham White. "Slave Clothing and African-American Culture in the Eighteenth and Nineteenth Centuries." *Past and Present* 148: 149–86.

Whitman, T. Stephen. *The Price of Freedom: Slavery and Manumission in Baltimore and Early National Maryland*. Lexington: University Press of Kentucky, 1997.

Windley, Lathan A. *Runaway Slave Advertisements: A Documentary History from the 1730s to 1790*. Vol. 2. Maryland, Westport: Greenwood Press, 1983.

Winter, Susan E. "Antietam Furnace: A Frontier Ironworks in the Great Valley of Maryland." In *Historical Archaeology of the Chesapeake*, edited by P. A. Shackel and B. J. Little, pp. 205–18. Washington, DC: Smithsonian Institution Press, 1994.

Wood, Kirsten E. "Broken Reeds and Competent Farmers: Slaveholding Widows in the Southeastern United States, 1783–1861." *Journal of Women's History* 13, no. 2 (2001): 34–57.

Yentsch, Anne Elizabeth. *A Chesapeake Family and Their Slaves*. Cambridge and New York: Cambridge University Press, 1994.

INDEX

Teresa S. Moyer is an archaeologist with the National Park Service in Washington, D.C.

Cultural Heritage Studies
Edited by Paul A. Shackel, University of Maryland

The University Press of Florida is proud to support this series devoted to the study of cultural heritage. This enterprise brings together research devoted to understanding the material and behavioral characteristics of heritage. The series explores the uses of heritage and the meaning of its cultural forms as a way to interpret the present and the past. Books include important theoretical contributions and descriptions of significant cultural resources. Scholarship addresses questions related to culture and describes how local and national communities develop and value the past. The series includes works in public archaeology, heritage tourism, museum studies, vernacular architecture, history, American studies, and material cultural studies.

Heritage of Value, Archaeology of Renown: Reshaping Archaeological Assessment and Significance, edited by Clay Mathers, Timothy Darvill, and Barbara J. Little (2005)

Archaeology, Cultural Heritage, and the Antiquities Trade, edited by Neil Brodie, Morag M. Kersel, Christina Luke, and Kathryn Walker Tubb (2006)

Archaeological Site Museums in Latin America, edited by Helaine Silverman (2006)

Crossroads and Cosmologies: Diasporas and Ethnogenesis in the New World, by Christopher C. Fennell (2007)

Ethnographies and Archaeologies: Iterations of the Past, by Lena Mortensen and Julie Hollowell (2009)

Cultural Heritage Management: A Global Perspective, by Phyllis Mauch Messenger and George S. Smith (2010)

God's Fields: An Archaeology of Religion and Race in Moravian Wachovia, by Leland Ferguson (2011; first paperback edition, 2013)

Ancestors of Worthy Life: Plantation Slavery and Black Heritage at Mount Clare, by Teresa S. Moyer (2015)